DEMOCRACY PARADIGM SHIFTS

Dr. Lalith Kumar Dharavath

Professor of Public Administration
Osmania University, Hyderabadi-
Telangana State, India.500007

TANEESHA PUBLISHING

ISBN : 9789347259692
Edition : First, January 2026
Title : Democracy Paradigm Shifts
Author : Dr. Lalith Kumar Dharavath

Published by

TANEESHA PUBLISHING

An Imprint of **Taneesha and Prachi NextGen Publication**

Registered Office: Sunil Complex, 2nd Floor, Vijay Nagar,
Western Kutchery Road, Meerut - 250002, Uttar Pradesh, India
Website : www.taneeshapublishing.com
E-mail : support@tpnextpub.com
Phone : 0121 453 0364

Printed by :
Manipal Technologies Limited, Bengaluru - 560001, Karnataka

Table of Contents

Final Word

"A small group of thoughtful, committed citizens can change the world".

- Margaret Mead

The final word on "paradigm shifts in democracy" is that this form of government is currently in a state of dynamic tension, marked by widespread democratic backsliding but also persistent citizen demand for more responsive and inclusive governance. The traditional model is shifting from purely procedure-based, representative democracy toward a more integrated approach that emphasizes liberal rights, citizen participation, and tangible results. Key conclusions on the current paradigm shifts include: Many nations, including established democracies, are experiencing "backsliding" or a shift toward "electoral autocracy". This often happens not through sudden coups, but through the gradual weakening of institutions like the judiciary, free press, and civil society by elected leaders.

However, this trend often sparks opposition and a renewed push for democratic principles, demonstrating democracy's inherent resilience. A major paradigm shift involves moving from a "government-centric" to a "citizen-centered" view of democracy. Citizens, empowered by increased awareness and connectivity, are demanding a more active role than just voting. The focus is moving towards empowering local communities and fostering personal agency and associational life as the primary determinants of societal well-being. There is a growing recognition that democracy must deliver tangible outcomes for citizens in areas like health, education, the economy, and climate change mitigation to maintain legitimacy. When democratic processes become bogged down by excessive proceduralism or fail to address inequality, public discontent rises, making populations more susceptible to populist or authoritarian appeals. Technology is a double-edged sword in this paradigm shift. On one hand, it is used by repressive regimes for surveillance and control. On the other, the "democratization of technology" and the rise of digital public infrastructure are being used by governments to promote good governance and increase digital inclusion, changing how citizens interact with their state. Ultimately, the idea of a fully "achieved" democracy is a myth. Democracy is a fragile, dynamic social and political system that requires continuous protection, popular debate, and steadfast justification of its principles. Its future depends on the ongoing choices of political actors and citizens to protect and practice its core values of individual rights, rule of law, and mutual toleration.

The final conclusion regarding "paradigm shifts in democracy" is that a fundamental systemic change is not yet complete, but democracy is undergoing a profound period of in response to deep-seated crises. The prevailing liberal democratic model is challenged by internal weaknesses and external pressures, leading to a potential tipping point where a new paradigm may emerge. The prevailing view is moving away from seeing democracy as a fixed "thing done" and embracing it as a continuous, active process that a nation "must be doing". This ongoing nature inherently involves adaptation and evolution. The current "democratic recession" stems largely from the failure of established models (often tied to the neoliberal economic consensus) to address core issues like inequality, economic insecurity, and climate change. When governments fail to deliver tangible outcomes, public discontent rises, challenging the legitimacy of the system itself.

There is a clear, ongoing shift in focus from purely representative, procedure-based governance to models that demand more deliberative and participatory engagement. Innovations like digital tools and the increased role of civic groups are changing how citizens interact with the state and influencing policy formulation beyond traditional party politics. The future of democracy is being forged in a period of significant political and social stress. The outcome is not guaranteed; it depends on political actors and citizens making conscious choices to protect democratic values and find new ways to govern effectively and inclusively. Despite the rise of autogravitation and populism, there is a strong underlying human desire for freedom, knowledge, and self-expression. Societies where these "emancipative values" are widespread are more resilient to anti-democratic pressures, suggesting that a future paradigm will need to be deeply rooted in these principles to succeed.

In sum, the "final word" is that democracy is at a critical juncture, not in a state of terminal decline but in a necessary, painful transition period that demands innovation and active citizen engagement to determine its next, more responsive form.

Preface

Paradigm shifts in democracy involve fundamental changes in governing ideas, moving from traditional liberal models to new forms like "Dharmic democracy" or experiencing crises where established norms like fair elections, media freedom, and institutional independence erode, leading to concerns about rising electoral autocracy, majoritarianism, and personalized power, shifting focus from broad participation to potential (or performance-based) leadership, and confronting global issues like climate change that demand new transnational approaches beyond state-centric models. These shifts reflect evolving societal needs, technological impacts, and challenges to existing democratic structures, impacting everything from governance styles to voter engagement.

The concept changes in the prevailing models, theories, and practices of democratic governance. These shifts are driven by various factors, including evolving societal demands, technological advancements, and responses to crises, leading to new frameworks for how power is exercised and public goods are delivered. Key aspects and examples of these paradigm shifts include: From Government to Governance major shift has been the movement from a traditional, state-centric model of "government" (characterized by hierarchical, top-down command and control) to a more complex, participatory model of "governance". The modern governance paradigm involves: The inclusion of public, private, and civil society organizations in decision-making and implementation processes. Reliance on policy and operational networks, such as public-private partnerships (PPPs), to deliver services and achieve collective goals. A move toward "good governance" principles like transparency, accountability, rule of law, participation, and efficiency, often influenced by international institutions.

In political science, there is an ongoing discussion about whether the traditional, narrow liberal-procedural paradigm of democracy research (focusing heavily on elections and formal institutions) is sufficient to explain current global challenges. Beyond Institutions: Researchers advocate for an "opening" of the paradigm to consider the quality and legitimacy of institutions on the ground, focusing on the core principles democracy is meant to serve. Global Dialogue: This shift involves moving beyond a Western-universalist model to embrace a more pluralistic and global understanding of democracy, incorporating non-Western or indigenous governance models and bottom-up perspectives from citizens themselves.

Modern challenges are also driving shifts in practice: Digital Democracy: The rise of digital media, e-governance platforms, and data-driven decision-making presents opportunities for more inclusive and efficient participation, but also introduces new challenges related to data ethics, privacy, and digital exclusion. Events like the COVID-19 pandemic have highlighted the limits of democratic governance in some areas (e.g., implementing strict lockdowns) and spurred discussions about how democratic institutions can adapt to manage social anxiety and new types of crises. Specific national contexts illustrate these shifts in action. In India, for example, the 2014 elections were seen by some as a paradigm shift in politics and governance, moving toward majority rule, a strong focus on economic development and growth, and a significant use of digital media for communication.

Paradigm shifts in democracy are about fundamental changes in the underlying assumptions, values, and practices of governance, often triggered by crises or new societal demands. The most resonant and relevant quotation for understanding "paradigm shifts in democracy" in a modern context is by Archibald MacLeish: **"Democracy is never a thing done. Democracy is always something that a nation must be doing"** . This quote moves beyond simply observing change and offers a prescriptive view of the democratic project. It directly addresses the concept of a "paradigm shift" by defining democracy not as a stable end-state, but as a continuous, active process that requires constant engagement and evolution. The quote suggests that democracy must be dynamic and adapt to new challenges—whether social, technological, or political—to survive. A "paradigm shift" is the necessary mechanism through which this "doing" occurs; it is how a society re-evaluates and reinvents its approach to self-governance.

It highlights that relying. The quote implicitly critiques the idea of a finished or frozen democratic model, which is a key issue when discussing paradigm shifts. The founders of nations like the United States, for example, built systems that had the "capacity for self-repair" and evolution, acknowledging the need to adapt over time. A static democracy "murders itself" through atrophy and an inability to respond to the needs of a changing populace, as John Adams warned. MacLeish's words place the burden of democracy squarely on the citizens. It is "something that a nation must be doing," implying an ongoing, active responsibility rather than a passive reliance on institutions alone. This resonates strongly with current shifts that emphasize the need for citizen participation beyond just voting. In an era of democratic backsliding and rising populism, this quote serves as a crucial reminder that democratic principles like the rule of law, individual rights, and free press need continuous protection and re-justification. The current paradigm is being forged in a "crucible of heat and stress," and only active commitment will ensure a successful transition to the next phase of stable, inclusive governance.

Acknowledgements

I would like to begin by expressing my profound gratitude to God, whose grace provided the strength and patience needed to bring this book to completion in a timely manner.

I am immensely grateful to my parents, my wife, my children, and my friends. Their constant support, encouragement, and belief in this project were my primary motivation.

I also wish to acknowledge and thank everyone else who was involved, whether directly or indirectly. The assistance I received from all quarters during the making of this book was vital, and I offer my heartfelt thanks once more to all who helped make this publication a reality.

Introduction book an overview

"Democracy is the government of the people, by the people and for the people." The evolution of governance models should pertinently adhere to this and investigate the underlying potential, opportunities, power, and capabilities of novel, emerging Internet technologies. The emergence of the social web and the exponential data generated consequently can be analyzed to give the human touch to governance. In this chapter we discuss the paradigm shifts from e-governance to s-governance characterizing a social model of governance that is envisioned to be democratic, transparent, and accountable. As a step toward intelligent governance, we expound a new perspective of "sentiment" in s-governance to understand the human element of Big Data. The impact of Big Data on governance facilitated by application of sentiment mining is exemplified by demonstrating its use in research and practice. Government refers to the formal institutions and body of people (legislature, executive, judiciary) empowered with the authority and coercive power to make and enforce laws. It often implies a centralized, bureaucratic structure. Governance is a broader concept that describes the process and manner of governing. It involves the interaction and coordination of various actors, including government, the private sector (market), and civil society (NGOs, community groups, citizens), in decision-making and implementation

The rise in the popularity of the term governance is closely linked with the redefinition of the state's role. In the post-World War II period, the state was seen as an engine of growth, but with the failures in development performance, it began to be blamed for all that had gone wrong. Ineffective development policies, poor implementation of these policies, and inefficient and incompetent absorption of international aid triggered the search for alternative frameworks for policymaking and institutions for delivering public services.

As the evidence of the ineffectiveness of public administration as an instrument of development mounted, the development strategy also began to emphasise freeing the market and liberalizing economic policies. Governance began to be closely linked with such policies of economic reforms, and the goal of public administration and that of the state began to be seen as one that supported the liberalization of the economy.

The introduction of economic reforms and acceptance of a neo-liberal ideology as a strategy of development in 1991 brought with it the impetus to transform government into what came to be known as governance. This move towards governance has changed India's entire context of public administration. It demands loosening the earlier view in which public administration was seen as a major instrument of delivering goods and services to the people. In this lesson, we intend to explore how governance within this neo-liberal framework impacts public administration in India and the kinds of tensions it has created between the demands of the new styles of government functioning and older traditional ways of doing work.

Governance is understood in many ways, but there is a baseline agreement that governance refers to developing governing styles in which boundaries between and within the public and private sectors have blurred. What previously was indisputably government roles are now increasingly seen as more common generic societal problems which political institutions and other actors can resolve. The main point is that political institutions no longer monopolies governance orchestration. The concept of governance indicates a shift away from well-established notions of how the government sought to resolve social issues through a top-down approach. The emphasis is on the reduced role of the state and the acknowledgement that it is no longer the only actor that steers society.

Network relationships of three actors – state, market and civil society became the core thrust of the idea of governance. Governance in its avatar during the neo-liberal era is seen as an interactive process where the government frames policies in collaboration with other non-state actors. There is a network of relationships; no one actor can easily dominate; it will depend on a particular exchange process. The monopoly of political institutions in providing services is diluted; the private sector and institutions of civil society fill in the space previously occupied by these institutions. New forms of institutions emerge, which find expression in blurring boundaries between the public and private sectors. A range of participative agencies that respond to collective concerns arise.

The focus is on the production of public policy and the contribution of public and private actors to it. As pointed out, 'policy networks are sets of formal institutional and informal linkages between governmental and other actors structured around shared if endlessly negotiated beliefs and interests in public policy making and implementation. These actors are interdependent and policy emerges from the interactions between them.'At the formal level, policy networks have emerged as public institutions where government, business and civil society interact. These interactions lead to policy outputs. In operational terms, governments have instituted advisory bodies and various kinds of Councils where representatives of government and two other actors – business and civil society are members. Such policy networks differ from lobby groups, whose role is influencing the government to get outputs in their favour.At the informal level, governance means opening up government activities to non-government actors. It is no longer a preserve of hierarchical decision-making, which is often secretive and closed. The three actors, state, market and civil society, interact more frequently in the public domain and attempt to formulate public policies together. This is distinct from an understanding of lobby groups who tend to influence the government to frame/bend policy in their favour. It is a fundamental change towards a more open government that is willing to listen and become one participant among the three in policy making.

Apart from policy networks, there can be operational networks too. These networks are implementation tools delivering public goods and services that one single actor cannot do. Increasingly, the government has adopted the mode of seeking cooperation from one or the other actors in implementing public interest programmes. Such cooperation has taken the form of what has come to be popularly known as public-private partnership. This type of partnership is widely being promoted as a strategy of governance in delivering goods and services in many sectors.

The governance agenda then underlines curbing the state's role and expanding the space for market and competition. Competition is accepted as a powerful tool and essential dimension of economic, political and social life. In extolling the virtues of the market and competition and laying stress on the past failures of the state, the governance agenda virtually condemns the state for having suppressed the energies of society. Because the state is an alien oppressor, the curtailment of state activities becomes a people-friendly, democratic venture, almost to the extent that state contraction or dissatisfaction is presented as synonymous with democratization. Its emphasis on civil society and its institutions has to be seen in this perspective of strengthening democracy and in constructing an informal sector that can harness people's entrepreneurship through community institutions and interpersonal relationships. In the good governance discourse, democracy emerges as the necessary political framework for successful economic development, and within this discourse, democracy and economic liberalism are conceptually linked: bad governance equals state intervention; good governance equals democracy and economic liberalism.

In this agenda of good governance, the conceptualization of civil society proceeds on the assumption that power and exploitation are associated with the state, while freedom and liberty fall in the realm of civil society. This leads to a kind of romantic view of civil society where the existence of institutions outside the state becomes a sufficient basis for assuming that state power is curbed and greater democratisation is taking place. In this perspective, the concept of civil society carries with it a notion of something worthy and of value. It is considered good in itself, and its creation is a worthy goal to be pursued.Those promoting the ideology of liberalization helped the international donors and governments of the Third World shape an uncritical view of civil society and persuaded them to believe that it can be created through their aid and support policies. The view that 'civil society could do no wrong and there was nothing it could not do' was widely accepted among donor agencies. Non-governmental organizations sprang up like mushrooms, offering to strengthen civil society and as civil organizations in their own right. In many cases, they claimed to speak on behalf of civil society at large.

In the development field, the role of NGOs was strengthened through donor aid and policies. Governance as a concept thus began to encompass a wide array of issues relating to the restructuring of state-market-society relationships. What all this has meant is that the governance reforms agenda is very wide and complex. It ranges from reforming the entire gamut of state machinery to improve the delivery of goods and services, strengthening civil society to become an effective partner in socio-economic endeavors, and strengthening market mechanisms for greater efficiency. Existing institutions needed to be improved, and new institutions needed to be created where none existed. This is a daunting challenge, a challenge that India is facing with uneven success. Across the world, partnership among the three actors – state, market and civil society is promoted as a good governance strategy. The partnerships promise to avoid duplication of efforts and are seen to draw on their complementary resources and capabilities to design more effective problem-solving mechanisms. They promise to increase the responsiveness of policies and create accountability by including other actors- market and civil society- in decision-making processes. They are also presumed to improve compliance with and implementation of political decisions.

In addition, the partnerships provide opportunities for the partners to learn from each other. It is widely believed that networks play a significant role in the processes promoting social and economic development. has argued that shared understandings are vital for the better functioning of economic decision-making. Shared understandings help overcome bureaucratic resistance and allow the state not to fall prey to social and political interests. Industrialists increase their ability to get necessary infrastructure and collective goods for future growth.

However, this optimism is not shared by many. Critics point out that these partnerships can be a strategy of the state to evade responsibility. Others point out that new institutions that lack democratic accountability can be created. Bureaucracy is responsible to the people's representatives, and networks risk weakening traditional accountability mechanisms by shifting policy decisions to the realm of partnerships that can circumvent parliamentary control. A fear is also expressed that the corporate sector can use partnerships to embellish its own power and resources. Despite these concerns, optimism about partnerships prevails, and a complex web of networks that has a far-reaching impact on the nature of the state and the functioning of democracy is emerging worldwide. The notion of governance is transforming the organization of the state and its relationships with private sector and civil society actors. A considerable amount of scholarly attention is now being devoted to analyzing and debating this transformation of state and democracy. Attention is being directed towards improving understanding of the wider public policy system in which the institutions of government appear to be involved in processes of negotiation, bargaining and compromise with a host of other actors.

The strategy of pursuing public-private partnership as a strategy of development has led to establishing new kinds of institutions that are not necessarily and not always part of the government hierarchy The fundamental concern here is that, with the formation of new institutions of policy-making and delivery of services and goods, how do the various actors with divergent orientations work together to achieve the goals of efficiency and equity. What is the impact of these new institutions on the functioning of democracy and the state? The issue of accountability is at the forefront of all academic and people's concerns. To whom are these partnerships accountable, and how? Who finds representation in these partnerships? Is the functioning of these partnerships transparent?

India's government adopted the new governance style enthusiastically as it began to prioritize the goal of raising the economic growth rate. In meeting this goal, the government saw its most important role in providing infrastructure, power, transport, roads, etc. However, these sectors demanded heavy investment, and the focus turned towards the corporate sector for financial and technological resources. The 11th Five-Year Plan emphasized the strategy of public-private partnerships for finding these resources. In a speech, the Prime Minister reiterated that a synergy between public support and private initiative could help multiply the productivity of resource mobilization. The government sought an alliance with the corporate sector to pursue this goal. Broad linkages between the government and the private sector began to be established by forging new institutions of consultation and advice. The Prime Minister headed a Council of Trade and Industry that had leading industrialists on board. Other economic ministries followed, and channels were opened up formally for advice. At the formal level, business organizations like FICCI and CII were represented in government advisory bodies, and these organizations reached out to policymakers to explain their demands. Liberal-minded prime ministers sought support for their policies from these organizations. In 2004, the Finance Minister requested 'the CII and FICCI to address some of our friends in the Left parties and convince them to increase the FDI cap'. In 2009, the finance minister, addressing a convention, exhorted CII to play a stellar role in making the Indian growth story a continuing one.

Other ministries, particularly those of Human Resource Development and Health, followed the economic ministries and established consultative bodies incorporating the corporate sector. Thus, at the policy level, the signal was clear. The role of the government had transformed itself; it was no longer to control the private sector to see that it works for the public interest. It was now to work with the private sector in public interest. In the shift of government to governance, the role of civil society has been very significant. There have been two kinds of strands in this role. One has been that of social movements that have taken the cause of the poor and the marginalized and made the government responsive to their needs through changes in institutions, laws, and procedures. The other has been the rise of what has come to be known as Non-Governmental Organizations that have taken upon themselves multifarious roles that include implementing governmental programmed as laid down in law. Social movements and Non-Governmental Organizations (NGOs) have carved out new spaces in the political processes and in delivering public services. While social movements have momentum of their own, NGOs have become partners in new policy networks. A National Advisory Council has been established under the chairpersonship of the President of the Congress party. This Council has civil society representatives and acts as a voice to influence government policy. It has specifically directed its attention to the social sector and has been influential in framing several policies in the arena.

The Council is not a constitutional body but wields influence because it is headed by the President of the party in power. The creation of such an institution is in keeping with the exhortation of The Eighth Five-Year Plan (1992-97) of re-examining and re-orienting the role of government by laying considerable stress on strengthening people's participatory institutions. It made a strong plea for a greater role in the private sector. It must be recalled that this Plan came at a time when economic reforms were being instituted, and a new governance style was being called for. Three Five Year Plans later, the Approach Paper to the Eleventh Five Year Plan has explicitly recognized that 'many civil society organizations have a proven track record of implementing programmes at the grass-roots level and they have shown impressive results in this area.'In May 2007, the Planning Commission announced the National Policy for the Voluntary Sector. This Policy is an expression of 'a commitment to encourage, enable and empower an independent, creative and effective voluntary sector, with diversity in form and function, so that it can contribute to the social, cultural and economic advancement of the people of India.' This policy further 'recognizes the important role that the voluntary sector has to play in various areas and affirms the growing need for collaboration with the voluntary sector by the Government, as well as by the private sector, at the local, provincial and national levels.

The Policy emphasizes the partnership of government with voluntary organizations and recognizes three instruments of partnerships: viz., (i) consultation, through a formal process of interaction at the Centre, State and District level; (ii) strategic collaboration to tackle complex interventions where sustained social mobilization is critical over the long term; and (iii) project funding through standard schemes. A significant achievement of the role of civil society has been the passage of the Right to Information Act in 2005. This has the potential to change the nature of governance in the country. Flowing from policy networks, the concept of partnership is also being applied at the level of providing public goods and services, which was the responsibility of public administration alone earlier. PPPs broadly refer to long-term contractual partnerships between the public and private sector agencies, specifically targeted towards financing, designing, implementing and operating infrastructure facilities and services that were traditionally provided by the public sector.

A Concept Note on Public- Private Partnerships prepared by the Planning Commission (2004) also points out that three things generally distinguish PPP from direct provision of services by governments, namely (i) a partnership based on well-articulated 'contract', (ii) a long term relationship between the public and private sector (iii) flexibility and responsiveness in decision-making. PPPs are embedded in the general idea they are the new implementing agencies replacing the ineffective and inefficient state and bureaucracy. The participation is being formalized in governance structures where the government and any of the other two actors in society can participate. These structures are not part of the government hierarchy and are being established as semi-independent institutions, though overseen by the government.

With all the caution about the power of the private sector to mould a PPP to its own interests, ambitious investment in PPP projects is planned in the 11th Plan and projected for the 12th Plan. In the infrastructure sector, the government relies on the partnership strategy for investment and technological resources. The investment in infrastructure is set to rise to Rs. 20,54,205 crores in the 11th Five-Year Plan period. During the 12th Plan, it is expected to be of the order Rs. 40,99,40 crores. (see GOI 2011) 136 projects had been approved by 2009. Several steps have been taken to facilitate the creation of agencies that can support this investment. The Prime Minister himself chairs the committee that looks after the implementation of PPP projects.

While most projects have not been evaluated, some infrastructure projects have come in for public scrutiny. The Joint House committee of Karnataka probing the construction of the Bengaluru International Airport has indicted several public functionaries and officials for faulty design and construction of the airport. The Committee on Public Undertakings of the Parliament has 'flayed' the National Highways Authority of India for irregularities in executing the traffic-intensive Delhi-Gurgaon highway, claiming that it made certain exceptions to the usual approach to projects to benefit the private concessionaire. (Indian Express, 17 December, 2009) For the first time, the Committee raised the question of how much should be the reasonable profit for the private investors which operate and collect tolls for periods extending to 20 years in such stretches. The private partner saw profit in light of the balance of risk and award and saw considerable risk in this case, thus pitching in a higher rate of profit. (Times of India, 9 October, 2009) While the challenge that the policymakers face in the infrastructure sector is that of creating a more favorable 'enabling state' to attract greater private sector investment, the story of PPP projects in the social sector has an additional challenge. This is concerned with not only creating the physical infrastructure that can provide health and education services but also providing them equitably. Public-private partnerships in the health and education sector appear to face problems that transport, roads or energy sectors in some ways do not face. These are in terms of reaching the poor and those who are deprived of these health and education services. However, in health or education, some innovations are taking place. Among the 16 case studies of public-private partnerships undertaken by Venkatraman and Bjorkman (2007), eight are those of the public sector and NGOs. Their analysis suggests that the most successful partnerships have been with NGOs despite the fact many terms and conditions have not been as favorable to them as to the 'for profit' sector. Poor patients seem to have benefited from the partnership arrangements. The NGOs have also succeeded in taking over the management of hospitals in partnership with the government. Another success story comes from Madhya Pradesh, where the government has encouraged the formation of Lok Kalyan Samitis, with representatives of civil society and hospital staff on board. They have been registered under the Madhya Pradesh Societies Registration Act 1973, with the mandate to manage the hospital and the powers to mobilize additional finances, apply them to local needs, hire staff on a contract basis and carry out other activities to improve hospital services.

Typically, the General Body consists of elected representatives, government officials, medical professionals, social workers and citizens. This kind of arrangement has had considerable influence on health reform. Institutions such as the Hospital Development Society in Kerala, the Medical Relief Society in Rajasthan, the Chikitsa Prabhandan Committee in Uttaranchal and Aspatal Kalyan Samiti appear to have roots in the experiment tried in Indore. Similarly, in the field of education in rural areas, the government has recognized the role of voluntary agencies in provisioning school education and enriching its quality. Network governance is assumed to contribute to the production of public purpose within a certain area. This public purpose expresses the social vision and the direction the policies should take to achieve this vision. But network governance is embedded in political and social processes at work in society, and they may not necessarily be conducive to producing public purpose on all occasions. Even the Prime Minister, speaking at a public function, has doubted the way we are going and has alerted the country to the growing symptoms of 'crony capitalism'. The reason is that in the Indian context, it is possible for big businesses to influence decisions in their favors and get away with it. The data on the Indian economy is a testimony to this view. This brings up the issue of the capacity of the state to negotiate and bargain in these networks. There is ample evidence to show that both political and bureaucratic leadership have not been too uncomfortable taking the personal advantages and benefits that liberalization policies have offered. Consequently, their capacity to negotiate is weakened. In addition, with the blurring of the boundaries of public and private interests, public servants may not feel the urge to pursue public interest alone. Thus, the partnerships are unequal and can allow certain private interests to dominate. While it is accepted that governance seeks to dilute the monopoly of political institutions in resolving societal problems and actively seeks other actors to play this role jointly or independently, the need to coordinate many players' roles remains. This coordination and coherence among a wide, disparate array of actors with different objectives and interests can only be brought about by the state and its institutions. In this emerging web of institutions, it should not be believed that the state has been rolled back and become ineffective. It remains a pivotal institution. Without the state playing its role and having the capacity to do so, the network of institutions cannot perform the functions they have been set up for. The state is the source of laws, and democracy legitimizes them. Laws are meant to resolve conflicts and maintain harmony in society. Together with making laws, the state is the only agency that can enforce them, for it has the monopoly on the use of coercive power.

Thus, a democratic state is based on the rule of law, and the critical question is its capacity to do so. This capacity does not stem from coercion alone but from legitimacy. With its extensive participative institutions, governance will presumably be better positioned to provide legitimacy than state-centric governance. Participative institutions help the state enforce laws cleanly and transparently; this is what the move towards governance does.

Democracy, meaning "power of the people," is a governance system where citizens hold ultimate authority, either directly or via representatives, focusing on participation, rights, and accountability, while paradigms refer to the differing frameworks (minimalist, liberal, social, participatory, deliberative) used to understand, measure, and implement democracy, addressing challenges like backsliding and the gap between ideals and reality by shifting focus from just procedures to citizen experiences. From Greek demos (people) + kratos (power), it's rule by the people, ensuring a voice in governance, equality, and accountability. From direct democracy (ancient Athens) to representative democracy (electing officials), evolving with Enlightenment ideals of rights and sovereignty. Free & fair elections, rule of law, free speech, association, and alternative information access. Major paradigm shifts in democracy's objectives have evolved from limited, exclusive self-governance to complex, inclusive systems focused on individual rights, economic welfare, and multi-stakeholder governance. Key shifts in objectives throughout history include1. From Oligarchy to Limited Citizen Rule (Ancient Greece) The initial objective was self-governance for a select group, moving away from aristocratic or tyrannical rule. While the model of governance by a single person or a small elite has largely been replaced by democratic systems, it still persists in various forms today, leading to ongoing crises concerning human rights and global stability. These systems are now categorized as autocracies or oligarchies, including absolute monarchies, dictatorships, and one-party states.

Persistence of Autocracy and Oligarchy

Modern Manifestations of Social Unrest Due to Inequality An intensifying concentration of wealth among the top 1% globally has occurred, with much of this wealth derived from inheritance or monopoly power rather than earned income. This dramatic rise in inequality often sees the rich accumulating wealth at rates far outpacing wage growth for the poor, fueling widespread discontent and movements questioning why they should obey the few without a fair reward. In many countries, the purchasing power of average wages is falling due to inflation and a lack of real wage growth, hitting low-income households particularly hard. This economic hardship makes basic needs like housing and healthcare inaccessible and can push even stable families into poverty, creating a backdrop of anxiety and social vulnerability significant crisis point is the rise of the "gig economy" and global supply chains where workers often lack formal contracts, social protections, and minimum wage guarantees. The demand for cheap goods and services in affluent nations can directly lead to the exploitation of underpaid workers in other parts of the world, with issues ranging from low pay in tea plantations to modern slavery conditions in other industries. In recent years, several countries have experienced widespread, often youth-led, social unrest and mass protests against ruling elites perceived as corrupt, gridlocked, and unresponsive to the needs of the general population. These movements are often sparked by specific economic triggers like punitive tax bills or food price spikes, which highlight the deep chasm between the political class and everyday citizens. Beyond direct financial exploitation, systemic exclusion based on race, caste, gender, and location continues to drive inequality and social friction. In India, for instance, the persistence of caste-based discrimination, a wide gender pay gap, and a significant digital divide contribute to ongoing social issues that disrupt harmony and hinder inclusive development. These modern examples demonstrate how the historical "crisis point" of social unrest stemming from the exploitation of the poor by the rich remains highly relevant, adapting to new economic and technological landscapes.

Dictatorships (Autocratic/Totalitarian): Rule by a single person or small group who seized power, often through military force, and suppresses opposition and civil liberties. North Korea (hereditary dictatorship with totalitarian control)Belarus one-party state, no elections since independence) Oligarchies and One-Party States: Power is concentrated in the hands of a small elite, such as a dominant political party or a group of wealthy individuals, even if nominal democratic institutions exist. China (one-party communist state)

Modern Crises and Challenges

These prior models face contemporary crises that challenge their legitimacy and stability: Democratic Deficit and Hybrid Regimes: Many countries exist as "hybrid regimes" or "electoral autocracies," where leaders hold elections but manipulate the process to ensure their power, creating a crisis of democratic standards and trust. Erosion of the Rule of Law: In many non-democratic states, there is a consistent decline in constraints on government powers, an erosion of fundamental rights, and a weakening of judicial independence, leading to human rights crises and internal instability.

The concentration of power and wealth often leads to social and economic inequality, which fuels internal conflict and mass protests, as seen in historical cases of revolution against absolute rule.: Modern autocratic regimes leverage technology for mass surveillance and propaganda, creating a crisis for freedom of information and expression, a challenge for global digital rights advocates. In the context of contemporary democratic objectives, the historical aim of "rule by the people" (demos) has undergone significant evolution, primarily focusing on radically expanding the definition of "the people" and deepening the practical application of civic engagement and equality before the law.The narrow historical definition limited to free, adult, male citizens has been systematically dismantled through several key movements and legislative changes that now constitute core objectives of modern democracy: A primary objective achieved in most established democracies is universal adult suffrage, ensuring voting rights for all adult citizens regardless of gender, race, property ownership, or social status. This was the culmination of long struggles, such as the women's suffrage movement and civil rights movements, that sought to make the "demos" truly universal. Modern objectives include robust legal protections to ensure that this right to vote can be exercised without interference or disenfranchisement. This involves legislation to prevent voter suppression tactics and ensure equitable access to the ballot box for marginalized communities.

Deepening Civic Engagement

Modern democracy aims for engagement that goes beyond simply voting every few years: There is a growing objective to move beyond "thin" electoral participation to "thick" engagement. This includes models of participatory budgeting (allowing citizens a direct say in public spending), citizen assemblies, and online deliberation platforms that seek informed public input on complex policy issues Modern systems aim for proactive transparency, making government data and processes easily accessible to the public (Open Government initiatives). E-governance tools are intended to lower barriers to interaction, allowing citizens to access services and monitor government activity more easily.

Realizing Equality Before the Law (Isonomia)

The objective of isonomic (equality before the law) has been broadened from a formal legal principle to a substantive social objective: The modern objective recognizes that simply having the same formal laws may not achieve true equality. It involves proactive measures like affirmative action, anti-discrimination laws, and social welfare policies designed to address historical disadvantages and systemic biases that prevent certain groups from achieving equal outcomes. A crucial objective is ensuring practical access to the legal system for all citizens, regardless of their economic means. This includes public defender systems, legal aid programs, and efforts to make the judicial system less intimidating and more efficient. The modern objective of "rule by the people" is to create a society where every individual is an equal and empowered participant in both the political process and the benefits of society, moving far beyond the exclusive clubs of ancient or early modern republics.

2. From Direct Participation to Representation (Roman Republic/Enlightenment)

As societies grew in size and complexity, the feasibility of direct democracy waned, leading to models of representation. The shift away from direct democracy (Athenian style) as a primary model of governance was driven by significant crises and systemic limitations, primarily the impracticality of scale and the potential for emotional, uninformed "mob rule" in large, complex societies. This led to the development of the more stable and manageable system of representative democracy. Crisis Points of Direct Democracy Ancient Athens was a city-state with a relatively small number of eligible citizens (around 30,000 to 60,000 adult males, excluding women, slaves, and foreigners) who could gather in one place (the Assembly or Ekklesia) to vote directly on all laws.

This model is logistically impossible for modern nation-states with millions of citizens spread across vast territories.: Philosophers like Plato and Aristotle, as well as historians like Thucydides, observed that large assemblies could be swayed by charismatic orators and collective passions, leading to impulsive and potentially irrational decisions (e.g., the Athenian Assembly's execution of generals after the Battle of Arginase, a decision later regretted).Citizens were expected to vote on complex military strategies, financial policies, and legal matters without specialized expertise or time for thorough research. This led critics to argue that the quality of governance suffered. The system of simple majority rule in the Assembly provided few formal safeguards for the rights of minority groups or individuals, a major concern that influenced later constitutional thinkers like James Madison. The Rise of Representative Democracy and Constitutional Republics The inadequacies of pure direct democracy in large nation-states led to the adoption of a new model: representative democracy (or a constitutional republic), which addressed the identified crises through delegation, professionalization, and structural checks and balances. The primary objective shifted to electing representatives who have the time and resources to study complex issues, deliberate, and make informed decisions on behalf of the citizenry. The U.S. Constitution, for example, was explicitly designed to be a republic with a system of elected representatives, not a direct democracy. Modern systems incorporate the separation of powers into legislative, executive, and judicial branches to prevent the concentration of power in a single body (like the Athenian Assembly) and safeguard against the "tyranny of the majority". While Athenian officials (magistrates) were often chosen by lot to prevent corruption, modern systems rely on elected or appointed professionals with relevant expertise (e.g., judges, financial officials, military leaders).While direct democracy at a national level is rare, its instruments persist as supplementary "corrective mechanisms" in modern representative systems, such as the frequent use of national and local referendums and citizen initiatives in Switzerland and New England town meetings in the U.S..

The shift to representative systems was a response to the inherent "crisis point" where direct governance models became inefficient and unmanageable for large, growing populations, frequently leading to internal conflict and instability. This crisis dynamic persists today, where modern states face similar challenges when their governance structures fail to manage complexity, diversity, and scale. The Modern "Crisis Point" in Large Populations Inefficient governance in the modern era can lead to a "failed state" where the government is unable to perform basic functions like providing security, essential services (water, education, healthcare), or levying taxes effectively. By 2030, more than half of the world's extreme poor are projected to live in countries characterized by such fragility, conflict, and violence. When large sections of a diverse population feel marginalized or excluded from decision-making processes and resource allocation, social tension and conflict risks increase. Inefficient distribution of resources, often exacerbated by corruption and weak institutions, fuels social resentment and can lead to mass protests or even armed resistance. Even in established democracies, governing large, diverse populations can lead to political paralysis and gridlock, where institutions move too slowly to address changing circumstances. This inefficiency in policy-making, such as an inability to pass a budget or address crucial problems like climate change or economic inequality, erodes public trust and can trigger widespread civil unrest. Population pressure combined with resource scarcity can lead to instability. For example, severe drought in Syria, linked to climate change, caused mass migration to cities, where people felt mistreated by the government, contributing significantly to the social instability that sparked the civil war. In multi-ethnic, large populations, governance failures often manifest as ethnic or communal conflicts when the state is perceived as biased or unable to manage competing demands for resources and recognition. The ongoing crisis in Manipur, India, illustrates how long-standing ethnic grievances, compounded by perceived government indifference and a lack of coherent policy, can spiral into widespread violence and a humanitarian crisis. These modern scenarios demonstrate that unmanageability in large populations remains a critical challenge, highlighting the ongoing need for effective governance models that can ensure inclusivity, accountability, and the efficient provision of public goods and services to maintain stability. The objective of using elected representatives and constitutional frameworks has been significantly refined in modern democracy to enhance efficiency, inclusivity, and accountability, moving beyond historical models like the Roman Senate.

Modern Objectives for Elected Representatives

The modern objective is to ensure that elected bodies reflect the diversity of the entire population, not just a narrow elite. This contrasts with the Roman Senate, which was largely aristocratic. Modern systems use various electoral methods (like proportional representation) to give weight to minority voices and ensure diverse interests are represented in policy-making. A core objective is holding representatives consistently accountable to the people they serve. This goes beyond periodic elections to include mechanisms like: Parliamentary procedures where the executive is directly scrutinized by the legislature. Laws ensuring public access to information about government decisions, spending, and operations to combat corruption and the misuse of power. Use of technology to enhance citizen engagement and monitoring of government activities. While efficiency was a goal in Rome, modern states emphasize the role of expert administrative staff and parliamentary committees who can deeply study complex issues like budgets, defense, and social impact assessments, ensuring more informed and effective governance than a general assembly of citizens or nobles could provide. Modern Objectives for Constitutional Frameworks and Checks/Balances Modern constitutions formalize the separation of powers into three distinct branches (legislative, executive, and judicial) to prevent the concentration of power, a principle articulated by Montesquieu. The objective is to establish an independent judiciary as a robust guardian of the constitution and individual rights. The power of judicial review allows courts to invalidate laws or executive actions that are deemed unconstitutional, a powerful check that was less defined in ancient systems. Modern constitutionalism aims to safeguard individual and minority rights against arbitrary state actions and potential "tyranny of the majority". This involves enshrining fundamental rights as justiciable, meaning citizens can seek legal remedies if their rights are violated. Beyond the three main branches, modern governance features numerous independent institutions (e.g., Election Commissions, human rights commissions, anti-corruption bodies) that provide additional layers of checks and accountability on the government's functions. the objective has evolved from merely managing a state efficiently to managing it efficiently, ethically, and inclusively, with robust institutional safeguards against the abuse of power.

3. From State Absolutism to Individual Rights (Enlightenment/Revolutions)

The objective of governance shifted from serving the monarch to protecting the inherent, natural rights of individuals. While the absolute monarchy model where power is concentrated in the hands of a single ruler is a historical precursor to modern democratic ideals, it has not been entirely eliminated. This "prior model" persists in the contemporary world in several nations, existing alongside modern representative democracies and often leading to significant internal and international crises regarding human rights and governance standards. Modern Manifestations of Centralized Absolutist Rule Today's examples of centralized, non-democratic power fall generally into two categories: remaining absolute monarchies and modern dictatorships/totalitarian states:

In these countries, the monarch holds supreme authority, unconstrained by a constitution, legislature, or other checks and balances, often ruling by hereditary right. Arabia. The King holds absolute power, governing based on Sharia law without a formal written constitution or an elected parliament: The Sultan acts as both Head of State and Head of Government with complete control, enabled by the nation's oil wealth to provide extensive social services without political opposition. Oman The Sultan has final authority over all military and political matters, though there is an advisory council (which cannot overrule his decisions). Eswatini (formerly Swaziland): Africa's last absolute monarchy, where the King holds near-total power, bans political parties, and appoints the prime minister. Vatican The Pope serves as an elected, non-hereditary absolute monarch of the city-state, wielding supreme legislative, executive, and judicial authority. United A federation of seven individual emirates, each of which is an absolute monarchy in its own right, with rulers retaining substantial powers. Dictatorships and One-Party States These regimes centralize power in a single person or a small elite group, often with no legal process for challenging their authority, creating systems that are effectively absolute in nature. These countries are ruled by single-party systems or long-standing autocratic leaders who face little to no political opposition.

Contemporary Crises Stemming from this Model

The persistence of these models leads to several contemporary crises: A lack of checks and balances often correlates with the suppression of fundamental freedoms, including freedom of speech, assembly, and the press. Instability and Unrest: Centralized, unaccountable power often leads to social and economic inequality, which can fuel mass protests, internal conflict, and civil wars when the populace demands change, as seen in various historical and modern contexts. Power transitions in absolutist systems are often fraught with instability, as there is no formalized, accepted process for succession, leading to internal power struggles or military coups. When a ruler is above the law, there is no legal mechanism for accountability for poor governance, corruption, or self-serving policies, which can have devastating economic and social consequences. The historical "crisis point" where perceived injustices, lack of individual freedoms, and intellectual challenges undermined centralized power is highly relevant today. While the "divine right of kings" is largely a defunct concept, modern authoritarian regimes face similar crises stemming from a lack of legitimacy, suppression of rights, and the rise of contemporary intellectual and digital movements.

Modern Manifestations of the Crisis Point

In many contemporary autocratic and one-party states, severe restrictions on freedoms of speech, assembly, and the press are common. Perceived injustices—such as arbitrary detentions, suppression of dissent, and lack of due process—fuel internal opposition and international condemnation. The internet has become a powerful tool for modern intellectual movements to question authoritarian rule. Social media platforms enable the rapid spread of information about government injustices and human rights abuses, circumventing state censorship and mobilizing populations in ways that parallel the circulation of Enlightenment-era pamphlets. The Arab Spring uprisings (starting in 2010), the protests in Belarus (2020), and movements in Hong Kong represent modern examples where perceived injustices and the demand for basic freedoms have brought citizens into direct conflict with entrenched power structures. These movements highlight the fragility of regimes that lack popular consent. In "hybrid regimes" where leaders claim a democratic mandate but systematically undermine the judiciary, legislature, and independent media, a crisis of legitimacy emerges. Citizens perceive the system as unjust and rigged, leading to cynicism and widespread social unrest. Modern civil society organizations, global NGOs (like Amnesty International and Human Rights Watch), and international organizations actively promote democratic norms and human rights as the legitimate standard for governance. Their reports and advocacy efforts function as a global "intellectual movement" that persistently challenges the legitimacy of non-democratic rulers. These contemporary challenges demonstrate that even in the 21st century, governments that fail to secure the consent of the governed, protect basic freedoms, and ensure justice for their citizens remain vulnerable to crises of legitimacy and social upheaval. The objective of enshrining individual rights, implementing the rule of law, and creating governments based on a "social contract" and popular consent has become the foundational model for most modern democracies. Originating from the Enlightenment and realized through revolutions, these concepts have evolved into robust international standards and ongoing governance objectives.

Modern Objectives of Individual Rights

The core rights of liberty, property, and freedom of speech have been expanded and deepened in modern governance: Beyond the foundational rights, modern objectives include socioeconomic rights (e.g., adequate standard of living, education, healthcare) as seen in documents like the Universal Declaration of Human Rights (UDHR). The focus has also shifted to protecting new rights, such as the right to privacy in the digital age. Modern objectives aim for substantive equality, actively combating discrimination based on race, gender, sexual orientation, disability, and religion through legislation and social programs. This moves beyond merely formal rights to ensuring equal opportunity and outcomes. Freedom of the Press: Freedom of speech has been bolstered by the explicit protection of a free press and independent media, viewed as crucial watchdogs against government abuse of power.

Modern Objectives of the Rule of Law

Implementing the rule of law involves ensuring everyone, including the government, is subject to the law. Modern objectives include: The objective is to ensure a judiciary that is truly independent from political influence, capable of impartially interpreting and enforcing the law against any party, including the state itself. Modern constitutional frameworks place heavy emphasis on due process rights, ensuring fair and transparent legal procedures for anyone accused of a crime, protecting individuals from arbitrary state power.A key modern objective in implementing the rule of law is the creation of strong, independent anti-corruption bodies that investigate and prosecute public officials, ensuring that no one is above the law.

Modern Objectives of the "Social Contract" and Popular Consent

The idea of a government deriving its legitimacy from popular consent has evolved into highly institutionalized forms: The objective is not just having elections, but ensuring they are free, fair, regular, and competitive, with independent electoral commissions overseeing the process to guarantee public trust and legitimate outcomes. Popular consent is now seen as requiring ongoing engagement, not just voting. This includes promoting high voter turnout, facilitating civil society involvement in policy advocacy, and providing mechanisms for direct citizen input (like referendums or public consultations). These principles have become international benchmarks for state legitimacy. Nations that systematically violate individual rights

4. From Elite Suffrage to Universal Inclusion (19th & 20th Centuries)

The core objective of "rule by the people" was challenged for its inherent exclusions, leading to movements for wider political inclusion. Historically, democratic citizenship was often restricted to elite classes, typically propertied men. This model has been largely abandoned in favor of the principle of universal adult suffrage in modern democracies, meaning all adult citizens have the right to vote regardless of their social, economic, or property status. However, elements of economic and social restriction, while rarely explicit in law, persist today through indirect means and elite-driven systems:

Modern Manifestations of Restricted Influence

Voter Suppression Tactics: While overt property qualifications are gone, subtle barriers can disproportionately affect lower-income and marginalized communities. These tactics include strict voter ID laws, purging voter rolls, closing polling locations in low-income areas, and limited voting hours, all of which make voting more difficult for the poor and working class. In several jurisdictions, particularly in the United States, individuals convicted of felonies may lose their right to vote, sometimes permanently. Because of socioeconomic disparities and biases in the criminal justice system, these laws disproportionately affect racial minorities and poor people, effectively disenfranchising specific social classes. A major contemporary concern is the immense influence of wealth in election financing and lobbying. The vast financial contributions from a small group of economic elites can distort the political process, meaning that while all citizens may have one vote, the "voice" of the wealthy is amplified, creating a de facto oligarchy or "elite democracy" where actual power rests with the affluent. The manipulation of electoral district boundaries to favor a particular political party or group can skew representation and dilute the voting power of specific communities, often impacting those with lower socioeconomic status. On an international level, some countries offer "citizenship by investment" programs, allowing wealthy individuals to essentially purchase citizenship and access to the benefits and travel rights of those nations. These schemes create a distinction in who can access full rights and mobility based purely on wealth.

Achieving substantive political equality is a key goal in modern democracies. This means ensuring that every citizen's voice and vote carry genuinely equal weight and influence in the political system, regardless of their economic background or social standing. The historical "crisis point" generated by social movements highlighting a "democratic deficit" and inequality is a cycle that repeats throughout history and remains profoundly relevant today. These movements emerge when the gap between the promise of "rule by the people" and the reality of exclusion and injustice becomes too great to ignore.

Modern Manifestations of Social Movements and the Democratic Deficit

Contemporary society continues to witness powerful social movements that mirror the suffragette and civil rights struggles, pointing out where modern democratic systems are falling short: The global Black Lives Matter movement highlights the persistent "democratic deficit" of racial inequality and police brutality. Protesters argue that the promise of equality before the law is not being met for Black citizens, demanding systemic reform and true justice. The movement challenges the state's legitimacy when it fails to protect all its people equally. Climate Action Movements (e.g., Fridays for Future, Extinction Rebellion): These movements argue that current democratic processes are inefficient and beholden to short-term political cycles, failing to address the existential crisis of climate change. They highlight a deficit in intergenerational justice, arguing that current decision-makers are disenfranchising future generations who cannot vote today.

This movement exposed systemic sexual harassment and power imbalances that persist even in modern, seemingly progressive societies. It highlighted a gap between legal equality and practical lived experience, pushing for cultural and institutional changes to realize true gender equality. Movements like Occupy Wall Street and various local living wage campaigns brought attention to the vast and growing wealth gap, arguing that political systems are skewed to favor corporations and the wealthy elite over the average worker. They underscore the "one person, one vote" deficit when wealth disparity translates to unequal political influence. Across the globe, Indigenous communities often use social movements to highlight a persistent deficit in their rights recognition, land claims, and self-determination within existing state frameworks. Protests often occur when governments approve resource extraction projects without proper consultation or consent, challenging the limits of popular sovereignty.

These movements are essential drivers of democratic evolution, serving as vital "crisis points" that force societies to confront their inequalities and redefine the objectives of a just and inclusive democracy. The objective of expanding the franchise to all adult citizens, regardless of gender, race, or economic status (universal adult suffrage), is now a foundational principle of modern democracy and a key international standard for legitimate governance. While nearly all countries have formally adopted universal suffrage laws, achieving truly mass participatory systems still faces significant contemporary challenges. The Universal Suffrage Norm The principle that every adult citizen should have one equal vote is widely accepted globally. Most nations have universal suffrage enshrined in their constitutions and electoral laws. For example, India adopted this principle from its independence in 1950, a revolutionary step at the time that empowered millions of marginalized people. Exceptions to the Rule: However, a few exceptions where universal suffrage is not fully implemented remain.In Saudi Arabia and Brunei, there are no national elections, and political participation remains highly restricted, functioning under absolute monarchies. Vatican City is an ecclesiastical state where voting rights are limited to a narrow body of cardinals. In other non-democratic states, such as North Korea and Eritrea, citizens are required to vote, but only one candidate or party is on the ballot, making the process a mechanism for state control rather than genuine political choice.

Modern Challenges to Mass Participation

The current objective has shifted from merely formal legal entitlement to ensuring substantive and inclusive participation. Challenges in 2026 include: Despite formal legal rights, informal restrictions hinder participation for marginalized groups. Issues like socioeconomic disparities, limited access to information, and discrimination can still limit who actually participates in the political process Modern tactics of voter suppression, such as complex registration rules, purging of voter lists, and limited polling station access, disproportionately affect low-income and minority voters in some democratic countries. While most countries grant women the right to vote, women remain underrepresented in political leadership roles. As of 2026, men continue to dominate top state positions and cabinet ministries, indicating a gap between voting rights and equal representation in power. The rise of sophisticated disinformation campaigns on social media can manipulate public opinion, making it harder for citizens to make informed decisions and undermining the quality of mass participation. Efforts are ongoing to ensure the full inclusion of specific groups, such as migrants, persons with disabilities, and those in conflict zones, who often face unique barriers to exercising their right to vote. The ongoing objective is to continuously refine the democratic process, using legal reforms, education campaigns, and technology to ensure that the principle of "one person, one vote" is fully realized in practice and all voices are heard.

5. From Minimal State to the Welfare State (Post-WWII)

Democracy's objectives expanded to include socioeconomic well-being and social justice. Classical liberalism, with its focus on "negative freedoms" (freedom from state interference), minimal government, and laissez-faire economics, was the dominant model through the 19th and early 20th centuries. This model was fundamentally challenged by the social and economic crises of the Industrial Revolution and the Great Depression. Crisis Points of Classical Liberalism Unfettered capitalism led to significant wealth disparities, worker exploitation, poverty, and poor working conditions. Critics argued that formal legal equality was meaningless without genuine equality of opportunity. The Great Depression demonstrated that unregulated markets could fail catastrophically, leading to mass unemployment, economic stagnation, and social misery that the minimal state was ill-equipped to address. Philosophers like T.H. Green argued that true freedom required not just the absence of constraints (negative liberty) but also the presence of opportunities and capabilities (positive liberty) for self-development, which sometimes necessitated state action.

The Rise of the Welfare State and Social Liberalism

The failures of classical liberalism led to a paradigm shift toward modern liberalism (or social liberalism/welfarism), which fundamentally redefined the state's role. The new objective was to balance individual freedom with social justice and equality through government intervention.

The government should actively promote individual welfare and create the conditions for human flourishing, not merely protect negative rights.: Addressing inequality through redistributive policies and social programs to ensure that all citizens have fair opportunities. Implementing oversight to prevent market failures, monopolies, and the exploitation of workers and the environment. Establishing a robust welfare state with government-provided healthcare, education, social security, and unemployment benefits to protect individual dignity and provide security against life's risks. This shift acknowledged that while markets are efficient, they require a legal and social framework to ensure fairness and stability, leading to the development of mixed economies and the expansion of civil and political rights that are characteristic of most Western democracies today. The Great Depression represented a profound "crisis point" that starkly exposed the vulnerabilities of purely market-based systems and the limitations of minimal-state governance. The resulting economic collapse, mass unemployment, and social misery created a void that contributed to the rise of authoritarian movements, including fascism.

The Failures of the Minimal State

Unregulated markets proved unable to self-correct in a timely manner. The widespread bank failures and mass unemployment (reaching 25% in the U.S.) demonstrated that the "invisible hand" could not prevent catastrophic human suffering. Without social safety nets (unemployment insurance, social security, public healthcare), millions were left entirely vulnerable to economic forces beyond their control. The failure of established democratic governments to effectively manage the crisis led to a widespread loss of faith in both democratic systems and capitalism itself.

The Rise of Fascism as a Response

In several nations, the perceived inefficiency and weakness of liberal democracies created an opening for fascist and authoritarian leaders who promised order, efficiency, and national revitalization: Fascist leaders like

Benito Mussolini in Italy and Adolf Hitler in Germany promised to end the political chaos and economic instability prevalent at the time. They advocated for a highly centralized, command-and-control economic system (though still working with private industry) that mobilized the nation's resources for state goals (e.g., rearmament, public works).Fascist movements capitalized on the social distress and national humiliation following WWI, promising to restore national pride and economic self-sufficiency (autarky).A Paradigm Shift to the Welfare State The response to this crisis fundamentally shifted the objectives of governance in democratic nations. The new paradigm, incorporating Keynesian economics and social liberalism, aimed to prevent a recurrence of such a catastrophe and counter the appeal of authoritarianism by:: Establishing robust systems of social security, unemployment benefits, and public assistance programs to provide economic stability and protect citizens from absolute poverty. Legitimizing an active state role in managing the economy, regulating financial markets, and undertaking massive public works to create jobs and stabilize the economic cycle. Reconciling the benefits of a market economy with the need for social welfare and justice to ensure all citizens had a stake in the system, thereby strengthening democratic resilience against authoritarian alternatives. This profound crisis redefined the "social contract," establishing the modern expectation that democratic governments are responsible for the economic well-being and security of their citizens.

The objective of the state actively managing the economy and implementing robust social welfare systems became the dominant paradigm after the mid-20th century. This "welfare state" model aimed to ensure social equality and well-being for all citizens, balancing market efficiency with social justice. While it remains a central objective in many modern democracies, this model now faces new crises and challenges that are driving a further evolution in governance objectives.

Current Challenges and Crises of the Welfare State Model

Many established welfare states are facing a crisis of sustainability. Aging populations in Europe and parts of Asia are increasing the burden on pension and healthcare systems, challenging governments to find the revenue needed to maintain current levels of service without causing excessive economic strain.

The rise of globalization and neoliberal economic thought from the 1980s onward has challenged the Keynesian consensus. The crisis here is that capital mobility and global competition have pressured governments to cut corporate taxes and deregulate markets, often leading to a reduction in social spending and a subsequent rise in inequality. The rise of the gig economy and non-traditional work arrangements has created a crisis for social security systems designed for full-time, stable employment. Many modern workers lack access to traditional benefits, highlighting a gap in the welfare state's coverage. Critiques of the welfare state often point to bureaucratic inefficiency and a lack of responsiveness to individual needs. This has led to calls for reform, including privatization of services or the implementation of market-based mechanisms within public services (e.g., healthcare vouchers).The funding and scope of the welfare state are a central point of political contention in many democracies, leading to legislative gridlock and a crisis in the ability to adapt social policies to new realities.

Emerging Objectives: A New Paradigm?

In response to these crises, new objectives are emerging in contemporary governance: The focus is shifting from direct provision of services to empowering individuals through education, skill development, and policies that encourage economic self-sufficiency and lifelong learning. There is a growing objective to move away from simply measuring how much money is spent on social programs toward measuring actual outcomes and using evidence-based policy-making to ensure efficiency. A new objective involves increased collaboration between the state, the private sector, and civil society to deliver public services and address complex social problems. In response to the precarity of the modern labor market and the potential impact of automation, several jurisdictions are experimenting with UBI as a potential new form of social safety net, fundamentally questioning the traditional welfare model. The current objectives are therefore a complex evolution, seeking to balance the core values of social well-being and equality with the demands for fiscal prudence, efficiency, and adaptability in a rapidly changing global economy.

6. From State-Centric "Government" to Multi-Actor "Governance" (Late 20th Century - Present)

The most recent shift involves a move away from the government as the sole provider of public goods to a more collaborative network. The model of top-down, bureaucratic, and state-centric "government" became dominant with the rise of the modern nation-state and the establishment of the welfare state objectives. This model is characterized by centralized authority, hierarchical decision-making, and specialized public administration. However, this traditional model has faced significant crises due to its inherent limitations in managing the complexities of the late 20th and 21st centuries.

Crisis Points of the Top-Down Government Model

Inefficiency and Red Tape: Centralized bureaucracy is often criticized for being slow, rigid, and inefficient. The volume of rules and procedures can hinder effective service delivery and responsiveness to local needs.: Hierarchical structures struggle to adapt quickly to rapid changes in technology, the economy, or unexpected crises (like pandemics or climate events). The top-down approach stifles innovation at lower administrative levels. Citizens often feel distant from decision-making centers, leading to cynicism, apathy, and a "democratic deficit." The model provides limited avenues for direct citizen input beyond periodic elections.

Inability to Address Complex, Cross-Border Issues: Global challenges like climate change, international financial crises, and cybercrime often require collaborative solutions that transcend national borders and involve non-state actors (NGOs, international organizations, private companies). The state-centric model is often too insular to manage these effectively. The Shift to "Governance" and Networked Management In response to these crises, a significant paradigm shift in objectives has occurred, moving from a rigid "government" model to a more fluid, multi-actor "governance" model. The new objectives include: Recognizing that the state is not the sole provider of public goods, the objective is to involve a wide range of actors—private companies, NGOs, civil society organizations, and international bodies—in policy formulation and service delivery. Moving away from strict hierarchy toward flexible networks and partnerships.

This involves decentralized decision-making and cross-sector collaboration to address complex problems that the state cannot solve alone.A core objective is enhancing transparency (Open Government initiatives) and creating robust accountability mechanisms that encompass all actors involved in public service delivery, not just traditional government departments. Leveraging technology to create more agile, efficient, and responsive public services and to open new channels for citizen participation and feedback, breaking down the top-down communication barriers. The objective has shifted from merely following established administrative processes to achieving specific, measurable public outcomes, often using performance metrics borrowed from the private sector. This paradigm shift aims to make the management of public affairs more effective, inclusive, and legitimate in a complex and interconnected world.

The traditional state models, characterized by top-down bureaucracy and state-centric approaches, face significant modern "crisis points" centered on issues of inefficiency, corruption, and the inability to effectively tackle complex, globalized challenges like climate change and financial crises.

The Modern Crisis of Governance

Traditional government bureaucracy often struggles to respond with the necessary speed and agility to rapidly evolving global problems. For instance, coordinating a response to a global pandemic or a rapid financial market crash often exposes the limits of slow-moving, siloed government departments. Perceived or actual corruption within state structures is a major crisis point that erodes public trust. When citizens believe resources are being mismanaged or stolen rather than used for the public good, the legitimacy of the entire state model is undermined, leading to social unrest and political instability. Transnational Challenges (Climate Change, Migration, Terrorism): Issues like climate change do not respect national borders. A purely state-centric approach often results in a "tragedy of the commons" or fragmented, insufficient responses. The inability to reach effective international agreements often highlights the failure of the traditional model to scale up to global challenges. The 2008 global financial crisis exposed how traditional regulatory frameworks were inadequate for overseeing highly interconnected global financial markets. The inability of single nations to manage cross-border capital flows and market volatility demonstrated a clear failure of the state-centric approach.

The Response: Objectives of "Good Governance"

In response to these pervasive crises, new objectives centered around the concept of "good governance" have emerged. These are intended to make governance more effective, accountable, and inclusive: A primary objective is to implement policies that make government operations and data publicly available (Open Government Data initiatives). This aims to combat corruption and allow citizens to monitor efficiency and decision-making processes. Recognizing the complexity of global issues, a key objective is to systematically involve civil society organizations, the private sector, and international bodies in policy design and implementation (multi-stakeholder governance): Governments are increasingly adopting objectives focused on "agile governance" and "policy labs" to encourage experimentation, rapid prototyping of solutions, and flexibility in response to complex challenges. The objective for tackling global challenges has shifted toward building stronger international regimes, treaties, and cooperative frameworks (e.g., the Paris Agreement on climate change), acknowledging that unilateral state action is insufficient. Modern objectives prioritize measuring and achieving specific outcomes (e.g., reducing carbon emissions by a certain percentage) rather than simply ensuring bureaucratic procedures are followed.

Achieving Transparency and Accountability

The objective of embracing "good governance" principles—transparency, accountability, multi-stakeholder involvement, and e-governance—represents the cutting edge of democratic evolution. This paradigm shift aims to make governance more effective, legitimate, and responsive to the complex demands of the 21st century. Governments are actively pursuing policies that make data sets publicly accessible, allowing citizens, journalists, and watchdog organizations to monitor spending, performance, and decision-making in real-time. The Open Government Partnership is a global initiative fostering this objective.: The objective involves strengthening the role of independent institutions, such as ombudsmen, auditor generals, and anti-corruption commissions, which operate outside of direct political control to ensure accountability across all levels of government.: Moving beyond financial compliance, modern objectives include regular performance audits that evaluate whether government programs are actually achieving their intended outcomes efficiently and effectively.

Involving Non-State Actors (Multi-Stakeholder Governance) Governments

increasingly work with the private sector to deliver infrastructure projects and public services (e.g., healthcare facilities, transport networks), leveraging private efficiency while requiring transparency and accountability mechanisms to protect the public interest. A key objective is the formal inclusion of civil society organizations (CSOs) and NGOs in policy development processes. This can range from public consultations and expert panels to formal roles in monitoring compliance with environmental or social regulations. For complex global issues like climate change or pandemic response, governance objectives now involve creating flexible, transnational networks of experts, private industry, and government agencies that share information and coordinate action, moving beyond rigid state-centric diplomacy.

Leveraging E-Governance for Efficiency and Engagement

E-governance aims to streamline and digitize public services (e.g., tax filing, license applications, benefit claims), making them more efficient, accessible 24/7, and reducing opportunities for corruption (e.g., India's digital identity system, Aadhaar). The objective is to use technology to facilitate citizen participation beyond elections. Tools like online town halls, e-petitions, and digital platforms for participatory budgeting (used in cities like Reykjavik and Paris) allow citizens to provide continuous feedback and directly influence local decisions. The use of data and technology in urban planning to manage resources efficiently (traffic, waste, energy) exemplifies how e-governance principles are applied practically to improve quality of life and citizen engagement in local governance.

Part I

Foundations and First Principles (Antiquity to the 18th Century)

The period from **antiquity to the 18th century** witnessed significant shifts in the foundations and first principles of political thought, moving from classical concepts of ethical rule and the ideal state to modern ideas centered on individual rights, the social contract, and limited, constitutional government. **Antiquity: Foundations of Ethical Governance**Political thought originated in ancient civilizations like Greece, Rome, and India, focusing heavily on ethics, order, and the "good life". **Ancient Greece (Plato & Aristotle):** Philosophers viewed politics as a branch of philosophy aimed at promoting virtue and achieving an ideal state.**Plato** proposed philosopher kings who would rule based on knowledge of virtue.**Aristotle**, considered the father of political science, brought practicality, analyzing various constitutions to find the best form of government that ensures stability and harmony. Athenian democracy, a direct form, was practiced but had limited citizenship.**Ancient India (Kautilya & Dharma):** Governance was rooted in *Dharma* (a code of duties and ethical responsibility). Treatises like Kautilya's *Arthashastra* focused on statecraft, efficient administration, and the king's duty to ensure public welfare and security.**Roman Republic:** Contributed practical aspects of governance, law, and the idea of a republic where power was distributed, influencing later Western thought.

The 18th Century: The Enlightenment and Modern Principles

The Enlightenment fundamentally challenged traditional structures, particularly absolute monarchies and the divine rights of kings, introducing concepts that form the basis of modern democracy. **Social Contract Theory:** Thinkers like Thomas Hobbes, John Locke, and Jean-Jacques Rousseau explored how governments derive their legitimacy from the "consent of the governed" through a social contract, replacing the idea of divinely ordained power.**Natural Rights and Liberty:** John Locke emphasized the inherent natural rights of individuals (life, liberty, and property) that the government is created to protect, laying the foundation for modern liberalism.

Separation of Powers: Montesquieu introduced the vital concept of dividing governmental power into legislative, executive, and judicial branches to prevent tyranny and ensure checks and balances.

Popular Sovereignty: The idea that the power to govern ultimately belongs to the people became central, culminating in revolutions in America and France that established new republics based on liberty, equality, and individual rights.

Would you like to delve deeper into a specific philosopher or explore the transition from these foundational ideas to modern **contemporary political theory**?

Classical political theory: foundations of ethical governance

Classical political theory spans from ancient Greece to the 19th century and is the bedrock of Western political thought. This era is characterized by an emphasis on ethical goals and the pursuit of the ideal state. Let's delve into some of the key contributions from this period.

Ancient Greece: the cradle of political thought

The origins of political theory can be traced back to ancient Greece, where philosophers like Plato and Aristotle laid the groundwork for future generations. Plato's "Republic" presents a vision of an ideal state ruled by philosopher-kings, emphasizing justice and the moral responsibilities of rulers. Aristotle, on the other hand, introduced the concept of empirical observation in politics with his work "Politics," advocating for a mixed government that balances different elements of society.

Roman contributions to political thought

The Romans continued to build on Greek ideas, introducing practical aspects of governance. Cicero's writings on natural law and justice influenced later thinkers, while Augustine's "City of God" juxtaposed the earthly city with the divine, adding a spiritual dimension to political theory.

Medieval political theory: blending faith and reason

The medieval period saw the integration of Christian theology with classical political thought. Thomas Aquinas, for instance, synthesized Aristotelian philosophy with Christian doctrine, arguing that reason and faith are complementary in understanding political order. His work laid the groundwork for the development of natural law theory.

The Renaissance and Enlightenment: reawakening and rationality

The Renaissance revived classical ideas, focusing on humanism and individual potential. Machiavelli's "The Prince" marked a departure from idealism, offering pragmatic advice on power and statecraft. The Enlightenment further advanced political thought with thinkers like John Locke and Jean-Jacques Rousseau, who championed natural rights, social contracts, and the concept of popular sovereignty.

Modern political theory: the rise of empirical and scientific approaches

The transition to modern political theory brought a shift towards empirical analysis and the scientific study of political institutions and power structures. This period is marked by a more systematic and data-driven approach to understanding politics.

The influence of the scientific revolution

The scientific revolution of the 17th and 18th centuries profoundly impacted political theory. Thinkers began to apply scientific methods to the study of society, leading to the development of political science as a discipline. Hobbes' "Leviathan" exemplifies this shift, using a mechanistic view of human nature to justify the need for a powerful sovereign to maintain order.

The emergence of liberalism and capitalism

Liberalism and capitalism emerged as dominant ideologies during this period. John Stuart Mill's "On Liberty" and Adam Smith's "The Wealth of Nations" explored the principles of individual freedom and economic markets. These ideas laid the foundation for modern democratic and capitalist societies.

Marxism: a challenge to the status quo

In the 19th century, Karl Marx introduced a radical critique of capitalism and liberal democracy. His theory of historical materialism argues that economic forces shape societal structures and political power. Marx's ideas inspired revolutionary movements and continue to influence contemporary political thought.

Contemporary political theory: integrating philosophy and empirical insights

Contemporary political theory seeks to synthesize the philosophical and empirical approaches of its predecessors, addressing complex issues like democracy, justice, and political value. Scholars such as Sheldon Wolin and David Held have contributed significantly to this ongoing dialogue.

The revival of normative political theory

Contemporary political theory has seen a revival of normative questions about what ought to be, rather than just what is. John Rawls' "A Theory of Justice" reintroduced the concept of justice as fairness, arguing for principles of equality and social justice that should guide the design of political institutions.

Feminist and postcolonial critiques

Feminist and postcolonial theorists have challenged traditional political thought, highlighting issues of gender, race, and colonialism. Thinkers like bell hooks and Frantz Fanon have expanded the scope of political theory to include marginalized voices and experiences, advocating for more inclusive and equitable societies.

Deliberative democracy and participatory politics

Contemporary theorists have also focused on enhancing democratic practices. Jürgen Habermas' theory of communicative action emphasizes the importance of rational discourse in democratic decision-making. Meanwhile, participatory democracy advocates argue for greater citizen involvement in political processes, beyond just voting in elections.

Globalization and cosmopolitanism

In an increasingly interconnected world, contemporary political theory must address the challenges of globalization. David Held's work on cosmopolitan democracy proposes global governance structures that can better manage transnational issues like climate change and economic inequality.

Environmental political theory

With the growing awareness of environmental crises, political theorists are examining the relationship between politics and the natural world. Theories of ecological justice and sustainability are becoming central to discussions about the future of political systems.

The evolution of political theory from classical to contemporary times reflects the changing concerns and complexities of human societies. From the ethical ideals of ancient philosophers to the empirical analyses of modern thinkers and the integrative approaches of contemporary scholars, political theory provides us with tools to understand and address the political challenges of our time.

What do you think?

How can contemporary political theory address the growing challenges of globalization and environmental crises? Do you believe that integrating normative and empirical approaches can lead to more effective political solutions?

Chapter 1

Defining Democracy and Paradigms

Defining democracy requires understanding its core principles and the various **paradigms** or models that have developed over time. At its core, democracy (from the Greek *demos* meaning 'people' and *kratos* meaning 'rule') is a system of government where power is vested in the people, who exercise it directly or through elected representatives. **Core Principles and Objectives**The fundamental objectives and principles of democracy include:

Rule of Law: Everyone, including government officials, is accountable under the law, which is supreme.

Equality: All citizens have equal rights, opportunities, and are treated with dignity and respect.

Individual Freedoms: Protection of basic human rights and liberties, such as freedom of speech, assembly, religion, and the press.

Participation and Accountability: Citizens actively participate in the political process (e.g., voting), and the government is responsible and accountable to the people.

Free and Fair Elections: Elections are held regularly, are accessible to all adult citizens, and ensure the peaceful transfer of power.

Necessity of Compromise: Given diverse interests, democracy requires negotiation and compromise for the common good and stability.

Paradigms and Models of Democracy

Different models of democracy emphasize these principles in distinct ways:

Paradigm/Model	Description	Key Focus
Classical/Direct Democracy	Citizens participate directly in decision-making and	High citizen participation, civic virtue.

	lawmaking.	
Representative/Liberal Democracy	Citizens elect representatives to make decisions on their behalf within a constitutional framework that limits government power.	Individual rights, rule of law, stability, efficiency through representation.
Participatory Democracy	Emphasizes broader and more direct citizen involvement in all aspects of decision-making beyond just voting.	Grassroots engagement, community deliberation, active citizenship.
Deliberative Democracy	Focuses on reasoned discussion and debate among citizens to reach consensus, valuing the quality of democratic participation.	Dialogue, public justification, informed and reflective decision-making.
Pluralist Democracy	Recognizes diverse interest groups that compete for influence, ensuring no single elite group holds all the power.	Distribution of power, group representation, competitive equilibrium.

The ultimate objective across these paradigms is to establish a system of governance that reflects the will of the people and promotes justice, liberty, and the common good.

What is democracy?

Democracy is often said to mean 'rule by the people'. An example of this is any system of government in which people vote their elected representatives into parliament.But simple definitions don't capture the complexity and opportunity of democracy.It's an ongoing conversation: robust discussion and debate that needs everyone's voices to work. That could mean voting, protesting, running for office or another of the many ways you can take part.Keep reading to explore how democracy evolved and the role you play in it.The word was first used in ancient Athens, which is considered the birthplace of democracy. It's a combination of two Greek words: demos, a citizen of a city-state, and kratos, meaning 'power' or 'rule'. Modern democracies took shape over many centuries. Citizens came together and worked towards a fairer society. They often had to fight to have their voices heard. This story of democracy continues today – most of the world's democracies are less

Democracy is a system of government where power is vested in the people, who rule either directly or through freely elected representatives [1]. Key characteristics include: Rule of the People: The citizenry holds ultimate power, typically through voting [1].Elections: Free, fair, and regular elections are held to choose leaders and representatives [1].Rights and Liberties: Fundamental individual rights and freedoms, such as freedom of speech and assembly, are protected by law [1].Rule of Law: All individuals, including government officials, are subject to the law, which is publicly promulgated, equally enforced, and independently adjudicated [1].

Governance

Governance refers to the process of governing—the way in which decisions, laws, and policies are made and implemented within a society, organization, or country [1, 2]. It encompasses the structures, processes, and traditions that determine how power is exercised, how citizens are given a voice, and how decisions are made and issues are addressed [2]. Governance is a broader concept than government, involving the interaction among the public sector, private sector, and civil society [2].

Effective governance is often judged on criteria like transparency, accountability, responsiveness, effectiveness, and inclusivity [2].

Paradigm Shift

A paradigm shift is a fundamental change in the basic concepts and experimental practices of a scientific discipline or, more broadly, in the fundamental approach or underlying assumptions of a system or society [3]. It describes a major change from one way of thinking to another, a transformation of a conceptual framework [3].A true paradigm shift is revolutionary and changes the basic assumptions, forcing a re-evaluation of existing rules, norms, or procedures [3].The term was popularized by American physicist and philosopher Thomas Kuhn in his 1962 book, The Structure of Scientific Revolutions [3].

Traditional Liberal Theory

Liberal democracy is a political ideology and form of government where representative democracy operates under the principles of liberalism. It emerged from Enlightenment thought and emphasizes protecting individual freedoms and limiting state power. Individual rights, liberty, and the consent of the governed Minimal or limited intervention in the lives of individuals and the economy. The state's primary function is to maintain law and order, enforce contracts, and protect natural rights (life, liberty, and property). Supports a market economy with strong private property rights and competition (capitalism/laissez-faire). Economic inequality is often seen as a natural outcome of individual ability and a free market. All individuals, including government officials, are subject to and protected by the law. Citizens choose representatives through regular, competitive elections with universal suffrage and secret ballots. Governmental power is divided among executive, legislative, and judicial branches to prevent a monopoly of power or tyranny. Constitutional principles and rights safeguard minorities from the "tyranny of the majority".

Social democracy is a political philosophy within the broader socialist movement that advocates for a peaceful, gradual transition to a more equitable society using established democratic processes. It evolved from a more radical 19th-century anti-capitalist stance to a reformist approach in the 20th century. Social justice, equality, and collective welfare. It recognizes that formal political equality may be insufficient without socioeconomic equality. An active, interventionist state that regulates the economy in the public interest and provides extensive social welfare. The state is seen as an agency for common good rather than a "necessary evil". Supports a mixed economy that combines private ownership with government intervention and robust social policies (e.g., progressive taxation, strong labor rights). Commitment to universal access to public services like education, healthcare, childcare, and social security, funded by progressive taxation Strong ties to labor movements and support for measures like collective bargaining and workers' co-determination to expand democratic decision-making into the economic sphere. Argues that democratic citizenship includes social rights, not just civil and political rights. Achieves goals through democratic means and legislative reform rather than revolution.

Summary of Differences

Feature	Liberal Democracy	Social Democracy
Primary Focus	Individual liberty and rights	Social justice and socioeconomic equality
Role of State	Limited, minimal intervention	Active, interventionist in social and economic affairs
Economic View	Laissez-faire/market economy with private property as a core right	Mixed economy, market regulation, and wealth redistribution
View of	Natural outcome of a free	A problem to be

Inequality	market	actively reduced through state action
Rights Emphasis	Civil and political liberties	Social and economic rights (e.g., healthcare, education)

Moments in history where existing models faced crises or became insufficient have been catalysts for major transformations across scientific, economic, and social fields. These periods of crisis, often marked by the accumulation of anomalies the current framework cannot explain, lead to intellectual upheaval and eventually a paradigm shift.

Geocentric to Heliocentric Model:

The Ptolemaic model, which placed the Earth at the center of the universe, was the accepted cosmological model for over a thousand years. However, as astronomical observations became more accurate, the model required increasingly complex additions (epicycles and deferments) to explain planetary motions, especially retrograde motion. The crisis intensified with Galileo's telescopic observations of Jupiter's moons (proving not everything orbited Earth) and the phases of Venus (proving it orbited the Sun). Nicolaus Copernicus' heliocentric model, which placed the Sun at the center, eventually provided a simpler, more elegant explanation, leading to a revolution in astronomy.

Classical Mechanics to Quantum Mechanics and Relativity:

By the late 19th and early 20th centuries, classical Newtonian physics, which had been the dominant paradigm for centuries, encountered numerous phenomena it could not explain. These anomalies included: Classical physics predicted an infinite energy output at short wavelengths (the "ultraviolet catastrophe"), which was inconsistent with observations. The energy of emitted electrons was dependent on the light's frequency, not its intensity, contradicting classical wave theory. Classical physics predicted that electrons in orbit around a nucleus would rapidly lose energy and spiral inward, causing atoms to be unstable. It also could not explain the specific, discrete wavelengths (line spectra) emitted by elements.

The Michelson-Morley experiment:

This "failed" experiment found no evidence for the luminiferous anther, a hypothetical medium believed to carry light waves. These crises paved the way for Max Planck's quantum theory, Albert Einstein's theory of relativity, and the development of modern quantum mechanics by physicists like Niels Bohr, Erwin Schrödinger, and Werner Heisenberg.

In Economics and Social Systems

The Malthusian model of population growth suggested that population growth would always outstrip food production, leading to eventual crisis (famine, disease). This model was largely rendered insufficient by the Industrial Revolution and subsequent agricultural and technological advancements that allowed for sustained, exponential population and economic growth not tied directly to land capacity. The crash of 1929 and the ensuing Great Depression exposed significant flaws in classical economic models, which assumed that markets naturally self-correct to full employment. The persistence of high unemployment and economic stagnation challenged these prevailing theories and led to the rise of Keynesian economics, which advocated for government intervention (through fiscal and monetary policy) to stabilize the economy. The abrupt collapse of market speculation, known in part as a "Minsky moment," highlighted the insufficiency of existing financial models that largely downplayed systemic risk and the potential for speculative bubbles to cause widespread financial instability. This crisis spurred new

Democratic Paradigms (Frameworks)

Focuses on competitive elections, freedom of expression/association, and information access as core components. Adds constitutional limits on state power and protection of individual freedoms (e.g., rights, rule of law). Integrates social justice, welfare, and economic equality alongside democratic processes. Creates avenues for broad citizen involvement beyond voting (e.g., protests, community forums). Emphasizes informed, rational, inclusive public discussion to reach decisions, aiming for transparent governance. New paradigms analyze democratic decline (illiberal, managed democracy) and the gap between citizen support and institutional failure, requiring focus on citizen experience beyond mere procedures.

"Democracy," "governance," and "paradigm shift" are core concepts in political science, sociology, and general discourse, defined as follows:Originating from the Greek words demos ("people") and kratos ("power" or "rule"), democracy is a system of government where power is vested in the people, who rule either directly or through freely elected representatives . Key characteristics typically include free and fair elections, the rule of law, protection of fundamental human rights, citizen participation, equality among citizens, and a system of checks and balances [1, 2]. Common forms include direct democracy (citizens make decisions directly, often in small communities) and representative democracy (citizens elect officials to make decisions on their behalf, the common model for modern nation-states) [1].

Governance refers to all processes of interaction, formal and informal, that determine how rules and collective actions are decided and implemented in a society, organization, or group [3]. It is a broader concept than "government" (which refers to the formal institutions of a state: Governance involves a wide range of actors besides the state, including non-governmental organizations (NGOs), civil society groups, corporations, and citizens [3]. Good Governance: Often used with the modifier "good," the term implies governance that is éffective, transparent, accountable, participatory, inclusive, and equitable [3].

Coined by the philosopher Thomas Kuhn in his book The Structure of

Scientific Revolutions, a paradigm shift is a fundamental change in the basic concepts and experimental practices that define a legitimate scientific discipline [4, 5]. In general usage, it describes a profound and often rapid change in a fundamental approach or underlying assumption that redefines how an entire field, society, or group of people perceives the world or solves problems [4]. It is a move from one dominant worldview to a completely new one (e.g., the shift from the geocentric model of the universe to the heliocentric model, or the societal shift brought about by the Internet) [4, 5].the interrelations, differences, and similarities between these three paradigms based on the information provided:All three paradigms share a foundational commitment to core democratic principles: They all originate from the core concept of demos (people) and kratos (power), meaning power is vested in the citizenry, either directly or via representatives. Each model incorporates competitive elections and provides avenues for citizen participation, though the emphasis and scope of this participation differ significantly. Fundamental freedoms like expression and association are considered vital components across all three frameworks to ensure a functional democratic system. The paradigms build upon one another sequentially. Liberal democracy incorporates and expands upon the competitive elements of procedural democracy, while social/participatory democracy integrates aspects of both while prioritizing broader societal outcomes and engagement.

Differences

The key differences lie in their primary focus, scope, and the range of actors and rights they emphasize:

Feature	Procedural/Competitive Democracy	Liberal Democracy	Social/Participatory Democracy
Primary Focus	Elections and procedures	Constitutional limits and individual	Social justice and economic equality

		rights	
Core Compone nts	Competitive elections, access to information, freedom of expression/associati on	Procedural components plus: Constitut ional limits, rule of law, protection of individual freedoms	Liberal components plus: Welfare, broad citizen involvement beyond voting (protests, forums)
Scope of Power	Focuses on how power is allocated and managed procedurally	Focuses on limiting stat e power to protect individuals	Focuses on broadening citizen power and ensuring equitable outcomes
Key Actors	Political parties, voters, electoral commissions	Government institutions, judiciary, individual citizens	Citizens, NGOs, community forums, government (as welfare provider)

Summary of Paradigms

1. Emphasizes the mechanics of democracy

Its success is measured by the existence of free, fair, and competitive elections, alongside basic freedoms required for political competition (like access to information and association).

Limitation: It is a minimal definition that often overlooks the quality of governance or the protection of citizens once elections are over.

2. Liberal Democracy

Builds on the procedural model by adding a crucial layer of constitutionalism and rights protection.It is defined not just by who rules, but by limits on that rule. Key elements include the rule of law, checks and balances, and robust protection of fundamental human rights, safeguarding the individual from state overreach.

3. Social/Participatory Democracy

A broad, inclusive framework that moves beyond procedure and individual rights into social outcomes and engagement.It integrates social justice, welfare, and economic equality as essential components of a true democracy. It actively encourages citizen involvement through diverse avenues beyond the ballot box (e.g., community forums, protests), aiming for informed public discussion and transparent governance. Traditional democratic theory encompasses two main perspectives: liberal democracy and social democracy. While both share a commitment to democratic processes, they differ fundamentally in their approach to the role of the state and the balance between individual liberty and social equality. Liberal democracy is a form of government in which representative democracy operates under the principles of classical and modern liberalism. It emphasizes individual rights and freedoms and a limited role for the government to prevent a "tyranny of the majority". Individual Rights and Freedoms: Strong emphasis on personal liberties, such as freedom of speech, religion, and assembly. Limited Government Intervention: The state's role is minimal, primarily to maintain law and order and enforce contracts, allowing individuals to pursue their self-interest and make their own choices with minimal interference (laissez-faire economics).All individuals, including government officials, are subject to the law, which is applied through fair and impartial processes and an independent judiciary.

Free and Fair Elections: A system of competitive, multi-party elections with universal suffrage ensures political equality and that the government derives its legitimacy from the consent of the governed. Constitutionalism and Separation of Powers: Power is distributed among different branches of government to prevent its abuse and protect individual autonomy. It generally supports a market economy with strong private property rights, viewing economic freedom as a complement to political freedom.John Locke (father of liberalism), Adam Smith, John Stuart Mill, Montesquieu, and Immanuel Kant.

Social Democratic Theory

Social democracy is a political, social, and economic philosophy that aims to achieve social and economic equality within a liberal democratic framework through gradual, reformist, and democratic means. Prioritizes social rights, such as universal access to education, healthcare, and social services, alongside civil and political rights. The government plays a significant, interventionist role in the economy to regulate capitalism, redistribute wealth, and promote the common good. Supports comprehensive social safety nets, including unemployment benefits, pensions, and public assistance programs, funded by progressive taxation. Emphasizes collective bargaining, trade union involvement, and workplace co-determination rights to protect workers from exploitation and ensure fair wages and working conditions. Accepts a market economy with a predominance of private property but uses state ownership or control of some strategic industries to benefit the public interest. Early proponents included August Bebel and Wilhelm Liebknecht; later influential figures include Eduard Bernstein, T.H. Green, and Anthony Crosland.

Summary of Differences

Feature	Liberal Democracy	Social Democracy
Primary Focus	Individual liberty and civil/political rights.	Socioeconomic equality and social rights.
Role of State	Minimal; limited to protecting rights and maintaining order.	Interventionist; used to regulate the economy and provide extensive social welfare.

Economic System	Emphasizes free-market capitalism and private property.	Supports a mixed economy with a regulated market and strong welfare programs.
Key Concern	Preventing the "tyranny of the majority" and state overreach.	Addressing the inequalities and social problems inherent in unregulated capitalism.

Historical Paradigms and Defining Crises

Democracy, derived from the Greek words demos (people) and kratos (rule), is a system of governance in which power is vested in the people, who exercise it either directly or through elected representatives. The history of democracy has been marked by different paradigms, each facing crises that eventually led to new models or expansions of democratic rights.

Historical Paradigms and Defining Crises

Paradigm	**Key Characteristics**	**Moments of Crisis and Insufficiency**
Ancient Direct Democracy (e.g., Athens, 5th Century BCE)	Citizens (limited to free, adult males) directly participated in assemblies to make laws and decisions.	Exclusion of most of the population (women, slaves, foreigners) exposed the model's inherent inequality and limitations of scale as political units grew.
Republicanism / Early Representative Democracy (e.g., Roman Republic, post-Magna Carta	Introduced concepts of representative government, constitutionalism, separation of	Internal instability, civil wars, and the initial restriction of voting rights to propertied elites highlighted the insufficiency of

England, US and French Revolutions)	powers, and the rule of law.	"republican" ideals to ensure universal political equality.
Modern Liberal Democracy (Post-19th/20th Century)	Characterized by universal adult suffrage, free and fair elections, multi-party systems, and the protection of fundamental human and minority rights.	Economic crises (e.g., the Great Depression, 2008 financial crisis), the rise of authoritarianism and populism, and the impact of globalization and information technology have exposed vulnerabilities in ensuring true equality, accountability, and the protection of rights for all citizens.

Key Moments Where Models Faced Crisis

Internal civil wars and instability exposed the weaknesses of its mixed government structure, leading to the rise of authoritarian rule. These conflicts set the stage for the shift of power away from an absolute monarchy towards a system where the monarch was subject to the law, as established by documents like the Magna Carta. While establishing foundational democratic principles, their initial models were insufficient, leading to subsequent struggles and amendments to expand participation and address systemic exclusions like slavery and women's suffrage. The Weimar Republic's collapse in 1933: Severe economic depression (hyperinflation and high unemployment), intense political polarization, and the use of constitutional emergency powers to allow the government to rule by decree (Article 48) created the conditions for the legal rise of Hitler and the end of democracy. The 1975-1977 Emergency in India: Widespread political unrest and a High Court verdict against the

Prime Minister led to the suspension of civil liberties and mass arrests, a crisis that emphasized the need to safeguard democratic institutions and led to a greater awareness of citizen's rights. The post-2000 "democratic recession" and modern challenges: A global decline in democratic quality, driven by a loss of trust in institutions, increased political polarization, disinformation via the internet, and economic inequality, has highlighted the insufficiency of existing models to address modern global challenges like climate change and the concentration of corporate power.

A book exploring paradigm shifts in democracy would typically be structured around historical transformations Paradigm shifts in democracy are indeed often structured around pivotal historical transformations. These shifts represent fundamental changes in the underlying principles, institutions, and practices that define democratic governance. Early models, particularly in Athens, featured direct participation by a limited segment of the population, often excluding women, slaves, and foreigners [1]. This was the initial "paradigm" of self-governance in Western thought. The transition from direct models to representative systems (republics and constitutional monarchies) was a major shift, necessitated by the size and complexity of modern nation-states [1]. This paradigm, formalized in the American and French Revolutions, centered on electing delegates to make decisions on behalf of the populace. Over the 19th and 20th centuries, waves of reform dramatically expanded who counted as "the people." Key shifts included the abolition of property requirements, universal male suffrage, and the women's suffrage movements [1]. This changed the very definition of a citizen within the democratic structure. This shift introduced the paradigm of constitutionally limited government, protecting individual rights (freedom of speech, press, religion) even from the majority [1]. This framework is foundational to most modern Western democracies. The collapse of the Soviet Union marked a significant geopolitical paradigm shift, leading to the rapid spread of electoral democracy to Eastern Europe, Latin America, parts of Africa, and Asia, cementing it as the globally dominant political system [1]. Contemporary discussions center on a potential emerging paradigm shift driven by technology, globalism, and concerns about democratic backsliding. This potential shift involves increased use of digital platforms for political engagement, "liquid democracy" models, and a greater emphasis on deliberative democracy to counteract polarization [1]. These transformations highlight how the structure of democratic ideals and institutions evolves in response to changing social, technological, and philosophical landscapes.

Challenges from Populism

Theoretical challenges to paradigm shifts in democracy in the 21st century center on the erosion of established liberal-procedural norms by internal and external pressures, particularly the rise of populism, the impacts of the digital age, and deepening economic inequalities. Populist leaders, often democratically elected, pose a theoretical challenge by exploiting democratic institutions to concentrate power and undermine checks and balances (e.g., judicial independence, media freedom), hollowing out liberal democracy while maintaining a facade of democratic rule. This challenges the traditional theory of "democratic consolidation," which assumed that once established, democracies would inherently stabilize. The challenge shifts from ensuring losing parties accept results (loser's dilemma) to preventing winning incumbents from permanently tilting the playing field and locking in advantages (winner's dilemma). Populism often mobilizes voters along exclusionary ethnic, religious, or cultural lines, which can lead to zero-sum political competition. This undermines the theoretical ideal of parties competing over broadly beneficial policies and compromises, fragmenting the political environment.

Challenges from the Digital Age

The digital revolution, while offering new avenues for political engagement, facilitates the rapid spread of misinformation, "fake news," and propaganda. This creates ideological "echo chambers" and deepens political polarization, challenging the theoretical ideal of an informed public sphere essential for rational deliberation. The use of "big data" and pervasive digital surveillance by both state and non-state actors raises profound theoretical questions about individual privacy and the potential for political manipulation through targeted messaging. The decline of independent, professional journalism, replaced by a fragmented and often partisan online media ecosystem, challenges the traditional role of a free press as a neutral gatekeeper and accountability mechanism in democratic theory.

Socio-Economic Challenges

Deepening economic insecurity and inequality challenge the theoretical link between economic well-being and democratic stability. When democracies fail to "deliver the goods" for a large segment of the population, citizens become disaffected, increasing vulnerability to anti-democratic alternatives and charismatic strongmen.: Economic globalization has increased capital mobility, which theoretically limits the ability of national governments to implement independent economic policies and taxation without risking capital flight. This challenges the autonomy of the nation-state, a core unit in traditional democratic theory. These contemporary issues force scholars to move away from linear, Western-centric models of democratization and consider more fluid, contested, and multi-causal explanations for democracy's evolution and resilience.

Network and Collaborative Governance

Emerging models of governance in democracy represent a paradigm shift from traditional, state-centric, hierarchical systems toward more collaborative, decentralized, and technology-driven approaches. These models often involve non-state actors and emphasize efficiency, transparency, and citizen participation to address the complexities of the

21st century. The recognition that governments alone cannot solve complex socio-economic issues has led to models of governance that emphasize networks and partnerships. This model involves collaboration among public, private, and civil society organizations in policy-making and service delivery. Power is interdependent, requiring negotiation and resource exchange among various autonomous actors. There is a significant movement toward devolving power and decision-making authority to local bodies (e.g., municipalities, village councils/gram sabhas). This "bottom-up" approach aims to make governance more responsive to local needs and empower marginalized communities through direct participation in local planning and implementation.

Technology-Driven Governance

Technological advancements are driving a major shift, allowing for greater efficiency, transparency, and citizen engagement.

E-Governance/Government 4.0: This involves using information and communication technologies (ICTs) to provide public services, enhance government operations, and facilitate citizen interaction. Examples include online tax payments, single-window clearances, and the use of big data for informed decision-making. Introduced in the context of the Fourth Industrial Revolution (AI, big data, IoT), this model advocates for adaptable, human-centered policymaking that involves rapid iteration and collaboration between government, business, academia, and the community." S-Governance" (Social Governance): This concept leverages social media and sentiment analysis of large datasets to incorporate the human element of public opinion into governance, aiming for a more transparent and accountable social model. Blockchain is being explored for its potential to ensure secure, transparent, and immutable record-keeping in governmental operations, which can help reduce corruption and enhance trust in processes like voting.

Participatory and Deliberative Models

These models aim to deepen democracy by moving beyond the act of voting to more direct and ongoing citizen involvement. This model focuses on inclusive and reasoned public dialogue among citizens to reach collective decisions, prioritizing open-mindedness and critical thinking in the public sphere. This advocates for direct citizen involvement in policy formulation, implementation, and evaluation through mechanisms like referendums, town hall meetings, and citizen assemblies. These emerging models collectively represent a move towards more fluid, accountable, and inclusive forms of democracy that seek to address the shortcomings of traditional representative systems in a rapidly changing world.

A table of contents designed to analyze major paradigm shifts in democracy would logically use both thematic and chronological organization to trace the evolution of governance. The structure would likely move from historical foundations to contemporary challenges and future models, effectively bridging traditional forms of governance with modern, and potentially post-national, democratic structures. Here is a proposed thematic and chronological structure: A Thematic and Chronological Analysis of Paradigm Shifts in Governance The concept of a "paradigm shift in democracy" appears in various academic contexts, often referring to a fundamental change in the dominant model of governance, theory, or practice. There is no single book with that exact title and structure; instead, several books and articles address different facets of this shift. Below are the structures and chapters from two relevant academic works that discuss the evolution and new paradigms of democracy and governance:

Example 1: Structure from Democratization: A Critical Introduction

This structure outlines a critical approach to understanding how the process of democratization has evolved and the various contemporary theories that represent a shift from traditional liberal democracy. Paradigm Shifts from E-Governance to S-Governance The provided text is an abstract for a book chapter titled "The text starts by quoting Abraham

Lincoln's famous definition of democracy: "Democracy is the government of the people, by the people and for the people. "It argues that the evolution of governance models should leverage emerging Internet technologies and the data from the social web to bring a "human touch" to governance. Shift to S-Governance: The text discusses a paradigm shift from traditional e-governance to s-governance (social governance), which is envisioned as more democratic, transparent, and accountable. As a step toward intelligent governance, it introduces the concept of "sentiment" in s-governance, utilizing sentiment mining and Big Data analysis to understand the human element and impact on governance. The impact of this approach is demonstrated through its use in research and practice.

"E-governance" refers to the use of Information and Communication Technology (ICT) to transform how a government operates and delivers services, while "governance" is the broader concept of how a government makes and enforces decisions. The transition from "e-governance" to "governance" implies moving beyond just implementing digital tools to achieving the higher-level goals of transparent, accountable, and responsive government. Essentially, e-governance is the "how" (using ICT) and governance is the "what" and "why" (achieving good governance outcomes). Definition: The application of ICT to streamline government functions and improve public services. Includes interactions between government agencies (G2G), with businesses (G2B), and with citizens (G2C). Digitizing records, providing online services, and improving communication and data exchange. To make government processes more efficient, effective, and transparent. The outcome and purpose The overall process of making and implementing decisions, and the results of those decisions from the perspective of those impacted. To achieve a better result, which is often defined as "SMART" governance: simple, moral, accountable, responsive, and transparent. Reduced corruption, increased citizen participation, and improved service delivery are outcomes of good governance. E-governance as a path to good governance E-governance is the method used to achieve good governance. By implementing e-governance, governments can create systems that make it easier to be accountable and transparent. The ultimate goal is not just to have e-governance, but to use it to transform the government into a responsive and participatory body. This goes beyond simple digital transactions to creating a fundamentally better system. "S-governance" most commonly refers to the "S" in ESG (Environmental, Social, and Governance) criteria, which focuses on how a company is run and its impact on people and society. This includes aspects like employee relations, diversity, fair wages, and labor standards. It can also refer to "Strategic public value(s) governance," a term from academic literature about public organizations and collaboration, or "Salience," a concept in sustainability governance related to the importance of science in decision-making, though these are less common. The "S" in ESG evaluates a company's relationship with its employees, customers, and the communities where it operates. This includes how a company treats its workforce, such as with employee satisfaction, fair pay and benefits, and diversity and inclusion. Companies measure and report on these social factors through metrics like employee satisfaction surveys, staff diversity data, and pay gap analysis.

Other uses of "S-governance"

Strategic public value(s) governance: This is a term found in academic research that examines how public sector organizations enhance public value through collaboration with various stakeholders. In the context of sustainability, "salience" refers to the importance of science-based information for decision-makers in governance. It's not a standard governance model but a concept about how scientific knowledge can be made more relevant and influential in decision-making processes, says ScienceDirect.com. A paradigm shift in democracy involves a fundamental change in its underlying principles or how it is practiced, moving from one dominant model to another, such as a shift from a purely representative model to one that incorporates more direct or deliberative forms of participation. Examples include a move from a focus on state control to a "good governance" model emphasizing transparency and citizen participation, or a shift in citizenship from being obligation-based to rights-based and socially engaged.

Forms of democratic paradigm shifts

The shift is from a model where citizens elect representatives to make decisions for them, to a model where citizens are more directly involved in policy-making and governance. This includes incorporating elements of direct democracy (e.g., referendums) and deliberative democracy (e.g., public forums).

This involves a move away from a purely top-down, state-led model of governance to one that emphasizes accountability, transparency, and efficiency in public services. It highlights the importance of civil society and the private sector in shaping public policy and managing society's affairs. The shift is from a model of citizenship that emphasizes obedience and moral obligations to one that stresses individual rights and critical thinking, while also fostering social responsibility and participation. This can be seen in educational curricula that move away from a focus on duty towards one that encourages human agency and social engagement. This represents a shift in how political and social movements operate. Instead of relying solely on large-scale mass mobilization, it involves a focus on micro-politics, which uses information and communication to influence behavior and shape public opinion on specific issues, as seen in public health campaigns.

A paradigm shift in democracy in developing countries

A paradigm shift in democracy in developing countries involves a fundamental change from traditional models to new forms focused on developmental goals, post-colonial self-determination, and different approaches to governance and citizenship. These forms often incorporate elements like developmental democracy, which prioritizes economic and social progress alongside political freedom; Afro-centric or post-colonial governance, which seeks to establish models rooted in local histories and cultures; and a shift from elite-focused to citizen-centric participation. Other emerging forms include a greater emphasis on local self-governance, integrating non-state actors, and a move toward negotiation rather than command-and-control state activity. This model views democracy not just as political freedom, but as an instrumental tool for development and enrichment. It seeks to address the failures of models that were ineffective in promoting social and economic well-being, as seen in countries where "bread is a rare commodity". Post-Colonial and Afro-Centric Governance: A rejection of Western-imposed models in favor of systems that are self-determined and rooted in the specific context of developing countries, particularly in Africa. This involves questioning imposed agendas and building a governance paradigm that aligns with local, non-Western values and historical experiences. Shift from Elite Rule to Broader Participation: A move away from a model that often empowers elites towards one that requires broad-based public participation from ordinary citizens to be truly democratic and effective. Decentralized and Multi-level Governance: A move away from a monolithic, bureaucratic state towards a system of multi-level governance that includes greater public involvement at the local level. This involves the incorporation of non-state actors into the policy-making process. From Command to Negotiation: The state's role shifts from a command-and-control hierarchy to one that engages in more negotiation and diplomacy with civil society and other actors. New Citizenship Models: A transition from citizenship defined primarily by obligation to one that emphasizes rights, individual agency, and social participation, as seen in the shift in educational curricula away from purely "obligations-oriented" models.

A major paradigm shift in democracy, moving from the traditional state-centric model to networked governance, involves a broader set of actors including non-governmental organizations and private companies in public service delivery. This shift, sometimes influenced by neoliberalism and a focus on efficiency, challenges traditional top-down, hierarchical government by emphasizing collaboration and interdependence among public, private, and civil society actors to achieve policy goals. This contrasts with earlier models where the state was the primary actor, such as the "transition paradigm" of the 1980s and 1990s, which focused primarily on a linear path to democracy through free elections.

Shift from state-centric to networked governance

From hierarchical to networked: The traditional model was a top-down, hierarchical system where the government was the sole provider of public goods and services. The new paradigm sees governance as a collaborative network of institutions and actors, both inside and outside the government. The new approach involves a wider range of actors, including citizens, community organizations, and the private sector, in shaping public policy and delivering services. The governance paradigm recognizes the interdependence of power and necessitates negotiation and resource exchange among various stakeholders to achieve collective goals.

Examples of different forms in developed countries

Public-Private Partnerships (PPPs): Developed countries increasingly use PPPs to deliver public services, from infrastructure projects to healthcare. Technologies are enabling new forms of citizen engagement beyond traditional elections, such as participatory budgeting and online forums for policy input. Non-governmental organizations and community groups play a larger role in areas like social care, environmental protection, and advocacy, working in collaboration with government agencies. Many developed countries are decentralizing power to regional and local levels, allowing for more flexible and responsive governance tailored to specific community needs.

Implications of the shift

The lines between the public and private sectors become less distinct as responsibilities are shared and collaborative partnerships become common. The shift is often driven by a desire for greater efficiency and innovation, drawing on the expertise and resources of non-state actors. This new model introduces challenges related to accountability, transparency, and ensuring that the interests of all citizens are represented when power is dispersed among many actors.

Key Concepts in the "Paradigm Shift"

The shift involves changes in emphasis in developed countries: The traditional model relies heavily on elected representatives. The new paradigm emphasizes more dircct involvement of citizens in decision-making processes, often through digital platforms (e-democracy). The "open government" movement, involving initiatives like the Open Government Partnership, pushes for greater transparency, accountability, and the inclusion of civil society organizations in governance debates. Role of Technology: Information and Communication Technologies (ICTs) are seen as catalysts for this shift, enabling new forms of citizen-government communication and engagement that challenge traditional democratic structures. Discussions in political philosophy touch on different interpretations of liberal democracy, including "liberal" versus "democratic-majoritarian" approaches, reflecting the complexity of modern democratic forms.

The provided text is an excerpt from a Wikipedia article titled "Types of democracy," which outlines various models of democratic governance and organization. The excerpt covers key classifications such as: Where citizens vote directly on laws and policies, including variations like participatory and industrial democracy. Where elected representatives make decisions on behalf of the people, encompassing forms like liberal, illiberal, parliamentary (e.g., Westminster), and presidential systems. Party Systems: Different structures within representative democracies, such as two-party, multi-party, and non-partisan systems. Types Based on Specific Influences: Categories based on location (workplace), ethnicity (ethnocracy), or religion (Islamic democracy, Christian democracy). Other

Types: A broad list including terms like consensus democracy, constitutional democracy, deliberative democracy, and democratic socialism.

The full article provides a comprehensive overview of how democratic principles ("rule by the people") are applied across different contexts, from governments to workplaces. The four common types of democracy are direct democracy, where citizens vote on laws themselves; representative democracy, where citizens elect officials to make decisions for them; constitutional democracy, which uses a constitution to limit government power and protect rights; and presidential democracy, where a president is elected to lead the executive branch, distinct from the legislature.

Direct Democracy:

Citizens participate directly in making and voting on laws, rather than electing representatives. This was practiced in ancient Athens and is seen today in forms like referendums and initiatives.

Representative Democracy:

Also known as indirect democracy, this is the most common form today.

Citizens elect representatives to make political decisions and laws on their behalf.

Constitutional Democracy:

A form of government where a constitution limits the power of the government and protects the rights of individuals.

This means the government must operate within the framework of the constitution, ensuring a balance of power.

Presidential Democracy:

In this system, the president is both the head of state and the head of government.

Voters elect the president separately from the legislature, and the president's power is separate from the legislative branch.

Parliamentary Democracy:

In contrast to a presidential system, the head of government (like a prime minister) is not directly elected by the people but is chosen from the legislature. The parliament has the main authority to carry out state tasks.

What are the three types of democracy in the world?

Constitutional democracy – governed by a constitution. Defensive democracy – a democracy that limits some rights and freedoms in order to protect its existence. Deliberative democracy – in which authentic deliberation, not only voting, is central to legitimate decision making. The Ship of Theseus paradox describes a ship that has had all its original parts replaced over time, questioning whether it is still the same ship. There is no single ship with this name that has a known history of democracy; instead, related concepts include a podcast titled "Democracy Paradox" and historical analyses of democracy's challenges, such as the "ship of state" analogy from Plato.

The Ship of Theseus paradox

Origin: The paradox was famously recorded by the ancient Greek philosopher Plutarch in his "Life of Theseus".: The Athenians preserved the ship that Theseus used to return from Crete by replacing its planks one by one as they decayed. The question arises: if all the original planks are replaced, is it still the same ship? This thought experiment is used to discuss the philosophical concept of identity over time, with philosophers like Thomas Hobbes and John Locke also contributing to the discussion. Not a single historical ship: There is no historical vessel called the "Democracy Paradox Ship." The term likely refers to the philosophical paradox applied to the concept of democracy or a podcast with that name. Plato's "Ship of State": Plato used a similar analogy to discuss the paradoxes of democracy. In this analogy, the ship's captain is the true expert, but the mutinous crew (the people) can be swayed by charismatic leaders to take control and steer the ship poorly.

"Democracy Paradox" podcast: A podcast named "Democracy

Paradox" explores the complex and often paradoxical nature of democracy in a modern context, discussing topics like civil resistance, populism, and political systems

The "democracy paradox" refers to the tension between democracy's ideals and reality, such as citizens voting for anti-democratic parties or the state itself controlling the process of choosing leaders. The "shift paradox" likely refers to the observation that the conditions necessary to establish a democracy may differ from the conditions needed to maintain it, a concept discussed in relation to democratic emergence versus backsliding, say scholars on the Democracy Paradox podcast.

Democracy paradox

Voting against democratic values: A key paradox is that democracy empowers people to vote for parties or leaders who may seek to undermine core democratic values like liberty and equality. This can be a reaction to the inclusion of previously marginalized groups, leading to support for majoritarian parties. The paradox is also seen in how current officeholders control the very process of elections. This can involve defining who is a voter, limiting access, and manipulating electoral districts, which means the leaders choose their electorate. Another aspect is that many citizens do not actively participate in political life beyond voting, yet they may still support democratic principles. This raises questions about what constitutes true democratic engagement. While democracy is based on deliberation, it can lead to slow decision-making because many people must be consulted. This process can also become focused on power struggles rather than morality.

Conditions for establishing versus maintaining democracy: The "shift paradox" highlights that the factors needed to start a democracy (democratization) might be different from those needed to prevent its decline (democratic stability). The conditions that explain the rise of a democracy are often different from those that explain its subsequent backsliding or setbacks. For instance, overcoming counter-revolution in an established democracy requires different strategies than achieving initial democratic gains. The focus of political science needs to shift from simply explaining why democracies emerge to also understanding the distinct causes and patterns of democratic decay. Democracy's Paradox: Social Hierarchies, Majoritarian Politics, and Inclusion

The paradox of people voting for parties that go against core democratic values like liberty, equality, and fraternity is a growing concern. This is seen in India and other democracies where many are attracted to strong leaders, free-market policies, and nationalist promises. This trend is partly a reaction to democracy empowering marginalized groups, which has triggered resistance from established social hierarchies. This resistance creates opportunities for majoritarian parties to gain support.

Additionally, other major political parties have failed to keep up with social changes, making old ideas about secularism seem outdated. To move forward, it's suggested that society should go beyond just tolerating minorities and actively embrace the diversity that reflects the majority's lived experiences.

What factors have helped social hierarchies stay strong even as democracy expands? How can other major political parties change to effectively oppose majoritarian ideologies? What can be done to promote a more inclusive approach to diversity in today's democratic societies?

Examples of paradigm shifts in democracy:

paradigm shift in democracy refers to a fundamental change in the dominant way of thinking about and practicing democratic governance, moving away from traditional models like liberal-procedural democracy towards new frameworks. This can manifest as a shift in national political paradigms, such as a move from pluralistic democracy to more majoritarian systems, or in new approaches to governance itself, like incorporating more participatory development and civil society engagement. It also includes changes in research and political theory, moving beyond just elections and institutions to consider broader social and cultural factors.

From liberal-procedural to other models: Many democracies are experiencing a shift away from a focus on just the formal processes (elections, institutions) to a broader understanding of democracy. This includes challenges to the traditional "liberal-procedural" model. Rise of majoritarianism: Some nations have seen a shift towards majoritarian politics, where the interests of the majority group become a primary focus, sometimes at the expense of minority rights, leading to changes in secularism, pluralism, and the rule of law.

Incorporating new forms of participation: There is a move to integrate more direct citizen participation into governance, sometimes through mechanisms like citizens' assemblies or other forms of deliberative democracy, which focus on collective decision-making based on evidence.

Re-evaluation of governance models: Some countries are moving away from purely Western-inspired liberal democracy models and developing unique, alternative models that incorporate local values and historical context.

Evolving voter behavior: Demographic shifts, like a younger electorate, along with the influence of the internet and changing aspirations, are changing how people vote and what they expect from the government.

Focus on good governance: Shifting the focus from just democratic ideals to the practical outcomes of governance, such as efficiency, accountability, and the effective delivery of public services.

Key Themes in the Paradigm Shift of Democracy

The shift itself is often discussed in terms of moving away from traditional, state-centric, or purely liberal-democratic models toward more inclusive, participatory, or global forms of governance. Common themes include:

From "Change-Oriented" to "Governance-Oriented": A focus on practical state governance and administration rather than just the process of transitioning to democracy.

From State-Centric to Post national: Recognizing global issues that transcend national borders (climate change, financial crises) requiring supranational or transnational democratic models.

Emphasis on Good Governance: A move toward principles of efficiency, effectiveness, accountability, and public service, often involving the integration of private-sector management styles (New Public Management).

New Forms of Participation: Exploring alternative democratic practices like deliberative democracy, e-governance, and various forms of social innovation and community empowerment.

"Democracy paradox" and "democratic paradigm" refer to distinct concepts in political theory. A paradigm in this context is a prevailing framework or model of democratic governance, while a paradox is a seemingly self-contradictory aspect of democracy that challenges existing assumptions.

The Democratic Paradigm

A democratic paradigm is a model or framework that shapes the understanding and implementation of democracy in a society. The dominant model today is often liberal democracy, which combines majority rule (democracy) with the protection of individual and minority rights, the rule of law, and institutions like a free press and an independent judiciary.

Key aspects of this paradigm include:

Elections and Representation: Regular, free, and fair elections are a core mechanism for citizens to express their preferences and hold leaders accountable.

Constitutionalism: The belief that a constitution, which may be established by consensus, provides a foundational standard for legitimate rule and protects fundamental rights.

Informed Citizenship: The idea that a functional democracy requires a well-informed citizenry capable of making rational choices and participating in public deliberation.

This paradigm provides a general framework for how a democratic system should ideally function, though its practical application faces ongoing challenges.

The Democracy Paradox

The term "democracy paradox" refers to a number of inherent tensions or contradictions within democratic theory and practice. These paradoxes often highlight the fragility of democracy and the challenges in reconciling its core ideals.

Key paradoxes include:

The Paradox of the Founding/Sovereignty: This points to the challenge of establishing a purely democratic constitution, as the procedures to create legitimacy cannot be self-generated purely by the people without some prior framework or authority.

The Paradox of Majority Rule (Popper's Paradox): The possibility that a democratic majority might vote to end democracy itself or elect a tyrant, thereby using democratic means to undermine democratic principles. This highlights a tension between the principle of majority rule and the protection of a tolerant, open society against intolerant forces.

The Paradox of Representation: The dilemma where citizens rely on political parties to realize their preferences, yet the compromises inherent in a multi-party system or coalition government may lead to outcomes that contradict individual voters' original preferences.

The Paradox of Participation vs. Truncated Norms: As seen in contemporary India, a rise in voter participation can occur simultaneously with an erosion of substantive democratic norms (e.g., minority rights, institutional deference).

The Paradox of Liberalism and Democracy: The tension between the "democratic" element (will of the majority/popular sovereignty) and the "liberal" element (individual rights/rule of law), where one may constrain the other.

Understanding these paradoxes is essential for a complete theory of democracy, as it moves beyond idealized models to address the practical vulnerabilities and tensions that political systems face.

Key Themes in the Paradigm Shift of Democracy

The shift itself is often discussed in terms of moving away from traditional, state-centric, or purely liberal-democratic models toward more inclusive, participatory, or global forms of governance. Common themes include:

From "Change-Oriented" to "Governance-Oriented": A focus on practical state governance and administration rather than just the process of transitioning to democracy.

From State-Centric to Post national: Recognizing global issues that transcend national borders (climate change, financial crises) requiring supranational or transnational democratic models.

Emphasis on Good Governance: A move toward principles of efficiency, effectiveness, accountability, and public service, often involving the integration of private-sector management styles (New Public Management).

New Forms of Participation: Exploring alternative democratic practices like deliberative democracy, e-governance, and various forms of social innovation and community empowerment.

In India, the procedure of shifting the paradigm for good governance has been dynamic and continuing. A notion known as "good governance" includes a number of rules and procedures designed to guarantee the efficiency, effectiveness, and accountability of governmental institutions.

India's approach to governance has gone through numerous stages of evolution over the years. The shift in the good governance paradigm in India is a result of on-going efforts to adapt to shifting economic and sociological circumstances while respecting democratic ideals and enhancing the provision of public services. It is a dynamic process that adapts to the demands and difficulties of a varied and rapidly modernizing country. The combined result of the two - open and accountable executive governance while concurrently involving. The participation of the people in the formulation of policies and in ensuring their efficient execution has been beneficial for the state of the nation as a whole.

A paradigm is a point of view, a way of conceiving, or a way of viewing social and natural phenomena. A nation's development can be understood using a variety of paradigms. Management specialists, such as Peter F. Drucker (1991), asserted that management factors were more to blame for the state's inability to bring wealth to its people. In accordance with this idea, the World Bank and UNDP created the notion that good governance, which places more emphasis on its components than on the entities or individuals who make up governmental institutions. In essence, "the way" or "the exercise" of management is good governance. Some people believe that countries emerge impoverished because they lack enough natural resources to serve as the foundational funding for construction. The creator of modern management, Peter F. Drucker (1991) later refuted that theory and asserted that the state's management was more to blame for the inability of the state to generate prosperity (causa prima). The UNDP and the World Bank expressed support for the proposal, which sparked the "good governance" paradigm, which is a governance reform.

New Public Management

Globalization has had a huge impact on public administration, stressing change and reinventing public administration with a managerial approach. Since the early 1980s, administration has faced significant hurdles in trying to lessen its reliance on bureaucracy, slow the growth of expenditures, and find innovative ways to provide public services. The New Public Management Perspective recommends a number of reform strategies for structuring and providing citizens with services through market mechanisms. As governments all over the world started consuming limited resources, there was a sweeping onslaught on the public sector and bureaucracy starting in the 1980s. The NPM perspective is the result of a number of things coming together. These consist of:

Influence of Neo Liberalism

There has been a powerful influence of nco-liberal political ideology during the 1980s and 1990s. Neo-liberalism favoured dominant presence of market forces than the state. Concepts such as efficiency, markets, competition, consumer choice, etc. had gained predominance. Neo liberalism favoured cutting back of welfare state, maximizing individual liberty and freedom, and encouraging market mechanisms leading to equitable outcomes. Free markets unrestrained by government, removal of barriers to facilitate the free flow of goods and money and privatization were considered significant measures for economic growth. The then prevailing scenario favoured roll back by the state and the space created by it to be filled with the private sector. The state was expected to promote the efficient functioning of markets.

Public Choice Approach

The development of the new public management approach was significantly influenced by the public choice methodology. It was proposed by economists like Tullock, Niskanen, and Buchanan, and its main assumption is that 'self-interest' drives all human conduct. NPM aims to spread a new way of thinking that emphasizes the following:

- The current changing environment necessitates government reforms;
- There is a need to shift government mindset from merely carrying out obligations to performance direction; and
- Public organizations must be risk-taking, mission-oriented, and

service-oriented.

Nuances of Governance in Sarkar

"We are modernizing governmental processes and incorporating modern technology in order to make institutions more accountable, efficient, and participatory. India's entire population will gain from this.

In modern India, good governance is a dynamic idea and a crucial component of the socio-political environment of the nation. It includes a variety of values and procedures designed to guarantee the effectiveness, productivity, openness, and attentiveness of governmental institutions. The government's processes and procedures need to be simplified in order to improve good governance and speed up the entire system. Another sign of the public's faith in the government is the movement toward self-certification in place of affidavits and attestations. Another area of concentration is the elimination of onerous, antiquated laws that are no longer necessary. In modern India, efforts are made to address problems and enhance the provision of public services while respecting democratic norms and principles. This process is dynamic and continuing.

Political governance must be strengthened by implementing the proper decentralization strategies, making elected officials responsive to and accountable to the people, building their capacities through education, awareness, and training, holding periodic elections that are free and fair, ensuring an impartial judiciary, and enhancing the efficiency of the civil service. Economic governance must be given priority through adequate budgetary support to socially important areas like housing, health, and education, as well as through effective tax and subsidy systems. Additionally, the government must support the growth of the private sector by establishing sound business practices, a stable economic climate, an effective regulatory framework, and the preservation of the interests of all parties involved, including workers, consumers, and society at large.

Civic governance entails utilizing people's inherent initiative, enhancing their capacity to manage their own lives, and educating and empowering them to actively participate in democratic governing processes. Any nation pursuing good governance must take steps to ensure a proper balance between the public, private, and civic sectors, as well as between economic growth and social justice. To achieve good governance, the government, business, and civil society must strike the right balance between their respective responsibilities to guarantee development that is focused on the needs of the people.

Reforms must be made in the political, economic, social, and administrative spheres in order to achieve good governance. Investing appropriately in human needs and providing social security systems for the underprivileged and marginalized are only two of the many strategies used to promote good governance. Enhancing the capability of the civil services using appropriate reform measures that match performance and accountability; strengthening the state institutions; introducing appropriate reforms to improve the effectiveness of the parliament; a new structure for government-business cooperation is being developed, along with new alliances being formed with the civic society.

Reforms are necessary for good governance on a number of levels, including the political, economic, social, and administrative. The pursuit of good governance is a multi-pronged strategy that includes: Reorienting the priorities of the State through appropriate investments in human needs and the establishment of social safety nets for the poor and marginalized; Strengthening the State institutions; Implementing suitable changes in enhancing the operation of parliament and increasing its effectiveness; and Increasing the capacity of the civil services through appropriate reform measures that match performance and a competitive compensation system.

- Creating new partnerships involving civil society; and
- Creating an innovative structure for cooperation between the government and business.

In order to respond to the shifting demands and ambitions of its varied people, the government keeps modifying its policies and procedures. The government views public grievance redress as a crucial element of a responsive administration. I have given orders to all the Ministries to make sure that public issues are given first consideration. To promote holistic development, "good governance" aims to combine political, economic, and social processes. The interaction between globalization and good governance, if properly handled, might become a transformative process to stabilize society. Improvements in public security, economic management, and public administration; shared systems of values through key public and private sector institutions; development of civil society and indigenous executive, legislative, judicial, and administrative institutions; and good governance, democratic development, and an effective capacity for development are all ways to achieve this type of stabilization (Kiggundu, 2002).

The government would operate as a SMART (Simple, Moral, Accountable, Responsive and Transparent) Government as part of a good governance strategy. While increasing its skills, promoting and supporting policy making and performance in the public sector, it would serve as a growth facilitator and catalyst, remain sensitive to the need for social equality and well-being, and operate as a catalyst for growth. As power and authority shift from governors to the governed, governance is no longer governor-centric.

Governance in Society

Governance in society encompasses a wide range of activities, processes, and structures that involve decision-making, authority, and the management of resources to ensure the well-being and functioning of a community or nation. The nuances of governance are complex and multifaceted, and they can vary significantly from one society to another. Here are some key nuances of governance in society:

Democratic vs. Authoritarian Governance

One of the fundamental nuances of governance is the type of political system in place. Democracies emphasize citizen participation, rule of law, and accountability, while authoritarian regimes are characterized by centralized power and limited political freedoms.

Legal Framework and Rule of Law: Governance is often defined by the legal framework that guides it. Rule of law ensures that government actions are consistent with established laws and principles, protecting individual rights and providing a framework for resolving disputes.

Accountability and Transparency: Good governance includes mechanisms for holding public officials accountable for their actions. Transparency in government operations, decision-making, and financial matters is crucial for building trust and preventing corruption.

Civil Socicty Engagement: Civil society organizations, including NGOs and community groups, play a significant role in governance by advocating for specific issues, monitoring government activities, and providing checks and balances to the government's power.

Decentralization vs. Centralization: The distribution of governance authority can vary, with some societies favoring centralized decision-making and others opting for decentralization, which allows local governments or communities to have more autonomy in decision-making.

Governance in Market

The governance of markets involves a complex interplay between government regulations, industry standards, corporate governance, and various stakeholders. It encompasses the rules and mechanisms that govern economic activities within a market system. Here are some of the key nuances of governance in markets:

Regulation and Compliance: Government regulations play a critical role in governing markets. These regulations can cover a wide range of areas, including consumer protection, competition, environmental standards, and financial stability. Market participants, such as businesses, must comply with these regulations, which are often enforced by government agencies. Compliance ensures fair competition, consumer safety, and the overall stability of the market.

Market Competition: Healthy competition is a fundamental aspect of market governance. It encourages efficiency, innovation, and better outcomes for consumers. Regulatory bodies often monitor and intervene to prevent anti-competitive practices, such as monopolies or price-fixing that can harm competition. Corporate Governance: Within individual companies, corporate governance refers to the rules, practices, and processes by which a company is directed and controlled. It involves the board of directors, shareholders, and management, and it aims to ensure transparency, accountability, and ethical behaviour within the organization.

Chapter 2

The Republican Turn: From Polis to Respublica

The shift from the Greek polis to the Roman res publica represents a fundamental paradigm shift in the conceptualization of democracy and political life, moving from a model of direct, local participation to one of representative governance over a vast territory. The Polis (Greek City-State) The Greek polis, such as ancient Athens, was a small-scale, organic community that was a way of life as much as a political entity.

This description accurately summarizes the system of direct democracy practiced in ancient Athens. Key aspects included:

Direct Participation: Citizens were expected to actively participate in the political life of the polis (city-state).

Assembly Voting: Eligible male citizens gathered in the Assembly (Ecclesia) to directly debate and vote on legislation, treaties, and other major decisions.

Jury Duty: Citizens also served extensively on large juries (dikasteria) to decide legal cases, further distributing judicial power among the people.

Holding Office: Many public offices were filled by lot (sortition), a practice intended to ensure broad citizen participation and prevent the concentration of power among a small elite.

This model contrasts sharply with modern representative democracy, where citizens elect representatives to make decisions on their behalf

Emphasis on Virtue: The good life (eudaimonia) was only possible within the polis, and a key objective was the cultivation of civic virtue, where citizens actively shaped their collective destiny.

Limited Scale: The system was only viable due to the limited size and population of the city-state, enabling face-to-face interaction and high levels of personal engagement.

The Res Publica (Roman Republic/Public Affair)

The Roman res publica ("public thing" or "commonwealth") emerged as a system capable of governing a much larger and expanding territory, necessitating a more complex constitutional framework.

Representation: A primary objective was to replace direct democracy with a system of representation where elected officials, magistrates, and the Senate managed public affairs on behalf of the citizens.

Rule of Law and Stability: The Romans prioritized a stable, legal, and constitutional framework (mixed government with checks and balances) designed to prevent dictatorship and ensure the continuity of the state across a vast empire.

Inclusion and Expansion (Relative): Unlike the exclusive polis, the res publica developed methods to incorporate conquered territories and a wider (though still limited) voting populace into its constitutional framework, allowing for pragmatic expansion that the Greek model lacked the institutional capacity for.

This "republican turn" introduced concepts like representation and constitutional checks that remain foundational to modern representative democracies.

Would you like to examine how these ancient ideals influenced modern thinkers like the Founding Fathers of the United States?

The Shifting Landscape of Democracy: A Thematic and Chronological Analysis of Paradigm Shifts in Governance would explore how governance models have evolved from ancient, limited forms to complex, modern systems, using both historical timelines and key themes to structure its arguments. The core argument would be that democratic paradigms are not static but are constantly shifting in response to new social, economic, and technological pressures. The analysis would likely be structured around the following key themes and their chronological development:

I. From Direct to Representative Rule

This section would cover the initial paradigm shift driven by scale and complexity. The impracticality of direct democracy in large nation-states.The rise of representative democracy, where elected officials make decisions on behalf of citizens, becoming the dominant traditional model of governance.

The shift from direct to representative rule was a paradigm change in governance driven by the impracticality of direct democracy in large and complex societies. The traditional model, where citizens elect officials to make decisions on their behalf, became dominant because it offered a more efficient and manageable form of government for modern nation-states.

Key factors driving this transition include:

Large Population and Geographic Scale: In modern countries with millions of citizens spread across vast areas, it is physically impossible for all people to gather in one place to debate and vote on every issue, as was the case in ancient Athens.

Complexity of Issues: Modern policy decisions often involve intricate details in law, economics, and various social sciences that require specialized knowledge and expertise. Elected representatives can dedicate the necessary time and resources to understand these complex matters, which the average citizen may lack the time or skill to do for every single decision.

Efficiency and Stability: Continuous, frequent voting on every policy would be time-consuming, expensive, and could slow down essential governance, leading to potential instability. Representative democracy allows for a more streamlined and stable decision-making process.

Risk of "Mob Rule" and Minority Rights: Direct democracy can sometimes lead to decisions based on emotion or short-term thinking, potentially resulting in the "tyranny of the majority" that could marginalize or harm the rights of minority groups. Representatives can act as a filter, engaging in deliberation and compromise to protect diverse interests.

Division of Labor: Representative government enables a division of labor in politics, relieving the ordinary citizen of the constant burden of governance while still holding their elected officials accountable through regular elections.

While some elements of direct democracy, like referendums and citizen initiatives, exist in many systems (such as in Switzerland), representative democracy has become the universal norm for national governance due to its scalability and practicality.

II. The Expansion of Inclusion and Rights

This theme traces the evolution of who is included in "the people" and the scope of individual rights. The fight for universal suffrage and civil rights, challenging the limited, often exclusionary, nature of early liberal democracies.: The entrenchment of liberal democracy, characterized by constitutionally protected freedoms (e.g., speech, press, assembly) and the rule of law, creating an environment for the effective realization of human rights.

The expansion of inclusion and rights in liberal democracies has been characterized by ongoing efforts to broaden the definition of "the people" and secure equal treatment for all individuals [1]. This historical evolution has seen the initial, often exclusionary, scope of early liberal thought—which frequently limited rights to propertied men—challenged and changed through sustained social movements and legal reforms [1].

Key milestones in this history include:

The Fight for Universal Suffrage: Gradually extending the right to vote to include working-class individuals, women, and racial minorities, thereby making political participation a right rather than a privilege [1].

The Civil Rights Movement: In many countries, most notably the United States, this movement directly confronted entrenched systems of racial segregation and discrimination, leading to landmark legislation that enforced equal protection under the law [1].

These struggles have worked to entrench the core tenets of liberal democracy, which are defined by:

Constitutionally Protected Freedoms: Safeguarding fundamental liberties like freedom of speech, press, and assembly, which are essential for individuals to participate in society and hold power accountable [1].

The Rule of Law: Ensuring that all people, including government officials, are subject to and accountable under the law, preventing arbitrary use of power and providing a framework for justice and the effective realization of human rights

III. Governance Beyond the State

This theme addresses the modern challenge to the nation-state as the sole locus of authoritative decision-making. The rise of complex interdependencies (globalization, transnational issues, multi-national corporations). Emerging models of multi-stakeholder and network governance, where non-state actors (NGOs, private sector, international bodies) collaborate in policy-making and service delivery, moving towards potentially post-national models of democracy.

The provided text is an excerpt describing the concept of "Governance Beyond the State" and does not contain a question or answer options to choose from. It seems that the prompt is missing the actual multiple-choice question.

However, based on the provided text, here is an overview of the key concepts of Governance Beyond the State:

Challenge to the Nation-State: The modern nation-state is no longer the sole source of authoritative decision-making.

Rise of Interdependencies: This shift is driven by global challenges that transcend national boundaries, such as globalization, transnational issues, and the rise of multi-national corporations.

Emerging Models: New models like multi-stakeholder and network governance are emerging.

Role of Non-State Actors: Non-state actors, including NGOs, the private sector (multinational corporations), and international bodies (UN, IMF, etc.), collaborate in policy-making and service delivery.

Post-National Democracy: This points towards potentially post-national models of democracy, where governance occurs on multiple levels and in hybrid forms beyond traditional state control.

For the most accurate answers, try including the answer options, the specific question asked about the passage, or the full context in your query.

IV. The Digital Age and Deliberation

This contemporary theme examines the newest wave of potential changes driven by technology.The impact of the internet, social media, and AI on the public sphere, including both opportunities for participation and challenges from disinformation and polarization.The exploration of participatory and deliberative democracy models, using technology to enable more direct, ongoing, and informed citizen engagement to enhance accountability and counter disaffection.

V. The Challenge of Backsliding and Resilience

This concluding theme analyzes the fragility of the current paradigm.

Internal pressures like economic inequality, polarization, and populism that lead to "democratic backsliding" and "hollowing out" of democratic institutions.: The re-evaluation of democratic theory to focus on resilience, the importance of civic education, and the need for adaptable ("agile") governance approaches in a rapidly changing and uncertain world.

Chapter 3

The Birth of the Modern Nation-State

The Peace of Westphalia, a series of treaties signed in 1648, is widely considered the foundational moment for the modern concept of state sovereignty and the international system of states [1]. This era established a framework for international relations that moved away from the authority of the Holy Roman Empire and the Papacy towards independent, self-governing states.

Key aspects of the Peace of Westphalia and the rise of state sovereignty:

Sovereignty: The treaties formalized the principle of cuius regio, eius religio ("whose realm, his religion"), allowing rulers to determine the official religion within their own territories without external interference [1]. This reinforced the idea that political authority resided within the state's borders, independent of the Church or other external powers.

Territorial Integrity: The Peace affirmed the territorial integrity and political independence of member states of the Holy Roman Empire, as well as the full sovereignty of the Dutch Republic and the Swiss Confederacy [1].

Diplomacy: It established the basis for modern diplomacy through the recognition of a system of coexisting sovereign states interacting through formalized diplomatic channels and international law [1].

Absolutism as a precursor to liberal reactions:

The rise of the sovereign state during and after the Westphalian era often manifested internally as absolutism, a system where the monarch held supreme, unchecked power over the state and its subjects [1, 2]. Rulers like Louis XIV of France became the embodiment of the state, governing by divine right.

This concentration of power, characterized by heavy taxation, lack of political rights for common people, and restrictions on individual liberties, directly fueled the liberal reactions of the Enlightenment and the revolutionary era [2, 3]:

Enlightenment Thought: Philosophers such as John Locke, Jean-Jacques Rousseau, and Montesquieu challenged the divine right of kings and absolute authority [2]. They championed ideas of natural rights, the social contract, and the separation of powers, arguing that government legitimacy came from the consent of the governed, not divine decree [3].

Revolutions: These liberal ideas provided the ideological foundation for major upheavals, including the American Revolution and the French Revolution [3]. These movements sought to replace absolute monarchies with constitutional governments, republics, and systems that protected individual freedoms and limited state power.

Constitutionalism: The ultimate liberal reaction was the development of constitutionalism, which institutionalized limits on government power and established frameworks for representative governance and the rule of law [3].

The objectives regarding the birth of the modern nation-state involve understanding two key historical developments: the establishment of state sovereignty through the Peace of Westphalia and the role of absolutism in sparking liberal reactions. The Peace of Westphalia (1648), a series of treaties that ended the Thirty Years' War, is a crucial benchmark in the development of the modern state system. It established the principle of state sovereignty, meaning that rulers had supreme authority over their territories and populations, free from external interference, particularly from religious authorities or the Holy Roman Empire [1]. This shifted the focus of European politics from religious conflict toward secular statecraft and diplomacy.

The second key development involves the rise of absolutist monarchies in the centuries following Westphalia. These regimes concentrated power in the hands of the monarch, leading to centralized administration and standing armies, but often at the expense of traditional rights and representative bodies [2, 3]. The perceived excesses and inefficiencies of absolute rule—exemplified by monarchs like Louis XIV of France—provoked significant opposition. This opposition fueled liberal movements and revolutions, most notably the American and French Revolutions, which championed concepts such as popular sovereignty, constitutionalism, and individual rights, fundamentally reshaping the modern nation-state's relationship with its citizens [2, 3].

You've accurately described the core principle of Westphalian Sovereignty, established by the 1648 Peace of Westphalia treaties, which ended the Thirty Years' War and founded the modern state system by affirming each state's exclusive control over its territory and internal affairs, free from outside interference, making them equals on the global stage.

Key Aspects of Westphalian Sovereignty:

Territorial Integrity: Each state has supreme authority within its defined borders.

Non-Interference: Other states or powers cannot meddle in a sovereign nation's domestic matters.

Equality of States: All sovereign states, regardless of size or power, are considered equal under international law.

Foundation of Modern System: It shifted power from empires/church to individual states, creating the basis for today's international relations.

In essence, it's the bedrock idea that independent nations govern themselves without external control, a cornerstone of international law today, though challenged by globalization and humanitarian concerns.

The given statement accurately describes a key outcome of the Peace of Westphalia, a series of peace treaties signed in 1648 that concluded the Thirty Years' War in the Holy Roman Empire and the Eighty Years' War between Spain and the Dutch Republic [1].

Key aspects of this shift included:

Sovereignty: The treaties established the principle of modern state sovereignty, recognizing states as independent entities with authority over their own territories and domestic affairs, free from external interference, particularly from the Church [1].

Religious Determination: It formally reaffirmed the principle of cuius regio, eius religio ("whose realm, his religion"), first introduced by the Peace of Augsburg (1555). This allowed the secular ruler of a state within the Holy Roman Empire to choose either Lutheranism or Catholicism as the official religion of their territory [1].

Decline of Transnational Authority: The Peace significantly diminished the political power of the Pope and the Holy Roman Emperor in secular European politics, paving the way for the rise of sovereign nation-states and the modern international system [1].

This foundation refers to the Peace of Westphalia (1648), which established the "Westphalian system" of sovereign states.

Key Principles of the Foundation

Westphalian Sovereignty: This principle dictates that each state has exclusive sovereignty over its territory and domestic affairs, prohibiting external powers from interfering in another state's internal matters [1, 2].

Legal Equality of States: Regardless of a nation's military or economic power, all sovereign states are viewed as legally equal under international law [2, 3].

Territorial Integrity: States have the right to maintain their borders without external aggression or encroachment [1, 4].

Modern Application

These 17th-century concepts remain the core of the United Nations Charter, specifically Article 2, which protects the "sovereign equality" of all members and restricts the use of force against the territorial integrity of any state [3, 5]. Over time, this foundation has evolved to include universal standards, such as the Universal Declaration of Human Rights, which allows for international scrutiny when a state fails to protect its own citizens

Absolutism inadvertently created the infrastructure for the modern state, which later became the target of liberal reforms and revolutions.

The Role of Consolidation

By centralizing authority, absolute monarchs—such as Louis XIV of France—standardized laws, created professional standing armies, and established unified bureaucracies. These actions effectively ended the fragmented power of the feudal nobility and the political dominance of the Church, creating the first recognizable sovereign nation-states.

The Shift to Liberalism

The transition from Absolutism to Liberalism was driven by the "Concentration-Reaction" dynamic:

The Intellectual Backlash: Enlightenment thinkers like John Locke and Montesquieu argued that if power comes from a social contract rather than "Divine Right," it must be limited to protect natural rights (life, liberty, and property).

Economic Friction: The heavy taxation required to maintain absolute rule and royal bureaucracies frustrated the rising merchant class, who demanded political representation in exchange for financial support.

Constitutionalism: The excesses of absolute power led directly to the development of Constitutionalism, shifting the source of law from the "Will of the King" to the "Rule of Law."

This friction culminated in pivotal historical shifts, most notably the Glorious Revolution (1688) in England and the French Revolution (1789), which replaced absolute authority with parliamentary systems and declarations of individual rights

Mechanisms of Centralization

Absolutist rulers in the 17th and 18th centuries utilized centralization to transform fragmented feudal territories into organized, modern states. This process laid the groundwork for contemporary governance but also created systemic social friction.

Bureaucratic Expansion: Monarchs created professional, loyal administrative systems to bypass the influence of the traditional nobility.

Louis XIV utilized "intendants"—royal officers dispatched to provinces to enforce laws and manage economic development.

Peter the Great introduced the Table of Ranks, a merit-based hierarchy that allowed individuals to earn status through service rather than birthright, effectively subordinating the "boyar" nobility to the state.

Standing Armies: Rulers established permanent, state-funded military forces that were loyal to the crown rather than local lords. By 1715, France's army had grown to 350,000 troops, ensuring internal stability and facilitating territorial expansion.

Symbolic Control: Grand architecture served as a tool of political control. The Palace of Versailles forced nobles to live under Louis XIV's direct supervision, while the construction of St. Petersburg acted as Peter the Great's "window to the west," symbolizing a modernized, centralized Russia.

Consequences and Abuses

Social Inequality: Centralization was funded by aggressive taxation, which fell disproportionately on the peasantry and middle classes while often exempting the nobility.

Suppression of Dissent: By declaring "L'état, c'est moi" (I am the state), Louis XIV embodied the lack of checks and balances; any opposition was often treated as a crime against the state.

Precursor to Revolution: While these reforms provided the political stability necessary for national growth, the resulting social tensions and "absolute" nature of the authority fueled the Enlightenment's push for individual liberties and the eventual French Revolution.

For more on the evolution of state authority, you can explore the United

Nations World Social Report 2026, which discusses how historical concentrations of power still influence modern global inequality.

Core Theories and Responses to Absolutism

The Enlightenment (17th–18th centuries), or the Age of Reason, was a transformative intellectual movement that directly challenged absolute monarchy by prioritizing reason, individualism, and skepticism of traditional authority. It provided the philosophical "ammunition" for the transition from despotism to modern liberal democracies.

Natural Rights: Intellectuals like John Locke argued that all individuals possess inalienable rights to life, liberty, and property. Unlike the "Divine Right of Kings," which placed monarchs above the law, Locke posited that these rights are inherent and cannot be surrendered to any government.

The Social Contract: Thinkers such as Locke and Jean-Jacques Rousseau redefined the state as a "contract" between the ruler and the ruled.

Locke's View: Government exists solely to protect natural rights; if it fails, the people have a right to revolution.

Rousseau's View: Political authority must reside in the general will of the people rather than a single monarch.

Separation of Powers: To prevent the abuses seen in absolute regimes, Baron de Montesquieu proposed dividing government into executive, legislative, and judicial branches. This system of "checks and balances" became a cornerstone of modern constitutions, including that of the United States.

Civil Liberties and Secularism: Voltaire was a fierce advocate for freedom of speech and religious tolerance, criticizing the "infamous" abuses of the clergy and royalty. He and other radicals pushed for the separation of church and state, arguing government has no authority over individual conscience.

Historical Legacy and 2026 Context

Revolutionary Impact: These ideals directly fueled the American (1776) and French (1789) Revolutions, replacing hereditary privilege with legal equality.

Evolution of Equality: While early Enlightenment thought often focused on landowning white males, its logic eventually inspired 19th- and 20th-century movements for women's suffrage, abolition, and civil rights.

Contemporary Challenges: In 2026, Enlightenment values face renewed pressure from "democratic backsliding" and the rise of authoritarian trends globally. Modern discourse on human rights, as seen in the UN Universal D

The transition from absolutism to modern representative governance was driven by two major waves of revolution that fundamentally redefined political legitimacy.

1. Foundations: American and French Revolutions

The American (1776) and French (1789) Revolutions acted as the primary catalysts for dismantling the "Divine Right of Kings".

The American Revolution: Advocated for "no taxation without representation" and established a republic with codified individual rights and a federal separation of powers.

The French Revolution: Introduced the Declaration of the Rights of Man and of the Citizen, championing "Liberty, Equality, and Fraternity". It replaced the hereditary monarchy with a system based on popular sovereignty, where power resides with the citizens.

2. The 1848 "Springtime of Nations"

Occurring across more than 50 countries, the Revolutions of 1848 were the most widespread revolutionary wave in European history.

Core Demands: Uprisings were driven by a mix of liberals seeking constitutional reform, nationalists wanting unified nation-states (especially in Germany and Italy), and socialists demanding economic rights for the working class.

Immediate Results: Most 1848 revolutions were eventually suppressed by conservative military forces. In France, the Second Republic briefly established universal male suffrage before falling to a coup by Louis-Napoleon (Napoleon III).

Lasting Legacy: Despite short-term failures, these uprisings made the transition to representative democracy inevitable. Key reforms included the abolition of serfdom in Austria and Hungary and the permanent shift to constitutional monarchy in Denmark and the Netherlands.

3. Influence on Global Governance (2026 Context)

In 2026, the principles born from these revolutions remain the standard for state legitimacy:

Constitutionalism: The shift from absolute rule to written constitutions is now a global norm, influencing frameworks like the UN Charter and the Universal Declaration of Human Rights.

Representative Systems: Modern democracies—from the United States to parliamentary systems like India's—trace their emphasis on the "consent of the governed" back to these historical uprisings.

The struggle against absolutism thus set the stage for the eventual emergence of constitutionalism and democracy, fundamentally shaping the political landscape of the modern world.

Would you like to dive deeper into the principles of the Westphalian system or the key thinkers of the Enlightenment who challenged absolutism?

Part II

The Great Democratic Waves (18th Century to Mid-20th Century)

The period from the 18th century to the mid-20th century saw two major "great democratic waves" and subsequent "reverse waves", driven by the objective of expanding political rights and establishing representative governments. First Wave of Democratization (c. 1820s–1920s) The primary objective of the first wave was the institutionalization of democracy through the gradual expansion of suffrage and the establishment of constitutional limits on power.

Period: Roughly from the 1820s to 1926.Widening Suffrage: The primary goal was the extension of voting rights, initially to a large proportion of the adult male population, beginning in the United States and spreading to countries in Western Europe and the British Commonwealth. The aim was to replace absolute monarchies with constitutional states where the rule of law was supreme, ensuring governments ruled within limits set by law and citizens' rights. National Self-Determination: Following World War I, the break-up of the Russian, German, Austro-Hungarian, and Ottoman empires led to the creation of new nation-states based on national identity, many of which adopted democratic republican forms of government. This wave peaked around

1926, bringing about 29 democracies into existence. First Reverse Wave (c. 1920s–1940s). A reverse wave began with the rise of Benito Mussolini in Italy in 1922, as fragile democracies collapsed and were replaced by aggressive fascist, militaristic, and communist authoritarian regimes. Second Wave of Democratization (c. 1940s–1960s) The objective of the second wave was largely to institutionalize democratic systems in the wake of war and decolonization, often under the influence of victorious Allied powers. Began after the Allied victory in World War II and crested around 1962.Post-War Reconstruction: Allied occupation forces worked to build strong, stable democracies in the defeated Axis powers (Germany, Italy, Japan). As European empires dissolved, many newly independent nations in Africa and Asia adopted democratic institutions upon achieving sovereignty. The establishment of these democracies was a strategic move in the developing Cold War context, aimed at preventing the spread of communism. This wave added many democracies, but an ebb began in the mid-1960s with a second reverse wave as many of these new, unstable democracies reverted to authoritarianism or military dictatorships. Would you like to focus on the specific outcomes of either the first or second democratic wave? To explain the importance of democracy some fundamental questions need to be answered: What exactly is meant when people say 'democracy'? Why is it assumed democracy should be the preferred form of government in the world? How does it compare to other models for political organization? And why is there such a widespread perception that democracy is under threat? When talking about the importance of democracy it is important to define it accurately. Democracy is popular sovereignty – in Abraham Lincoln's words, 'government of the people, by the people, for the people'. At its heart is the concept of the population choosing a government through regular, free, and fair elections.

In Europe and the English-speaking world it is often assumed democracy naturally takes the form of liberal democracy – popular sovereignty but limited by a constitution which guarantees individual freedoms (such as speech) and rights (such as to a fair trial). Crucially these essential freedoms are not subject to a democratic vote.In fact, democracy does not necessarily have to be liberal. Certain nations today have illiberal democracies where voting continues but liberal characteristics, such as an independent judiciary and free press, have been compromised. Defenders of liberal democracy say this actually makes these societies inherently undemocratic, as stripping away liberal guarantees leads to intimidation and coercion by the state, undermining elections. The guarantees of liberal democracy are intended to ensure no ethnic, geographic, class, or business interest dominates or exploits others to an unreasonable degree, and that there is fair and universal consent gained for government policies. Arguably the importance of liberal democracy is two-fold: no other system of government guarantees the right to free expression of political preference; and no other system promotes progress through peaceful competition between different interests and ideas.

This question is being asked a lot more as democracy is threatened by various forces around the world. Some question the value of the popular vote when it leads to seismic shifts such as Brexit, and the election of demagogues who threaten liberal values. Even the American system, for a long time the exemplar of democratic freedoms, seems so polarized that it is in danger of becoming impotent, its ability to endure technological, demographic, and cultural change in doubt. Meanwhile, over the last 30-50 years, a more technocratic, uniform form of politics has taken hold in the European Union (EU), where democracy is arguably less responsive to citizens and large elements of the population feel excluded from the process of government.

All this may question the need for democracy. But most authoritarian systems are hampered by structural weaknesses: large, disenfranchised minority groups foster a sense of injustice; reliance on 'strongmen' figures makes the transfer of power potentially violent; and vested interests are protected from popular demands for change. Liberal democracy, in theory at least, provides a mechanism for some form of rule by proportionate representation, with citizens empowered to bring about change through participation and persuade the powerful to act for the greater good. But democracy is a process, not a state. Countries such as the UK and the US were not true democracies until relatively recently. Britain's franchise was gradually extended from 1830 and it was only in 1918 that women were given the right to vote. In the US it was not until 1965 that African-Americans in its southern states gained a guaranteed right to vote. Democracy has endured in part due to its ability to accommodate change from below through expansion of voting rights, and greater protection of civil liberties. By contrast authoritarianism is, by its nature, centralized and limiting of free thought and expression. It can accomplish rapid change, but only ordained from above. Perhaps what has been witnessed in democracies since 2016 signals a need for further renewal and evolution of democratic systems. Because the more averse to change democracies become, the more likely it is they will wither. Democracy has played a vital role in the story of civilization, helping transform the world from power structures of monarchy, empire, and conquest into popular rule, self-determination, and peaceful co-existence. A direct form of democracy was initially practiced in ancient Greece, but there were many slaves in that society, and hardly anyone was a citizen and able to participate. Democracy then vanished until its re-emergence as 'representative democracy' in the late 18th century. Since then it has been generally understood that modern human history follows a trend towards greater democracy, with some scholars describing the phenomenon taking place in three waves.

The first wave, between the late 18th century and 1918, saw the American, French, and Haitian revolutions; the gradual emergence of democracy in Britain; Bolivarian revolutions establishing democracies in South America; and the break-up of the German, Ottoman, and Austro-Hungarian empires after World War 1 into democratic republics. The second wave, between 1945 and 1960, saw the reorganization of the defeated axis powers Germany, Italy, and Japan into strong democracies, and decolonization unfolding across the world, creating independent and largely democratic nations. The third wave from 1975 to 1991, saw the end of dictatorships in Portugal, Spain, and Brazil, democratic transitions in Taiwan and South Korea, and the eventual collapse of the USSR, creating free, democratic, Eastern European states.

But since 1991, by contrast, there has been what Larry Diamond calls a 'democratic recession', as ex-Warsaw Pact nations, such as Russia, Hungary and others have slid back into authoritarianism. The number of African countries that have adopted democratic systems of government has grown since decolonization, the collapse of communism and the ending of a number of civil wars. Some countries, such as Ghana, are seen as resilient democracies, while for others the democratic transition is more fragile. African states and societies are grappling with the dual complex challenges of democratizing and developing their economies – in the context of the most diverse continent in the world with some of its least developed countries. Progress towards democratic consolidation is therefore not linear and is threatened by populism, authoritarian leaders and divided societies. The COVID-19 pandemic gave rise to authoritarian opportunism but in 2019 Freedom House had already noted steep declines in freedoms in 22 African countries, especially in West Africa.

Some argue that development and poverty reduction should be prioritized over democracy. However, demand for democracy and political freedoms in Africa remains high, if often disappointed, as Afrobarometer data show. Positive changes to bring about or protect democracy have often been led by young people, women and increasingly well-established civil society groups and journalists. Over 60 per cent of the continent's population is under the age of 25, so demand for political freedoms as well as accountable governance for inclusive economic growth is likely to only grow. Thinkers such as Amartya Sen argue democratic values are essential to successful development, pointing out no substantial famine has ever occurred in an independent and democratic country with a relatively free press. He cites the example of India, where the last famine, in 1943, took place under British colonial rule. This perception of a link between democracy and development has ebbed and flowed over the last century, as communism rose and fell and the economic balance of the world shifted from West to East.

In the 1930s, 1940s, and 1950s communism seemed capable of lifting millions of people out of poverty while building vast new industries, winning wars, and delivering cutting edge science. But towards the end of the Cold War, the Soviet Union had stagnated and communism seemed doomed to stifle innovation and growth.

The idea that democracy and economic success go together has been thrown into doubt by the success of China's authoritarian capitalism, known as the 'Beijing consensus', which has developed a way to attain both military and economic superpower status, while restricting individual freedoms at home.The jury is still out on how China's story will develop. Only fifty years ago the country was in a state of near civil war during the cultural revolution. The more important question is whether other nations will strengthen or weaken their democracies in response.

Historically, many thinkers argued democracy can only be detrimental to a free and just society, characterizing rule by the majority as inherently unstable, irrational, and a threat to private property.

Plato's Republic rejects democracy and instead proposes the idea of rule by 'philosopher kings'. Tocqueville and others warned of the 'tyranny of the majority' democracy might bring. The Founding Fathers of the United States of America were acutely aware of this perceived threat and designed the constitution and electoral college to constrain popularly elected leaders with the liberal rights guaranteed by the constitution. Recent events have led some commentators to conclude that the system is broken. But when we question its merits and seek out its flaws, we should be acutely aware that we live in societies that permit us to criticise, and that this is in itself a crucial right. We should also question what our alternatives would be. We might imagine the landscape in an authoritarian or dictatorship state:

would we expect to receive a fairer trial? To find more balanced information on the internet? To see minority rights more protected? Would a settlement of World War Two imposed by fascist victors, rather than democracies, have created a more just and free peace? It is most likely that democracy needs to be further deepened, by reinvigorating the rights and guarantees enshrined in liberal democracy and making it more responsive and accountable however possible. Looking at the alternatives it is fair to conclude that people living in democracies have no alternative.

2024 saw a huge number of elections take place around the world, with over 50 polls in countries that together host nearly half the global population. Some elections, held in authoritarian regimes such as Russia and Venezuela, were not genuine democratic exercises. Instead they were designed to ensure victory for ruling elites, legitimizing and preserving their power. Other contests delivered surprises, or substantially altered governments. The Indian election saw Prime Minister Narendra Modi's BJP party achieve victory, but by a far smaller margin than was predicted. The UK election was called for July, months earlier than expected, delivering an historic victory for Sir Keir Starmer's Labour Party. In South Africa, the ANC finally lost its parliamentary majority, resulting in a switch to coalition government for the first time since Apartheid. One of the greatest surprises was in France, where snap parliamentary elections were called by President Emmanuel Macron, following his party's weak performance in June's European Parliamentary elections. A victory for Marine Le Pen's far-right National Rally (RN) party did not materialize, as some had predicted, but the inconclusive result created political mayhem in the country.

In the United States, following months of speculation that the US November presidential election would be very close, Donald Trump decisively beat Democratic Party candidate Kamala Harris and his Republican Party won majorities in both houses of Congress. During 2024 elections were held in countries of all sizes, for presidents and parliaments in both flourishing and flawed democracies – showcasing the extraordinary diversity of democratic processes and participation that exist around the world. Democracy has played a vital role in the story of civilization, helping transform the world from power structures of monarchy, empire, and conquest into popular rule, self-determination, and peaceful co-existence. A direct form of democracy was initially practiced in ancient Greece, but there were many slaves in that society, and hardly anyone was a citizen and able to participate.

Democracy then vanished until its re-emergence as 'representative democracy' in the late 18th century. Since then it has been generally understood that modern human history follows a trend towards greater democracy, with some scholars describing the phenomenon taking place in three waves. The first wave, between the late 18th century and 1918, saw the American, French, and Haitian revolutions; the gradual emergence of democracy in Britain; Bolivarian revolutions establishing democracies in South America; and the break-up of the German, Ottoman, and Austro-Hungarian empires after World War 1 into democratic republics.

The second wave, between 1945 and 1960, saw the reorganization of the defeated axis powers Germany, Italy, and Japan into strong democracies, and decolonization unfolding across the world, creating independent and largely democratic nations.

The third wave from 1975 to 1991, saw the end of dictatorships in Portugal, Spain, and Brazil, democratic transitions in Taiwan and South Korea, and the eventual collapse of the USSR, creating free, democratic, Eastern European states.

since 1991, by contrast, there has been what Larry Diamond calls a 'democratic recession', as ex-Warsaw Pact nations, such as Russia, Hungary and others have slid back into authoritarianism.

Some countries, such as Ghana, are seen as resilient democracies, while for others the democratic transition is more fragile.

African states and societies are grappling with the dual complex challenges of democratizing and developing their economies – in the context of the most diverse continent in the world with some of its least developed countries.

Progress towards democratic consolidation is therefore not linear and is threatened by populism, authoritarian leaders and divided societies. The COVID-19 pandemic gave rise to authoritarian opportunism but in 2019 Freedom House had already noted steep declines in freedoms in 22 African countries, especially in West Africa.

Some argue that development and poverty reduction should be prioritized over democracy. However, demand for democracy and political freedoms in Africa remains high, if often disappointed, as Afrobarometer data show.

Positive changes to bring about or protect democracy have often been led by young people, women and increasingly well-established civil society groups and journalists.

Over 60 per cent of the continent's population is under the age of 25, so demand for political freedoms as well as accountable governance for inclusive economic growth is likely to only grow.

Thinkers such as Amartya Sen argue democratic values are essential to successful development, pointing out no substantial famine has ever occurred in an independent and democratic country with a relatively free press. He cites the example of India, where the last famine, in 1943, took place under British colonial rule.

This perception of a link between democracy and development has ebbed and flowed over the last century, as communism rose and fell and the economic balance of the world shifted from West to East.

In the 1930s, 1940s, and 1950s communism seemed capable of lifting millions of people out of poverty while building vast new industries, winning wars, and delivering cutting edge science. But towards the end of the Cold War, the Soviet Union had stagnated and communism seemed doomed to stifle innovation and growth.

The idea that democracy and economic success go together has been thrown into doubt by the success of China's authoritarian capitalism, known as the 'Beijing consensus', which has developed a way to attain both military and economic superpower status, while restricting individual freedoms at home.

The jury is still out on how China's story will develop. Only fifty years ago the country was in a state of near civil war during the cultural revolution. The more important question is whether other nations will strengthen or weaken their democracies in response.

Historically, many thinkers argued democracy can only be detrimental to a free and just society, characterizing rule by the majority as inherently unstable, irrational, and a threat to private property.

Plato's Republic rejects democracy and instead proposes the idea of rule by 'philosopher kings'. Tocqueville and others warned of the 'tyranny of the majority' democracy might bring.

The Founding Fathers of the United States of America were acutely aware of this perceived threat and designed the constitution and electoral college to constrain popularly elected leaders with the liberal rights guaranteed by the constitution.

Recent events have led some commentators to conclude that the system is broken. But when we question its merits and seek out its flaws, we should be acutely aware that we live in societies that permit us to criticise, and that this is in itself a crucial right. We should also question what our alternatives would be.

We might imagine the landscape in an authoritarian or dictatorship state: would we expect to receive a fairer trial? To find more balanced information on the internet? To see minority rights more protected? Would a settlement of World War Two imposed by fascist victors, rather than democracies, have created a more just and free peace?

It is most likely that democracy needs to be further deepened, by reinvigorating the rights and guarantees enshrined in liberal democracy, and making it more responsive and accountable however possible. Looking at the alternatives it is fair to conclude that people living in democracies have no alternative.

2024 saw a huge number of elections take place around the world, with over 50 polls in countries that together host nearly half the global population.

Some elections, held in authoritarian regimes such as Russia and Venezuela, were not genuine democratic exercises. Instead they were designed to ensure victory for ruling elites, legitimizing and preserving their power.

Other contests delivered surprises, or substantially altered governments. The Indian election saw Prime Minister Narendra Modi's BJP party achieve victory, but by a far smaller margin than was predicted. The UK election was called for July, months earlier than expected, delivering an historic victory for Sir Keir Starmer's Labour Party. In South Africa, the ANC finally lost its parliamentary majority, resulting in a switch to coalition government for the first time since Apartheid.

Our flagship newsletter provides a weekly round-up of content, plus receive the latest on events and how to connect with the institute.

Top of Form

One of the greatest surprises was in France, where snap parliamentary elections were called by President Emmanuel Macron, following his party's weak performance in June's European Parliamentary elections. A victory for Marine Le Pen's far-right National Rally (RN) party did not materialize, as some had predicted, but the inconclusive result created political mayhem in the country.

In the United States, following months of speculation that the US November presidential election would be very close, Donald Trump decisively beat Democratic Party candidate Kamala Harris and his Republican Party won majorities in both houses of Congress.

During 2024 elections were held in countries of all sizes, for presidents and parliaments in both flourishing and flawed democracies – showcasing the extraordinary diversity of democratic processes and participation that exist around the world

Chapter 4

The Liberal Democratic Paradigm Shift

The American (1776) and French (1789) Revolutions represent a decisive "rupture point" in human history, marking the transition from hereditary rule and feudalism to the modern era of constitutional democracy. While both were fueled by Enlightenment ideals, they offered distinct models for state-building that continue to shape global politics in 2026.

The Rupture: From Subject to Citizen

Abolition of Divine Right: Both revolutions shattered the myth that monarchs ruled by "Divine Right," establishing the Constitution as the supreme source of political authority.

Popular Sovereignty: They shifted the seat of power from the crown to the people, fundamentally redefining individuals as "citizens" with rights rather than "subjects" with duties.

Global Catalyst: The success of the American Revolution proved a republic was viable, while the French Revolution's radicalism dismantled feudal structures across Europe, inspiring global movements for centuries.

Key Components of the New Order

These revolutions institutionalized three pillars that form the "bedrock" of modern liberal-democratic states:

Rule of Law:

Established the principle that every citizen, including government officials, is equal before the law.

Replaced arbitrary royal decrees with clear, predictable legal systems and codified constitutions.

Individual Rights:

Inalienable Rights: Based on the works of John Locke, the American Declaration of Independence (1776) asserted "natural" rights to life, liberty, and property.

Universal Proclamations: The French Declaration of the Rights of Man and of the Citizen (1789) proclaimed universal civil liberties, including freedom of speech, religion, and the press.

Separation of Powers:

Inspired by Montesquieu, both systems divided government into Executive, Legislative, and Judicial branches.

Checks and Balances: This structure was designed to prevent any single entity from gaining absolute control, serving as a safeguard against the return of tyranny.

In 2026, these revolutionary principles remain the standard for international legitimacy, directly influencing the UN Charter and the Universal Declaration of Human Rights. While modern states vary in their application—such as the strict separation in the U.S. system versus the functional overlap in India's parliamentary model—the core objective of limiting state power through law and rights remains a universal aspiration.

In 2026, Chapter 4 focuses on the transition from traditional monarchical rule to the modern liberal democratic framework. This paradigm shift, centered on the American and French Revolutions, established the ideological and institutional foundations of current global governance.

The Revolutions as a Rupture Point

The late 18th century served as a definitive "rupture point" where divine right and absolute monarchy were replaced by systems based on popular sovereignty.

The American (1776) and French (1789) Revolutions served as pivotal "rupture points" that shattered the Ancien Régime—the traditional social and political order of Europe—replacing monarchical absolutism with systems based on popular sovereignty.

The French Revolution: Dismantling Internal Feudalism

The French Revolution targeted the internal class structure of an established absolute monarchy.

End of Feudalism: On August 4, 1789, the National Assembly passed the August Decrees, which abolished feudal dues, serfdom, and tithes, effectively ending centuries of manorialism.

Destruction of Privileges: It eliminated tax exemptions for the nobility and clergy (the first two "Estates"), establishing that all citizens were equal before the law.

Secularization: The revolution nationalized Church property and subordinated religion to the state, breaking the political dominance of the Catholic Church.

The American Revolution: Challenging Colonial Authority

The American Revolution was primarily an anti-colonial war of independence against a foreign monarchy.

Rejection of Divine Right: By successfully defeating Great Britain, the colonists proved that monarchical power could be replaced by a republic where the head of state is not hereditary.

Establishment of Home Rule: It focused on removing the constraints of British mercantilism and "taxation without representation," asserting that government legitimacy derives from the consent of the governed.

Constitutional Template: It established the world's first written constitution, serving as a functional model for how to structure a government with limited, separated powers.

Global Legacy in 2026

Modern Statehood: These revolutions created the modern concept of citizenship, where rights are inherent to the individual rather than granted by a ruler.

Human Rights Standards: Foundational documents like the Declaration of the Rights of Man and of the Citizen and the U.S. Declaration of Independence remain the prototypes for 2026 human rights frameworks, including the UN Universal Declaration of Human Rights.

Rule of Law: The shift from the "will of the King" to codified constitutions is now a near-universal standard for legitimate governance.

This ideological transformation represents the most significant shift in political history: the transition from subjects of a crown to citizens of a state. By 2026, this "people-centric" model of authority remains the global standard for political legitimacy.

The Shift in Political Authority

From Divine Right to Popular Sovereignty: Before these revolutions, monarchs claimed authority through "Divine Right" or hereditary succession. The revolutions institutionalized Popular Sovereignty, the principle that the state's right to govern is created by and for the will of its people.

The Constitution as Supreme Authority: The source of law shifted from the arbitrary "will of the King" to written, codified Constitutions. This change ensured that power was bounded by law rather than personal whim.

Institutionalizing Enlightenment Ideals

The revolutions translated abstract philosophy into concrete government structures:

Reason over Tradition: Governance was reimagined as a rational system designed to serve the public good. This led to the creation of professional bureaucracies and merit-based systems, replacing the nepotism and "tradition" of the Ancien Régime.

Liberty as a Legal Right: Liberty was redefined from a "grant" given by a ruler to an Inalienable Right inherent to every human being. This included protections for speech, assembly, and conscience.

Equality before the Law: The revolutions dismantled the legal hierarchy of the Three Estates (Clergy, Nobility, and Commoners). The new standard established that all citizens are subject to the same laws and entitled to the same legal protections, regardless of birth.

In 2026, this ideological framework serves as the foundation for modern international governance:

Democratic Norms: The United Nations Charter begins with "We the Peoples," a direct linguistic and ideological heir to this era.

Human Rights: The Universal Declaration of Human Rights provides a 21st-century codification of the "reason and liberty" championed during the Enlightenment.

Global Citizenship: The shift to "the people" as the source of power remains the primary driver behind modern movements for transparency, anti-corruption, and democratic reform worldwide.

The American and French Revolutions acted as global catalysts, shattering the traditional order and initiating waves of reform that defined the 19th and 20th centuries. By 2026, their legacy remains foundational to the international order.

Global Waves of Influence

The success of these revolutions proved that traditional monarchies could be replaced with republics, inspiring subsequent movements across the globe:

The Atlantic Revolutions (1776–1824): The American victory immediately influenced the French Revolution (1789) and sparked the Haitian Revolution (1791), the first successful slave revolt leading to a republic.

Latin American Independence: Enlightenment ideals and Napoleon's disruption of European monarchies inspired leaders like Simón Bolívar and José de San Martín to lead independence wars across South and Central America.

European Liberalism (1848): Known as the "Springtime of

Nations," this wave of uprisings targeted absolutism across Europe, demanding constitutional rule and national self-determination.

Rise of Secular and Democratic Governance

The revolutions institutionalized a new relationship between the state, its citizens, and religion:

Secularization: The French Revolution established laïcité, the strict separation of church and state, which became a model for modern secular republics, including Turkey (1923) and India (1950).

Popular Sovereignty: These events replaced "Divine Right" with the principle that government legitimacy derives from the consent of the governed, a norm now embedded in the United Nations Charter.

Codified Law: Napoleon's Civil Code, a direct product of revolutionary ideals, spread across Europe and Latin America, establishing equality before the law as a universal legal standard.

political scientists continue to analyze these events as the "First Wave" of democratization. While the world faces modern challenges like "democratic backsliding," the core principles of reason, liberty, and equality established during these revolutions still serve as the primary benchmarks for human rights and constitutional governance globally.

The shift to the liberal democratic paradigm is built upon three core pillars designed to prevent the concentration of power and safeguard the individual: the Rule of Law, Individual Rights and Civil Liberties, and the Separation of Powers.

1. The Rule of Law

This principle ensures that governance is based on established legal codes rather than the arbitrary will of a ruler.

Supremacy of Law: All individuals and institutions, including the state itself, are accountable to laws that are publicly promulgated and equally enforced.

Due Process: Protects citizens from arbitrary state actions by requiring that legal proceedings follow fair and established rules, such as the right to a fair trial.

Consistency: Laws must be clear, stable, and applied consistently to ensure justice and predictability within society.

2. Individual Rights and Civil Liberties

Often considered the "cornerstone" of the paradigm, this pillar protects the inherent freedoms of the citizenry from government infringement.

Fundamental Freedoms: Includes essential civil liberties such as freedom of speech, expression, association, and religion.

Political Rights: Guarantees the right to participate in governance through free and fair elections, universal suffrage, and the right to run for public office.

Protection of Minorities: Liberal democracies emphasize the protection of individual and minority group rights against the "tyranny of the majority".

3. Separation of Powers

To prevent the abuse of power, authority is divided among distinct branches of government that operate independently yet provide a system of "checks and balances".

The Legislature: Responsible for creating and amending laws that reflect the will of the people.

The Executive: Charged with implementing and enforcing laws, as well as managing the daily operations of the state.

The Judiciary: Interprets laws and the constitution, ensuring that the other branches do not exceed their authority.

In 2026, these pillars face modern challenges such as political polarization and "democratic backsliding," making the maintenance of independent institutions—especially a free media and an independent judiciary—critical for their continued function.

In 2026, the Rule of Law remains the definitive mechanism for holding power accountable, ensuring that the state functions as a servant to the law rather than its master.

1. Universal Accountability

The core of this principle is that no one is above the law. Unlike absolutist regimes where the monarch was the source of law (and thus exempt from it), the liberal democratic paradigm subjects everyone—from the head of state to the average citizen—to the same legal standards.

Legal Equality: It guarantees that laws are applied without prejudice based on status, wealth, or political affiliation.

Governmental Constraint: It prevents officials from acting on personal whim, requiring that every state action has a clear legal basis.

2. Transition from "Rule by Men" to "Rule of Law"

This pillar represents a historical departure from arbitrary governance:

Predictability: By replacing "rule by men" (personal, unpredictable decrees) with rule of law (public, stable regulations), citizens can act with the certainty that their rights are protected by a known legal framework.

Due Process: It mandates that legal procedures—such as those found in the U.S. Bill of Rights—must be followed before the state can deprive an individual of life, liberty, or property.

3. The Constitutional Bedrock

A written or codified Constitution serves as the ultimate instrument of the rule of law.

Anti-Tyranny Mechanism: By defining the limits of state power, the constitution acts as a "shield" for the citizenry, preventing the return of tyrannical governance.

Institutional Integrity: In 2026, the rule of law is heavily dependent on an independent judiciary. Without courts that are free from executive interference, the rule of law risks collapsing into "rule by law," where the state uses the legal system merely as a tool of control.

According to the 2026 World Justice Project Rule of Law Index, maintaining these standards is currently the primary challenge for modern democracies facing "democratic backsliding" and the erosion of judicial independence.

In 2026, the protection of individual rights remains a cornerstone of the liberal democratic paradigm, acting as an essential buffer between state power and personal freedom. These rights are legally protected guarantees that the government cannot arbitrarily violate.

1. Enshrined in Landmark Documents

The modern concept of individual rights was formalized during the revolutionary era and codified in foundational texts:

Declaration of the Rights of Man and of the Citizen (France): Proclaimed in 1789, this document established that "Men are born and remain free and equal in rights." It served as a universal ideal for liberty that influenced constitution-making across Europe and beyond.

The Bill of Rights (U.S.): The first ten amendments to the U.S. Constitution (1791) specifically limit the power of the federal government. Key provisions include the First Amendment's protection of freedom of speech, press, and religion, and the Fifth Amendment's guarantee of due process.

These documents shifted rights from being "grants" given by a ruler to inherent, inalienable entitlements of citizenship.

2. Protection of Inherent Freedoms

These rights prioritize the private sphere of life, safeguarding individuals from government overreach:

Freedom of Speech and Expression: Essential for democratic discourse and holding power accountable.

Freedom of Religion and Conscience: Guarantees the right to worship freely or not at all, a direct response to historical religious conflicts and state-imposed faiths.

Freedom of Association and Assembly: Allows citizens to organize politically, form civil society groups, and protest without fear of state suppression.

Property Rights: A key focus for Enlightenment thinkers like John Locke, protecting individuals' ability to own and control their possessions and wealth.

3. Prioritizing Personal Autonomy and Equal Protection

The ultimate goal of enshrining these rights is to ensure personal autonomy and a level playing field for all citizens:

Equal Protection: The principle ensures that the law protects every citizen equally, regardless of their background, status, or beliefs. This is a direct repudiation of the Ancien Régime's system of hierarchy and privilege.

Mechanism for Justice: Rights act as a legal recourse. Citizens who believe the state has overstepped its bounds can seek protection and justice through an independent judiciary.

In 2026, the global respect for these rights is measured by indices like the World Justice Project's Rule of Law Index and the UN's Universal Declaration of Human Rights, which remain the international standards for legitimate governance.

The Separation of Powers is the final core pillar of the liberal democratic paradigm, a structural defense mechanism against the return of absolutist tyranny. It institutionalizes the principle that power should be a "check" on power.

1. Division into Independent Branches

Inspired by Enlightenment thinkers like Montesquieu, modern liberal democracies divide state authority into three distinct branches:

Legislative (Law-making): This branch (e.g., Parliament, Congress, or the Lok Sabha) is responsible for debating, creating, and passing laws that represent the will of the people.

Executive (Implementation): This branch (e.g., the President, Prime Minister, or Cabinet) is tasked with executing the laws passed by the legislature and managing the daily affairs of the state.

Judiciary (Checking Validity): This branch (the system of courts) interprets the laws and the constitution, ensuring that the other two branches act within their legal mandates.

2. Preventing the Concentration of Power

The primary goal of this division is to ensure that no single individual or group can seize total control of the state apparatus, a direct response to the absolute monarchies of the past.

Reducing Corruption: The transparency and oversight inherent in the system naturally reduces opportunities for unchecked corruption.

Preventing Abuse: By ensuring different institutions have different powers, it safeguards against the kind of abuses seen under rulers like Louis XIV or Peter the Great.

3. System of Checks and Balances

The separation of powers works in tandem with a system of checks and balances to maintain institutional equilibrium. Each branch possesses specific powers that allow it to limit the authority of the others:

Executive Veto: The executive can veto legislation passed by the legislature.

Legislative Oversight: The legislature can override a veto, impeach executive or judicial officials, and approve judicial appointments.

Judicial Review: The judiciary can declare laws passed by the legislature and actions taken by the executive to be unconstitutional.

In 2026, the independence and integrity of these separate powers—particularly the judiciary and free press—are considered critical metrics by the World Justice Project and the UN for determining a nation's democratic health.

Chapter 5

Expanding the Electorate: The Suffrage Revolutions

A chronological analysis of the expansion of the "demos" (the people) illustrates the transition from exclusive, property-based governance to universal participation. In the liberal democratic paradigm, this process has moved through several distinct waves of enfranchisement.

1. The Era of Property and Privilege (Late 18th – Early 19th Century)

In the early modern period, the "demos" was highly restricted, often limited to less than 5% to 10% of the adult population.

Property Qualifications: In the early United States and United Kingdom, voting was a privilege reserved for white, male property owners or taxpayers.

Religious and Racial Tests: Many early systems explicitly excluded non-Christians and non-white individuals from the political process.

Early Rupture (1792): The First French Republic briefly adopted universal male suffrage, one of the first national systems to abolish property requirements, though this was soon reversed.

2. The Rise of "Jacksonian" Democracy and Male Suffrage (1820s–1880s)

The mid-19th century saw the gradual dismantling of wealth-based barriers for men.

White Male Enfranchisement: By the 1830s in the U.S., most states had removed property requirements for white men.

British Reform Acts: The Reform Act of 1832 widened the pool to middle-class men, followed by the Reform Act of 1867, which included many urban working-class men.

The 15th Amendment (1870): In the U.S., this prohibited denying the vote based on "race, color, or previous condition of servitude," though systemic barriers like poll taxes and literacy tests often negated these rights in practice.

3. The "First Wave" of Universal Suffrage (1890s–1920s)

This period marked the inclusion of women and the formalization of universal male suffrage across Western democracies.

Pioneering Nations: New Zealand (1893) became the first self-governing nation to grant all women the right to vote, followed by Australia (1902), Finland (1906), and Norway (1913).

Post-WWI Shifts: The war served as a major catalyst. The 19th Amendment (1920) in the U.S. and similar acts in the UK (1918/1928) and Germany (1918) granted women the vote.

Standardization: By 1920, universal adult male suffrage was the norm across North America and Western Europe (with the notable exception of Switzerland until 1971).

4. Global Decolonization and Civil Rights (1945–1980s)

Following WWII, the "demos" expanded globally through decolonization and the dismantling of internal racial barriers.

International Norms: The UN Declaration of Human Rights (1948) established universal suffrage as a fundamental right.

Decolonization: Most nations gaining independence in Africa and Asia (e.g., India in 1947/1950) adopted universal adult suffrage immediately in their new constitutions.

The U.S. Voting Rights Act (1965): This landmark legislation finally removed the "Jim Crow" barriers (literacy tests, poll taxes) that had disenfranchised Black Americans for a century.

5. Contemporary Trends and Challenges (2000s–2026)

In 2026, the expansion of the "demos" continues to evolve, even as it faces modern "backsliding".

Lowering the Voting Age: Since the 1970s, many nations have lowered the voting age from 21 to 18 (e.g., U.S. in 1971) or even 16 (e.g., Austria, Brazil).

Participatory Democracy: New models, such as participatory budgeting and citizens' assemblies (pioneered in Brazil and recently used in Ireland and France), aim to deepen the public's role beyond simple voting.

Democratic Backsliding (2026): Recent data from 2024 and 2026 indicates a significant global trend of "autocratization," with a record number of countries (45 in 2024) experiencing declines in democratic rights.

The expansion of the "demos" (the people) progressed from a system of exclusive privilege to one of universal participation, primarily through the removal of wealth barriers and the inclusion of women.

1. Abolition of Property Qualifications

Historically, voting was tied to land ownership or income, based on the belief that only those with a "stake in the country" should have a voice.

United States:

Early Republic: Initially, most states required voters to be white male property owners.

Jacksonian Era (1820s–1830s): A major shift toward "universal white manhood suffrage" occurred as states dropped property and religious tests.

Final Abolition: North Carolina was the last state to remove property requirements in 1856, though some tax requirements remained.

United Kingdom:

Reform Act of 1832: Standardized a property qualification (e.g., owning property worth £10), which expanded the vote to middle-class men but still excluded the working class.

Representation of the People Act 1918: Finally abolished almost all property qualifications for men, establishing universal male suffrage based on residence.

British India: The Government of India Act (1919) maintained strict property and income qualifications, enfranchising less than 1% of the population.

2. Women's Suffrage Movements

The struggle for women's right to vote was a prolonged global movement that challenged traditional gender roles and demanded legal equality.

Pioneering Nations:

New Zealand (1893): The first self-governing nation to grant universal suffrage to all women.

Finland (1906): The first in Europe and the first in the world to allow women to both vote and run for office.

Major Landmarks:

United Kingdom: The 1918 Act gave the vote to women over 30 who met property qualifications. Equality was finally achieved with the Equal Franchise Act of 1928, which gave all women over 21 the vote regardless of property.

United States: The 19th Amendment (1920) prohibited denying the vote on account of sex, following decades of advocacy by leaders like Elizabeth Cady Stanton and Susan B. Anthony.

Global Expansion (Post-1945):

France (1944) and Italy (1945): Both countries granted women suffrage in the immediate aftermath of WWII.

United Nations: The 1948 Universal Declaration of Human Rights (Article 21) established universal and equal suffrage as an international standard.

Late Adopters: Switzerland (federal level, 1971) and Saudi Arabia (municipal level, 2015) were among the last to grant women the vote.

By 2026, while universal suffrage is a global norm, these historical movements remain critical case studies in the ongoing fight against systemic disenfranchisement.

The expansion of the "demos" (the voting public) in the United States and globally has been a gradual, often contentious process defined by major legislative shifts and social revolutions.

1. Chronological Expansion of the Electorate

Initially, the U.S. Constitution left voting qualifications to the states, which generally restricted the franchise to white, male property owners. The subsequent expansion followed this general timeline:

Late 1700s – Early 1800s: States began removing property qualifications, moving toward "universal white manhood suffrage".

1870: The 15th Amendment prohibited the denial of voting rights based on "race, color, or previous condition of servitude," though it did not effectively protect these rights for nearly a century due to state-level Jim Crow laws.

1920: The 19th Amendment guaranteed women the right to vote nationwide.

1965: The Voting Rights Act abolished discriminatory barriers like literacy tests and poll taxes, providing federal enforcement for minority voting rights.

1971: The 26th Amendment lowered the minimum voting age from 21 to 18.

2. Abolition of Property Qualifications

The requirement that voters own land or pay certain taxes was the first major barrier to fall.

Early 19th Century: Economic crises like the Panic of 1819 fueled demands for enfranchisement from propertyless men.

1820s–1840s: Most states repealed property requirements. For example, New York removed them for white men in 1821 (while maintaining them for Black men).

1856: North Carolina became the last state to officially abolish property ownership requirements for white men.

3. Women's Suffrage Movements

The struggle for women's enfranchisement was a multi-decade "revolution" characterized by both state-level successes and a national constitutional battle.

Seneca Falls Convention (1848): Often cited as the formal start of the movement, where Elizabeth Cady Stanton and Lucretia Mott drafted the "Declaration of Sentiments".

Western Successes: Territorial and state governments in the West led the way;

Wyoming

granted women the vote in 1869 while still a territory and became the first state with full suffrage in 1890.

Tactical Shifts: Groups like the National American Woman Suffrage Association (NAWSA) focused on state-by-state lobbying, while the National Woman's Party (NWP) used more militant tactics, such as picketing the White House.

Global Context:

New Zealand

was the first self-governing country to grant women national voting rights in 1893, followed by

Australia

(1902) and

Finland

(1906).

The Historical Expansion of Voting Rights in the United States

The Declaration of Independence famously reads, "all men are created equal," but all were not granted equal voting rights when the United States began. Many men could not vote for the leaders of their new nation. Women could not vote at all for some time after those words were written in 1776.

As the country grew, so did its voting rights, moving closer to the ideals of the Declaration. Today nearly all adult U.S. citizens have a legal right to vote. Read on to learn more about the expansion of voting rights throughout the country's history.

Voting rights in the United States have evolved over time with the passage of new election laws and Constitutional amendments.

In the late 1700s, most states restricted voting rights to white male property owners older than 21. They began to remove the property ownership requirement in the early 1800s, and by the 1820s, it was no longer common.

The next major change to voting rights came at the end of the Civil War. In 1865, the 13th Amendment to the U.S. Constitution ended slavery nationwide. The 14th Amendment then granted citizenship and equal protection under the law to "all persons born or naturalized in the United States," including former slaves.

In 1870, the 15th Amendment extended voting rights to Black men. They would face a long struggle before they could exercise it freely.

In the meantime, women were beginning their own fight for the right to vote. Wyoming was the first to grant it to women in 1869. One by one, more states allowed women to vote, but most still banned it during the 19th century.

While the expansion of voting rights had already begun, many Americans wouldn't see true change until the 1900s.

The women's suffrage movement in the U.S. began in the mid-1800s. Supporters protested, marched, and lobbied for women's right to vote. Women still could not vote nationwide the 19th Amendment was ratified in 1920. Even then, Black women still faced the same obstacles to voting as Black men did.

While Black men were granted the right to vote by law in 1870, most still could not vote well into the 20th century. Many states, especially in the South, quickly put up barriers to voting that targeted Black citizens. Poll taxes required payment to vote, and Black voters were less likely than white voters to be able to pay them. Literacy tests also disadvantaged Black citizens, whose educational opportunities were limited. The requirements were often waived for white voters. Some states enacted "grandfather clauses," which exempted people from these laws if they or their ancestors could vote before 1866 or 1867.

In the 1960s, the Civil Rights Movement challenged these and other discriminatory laws. Black Americans and their allies fought for equality through years of protests, marches, and civil disobedience. As a response, Congress passed the 24th Amendment to the Constitution, which banned poll taxes. Congress then got to work on civil rights legislation.

In 1965, President Lyndon B. Johnson signed the Voting Rights Act, which banned literacy tests and enforced the 15th Amendment. Johnson had told Congress that these "literacy tests" sometimes required Black voters to recite the Constitution or explain complex state laws. Since its passage, several amendments to the Voting Rights Act have extended it and added protections for voters. Notably, a 1975 change required districts with a significant non-English-speaking population to provide ballots and information in the language of that population.

Some Native Americans already had citizenship by 1924, but that year, the Indian Citizenship Act granted all Native Americans citizenship and the right to vote. Some states still prevented them from voting for a few decades.

The Magnuson Act of 1943 gave Chinese immigrants the right to citizenship and, thus, the right to vote. In 1952, the McCarran-Walter Act granted these rights to all Americans of Asian descent.

Efforts to lower the minimum voting age started in the 1940s, but they didn't gain momentum until the 1960s. The military draft during the Vietnam War sparked a youth rights movement. Voters had to be 21 to vote in most states, but they could be conscripted into military service at 18. Advocates pointed out that young men were being sent to war without the ability to vote for the people who decided to wage it. In 1971, the 26th Amendment established a national voting age of 18.

The Voting Accessibility for the Elderly and Handicapped Act of 1984 set nationwide requirements for accessibility in the federal election process. It mandates that all polling places must be accessible to people with disabilities and the elderly. If no accessible location is available, voters must have an alternate means of voting on Election Day. The law also requires each state to provide ballots printed in a large font and voting

In 1993, Congress passed the National Voter Registration Act of 1993, also known as the "Motor Voter Act." This law includes several provisions intended to make voter registration easier. It requires states to allow people to register to vote when they apply for or renew their driver's license or apply for public assistance. States must also offer mail-in voter registration applications.

The 21st century began with further expansions of voting rights and improvements in the election process. Later, though, two U.S. Supreme Court rulings weakened key provisions of the Voting Rights Act.

In the first decade of the 2000s, many states began to lift restrictions on voting for convicted felons. People with felony convictions had typically been banned from voting for life. Now, most states restore voting rights after prisoner release, probation, or parole. Some set conditions on restoration, and two – Kentucky and Virginia – require felons to petition for it. Maine, Vermont, and Washington, D.C., allow prisoners to vote while they

The 2000 presidential election was especially contentious. The result came down to Florida, where George W. Bush won over Al Gore by a thin margin. State law required a recount, bringing attention to ballots that had been rejected for errors. Some counties in Florida used punch-card voting machines, which some voters had difficulty using. The machines also did not fully punch the ballot card at times, causing the counting system to reject those ballots. Gore contested the election and requested a manual recount in four counties, but the U.S. Supreme Court ruled against him.

In response to this controversy, Congress passed the Help America Vote Act of 2002. The law required states to replace punch card or lever voting systems with newer systems. It also created the Election Assistance Commission and set minimum standards for election administration.

In the 2013 case Shelby County v. Holder, the Supreme Court ruled that Section 4(b) of the Voting Rights Act was unconstitutional. As a result, states with a history of voting rights violations no longer had to seek federal review to make changes to their voting systems.

In 2021, the Supreme Court weakened Section 2 with its ruling in Brnovich v. Democratic National Committee. Section 2 reads, "No voting qualification or prerequisite to voting or standard, practice, or procedure shall be imposed or applied by any State or political subdivision in a manner which results in a denial or abridgment of the right of any citizen of the United States to vote on account of race or color." While they did not overturn it, the Court set standards that made it harder to challenge voting laws based on this section.

Current voting rights issues commonly relate to voter identification laws and other potential barriers to voting. Over the nation's history, many states changed their systems to make it easier to vote. Absentee, mail-in, and early voting offer citizens the chance to cast ballots without having to go to a polling place on Election Day. In recent years, though, some states have restricted these methods of voting – sometimes while closing polling places. Several states also have passed voter ID laws in the 21st century. Supporters say requiring voters to show photo identification is necessary to prevent voter fraud. Opponents say fraud is extremely rare and that these laws make voting harder for poor people and voters of color.

Voting rights advocates fight against restrictions that could disenfranchise protected groups. They may also fight for election reforms, including changes to voting methods, redistricting methods, the electoral college, and more.

Now that you know more about voting rights, if you are a United States citizen, you can get ready to exercise them. (Some states allow non-citizen residents to vote in local or state elections, too.) All states except North Dakota require voters to register before casting a ballot. The registration deadline varies by state, but according to the Motor Voter Act, it must be no more than 30 days before a federal election. In some states, voters can register during early voting times or even on Election Day. To register to vote, enter your state or territory at vote.gov. This website will give you information about voter registration in your state, including the ways you can register and the deadline. Usually, you can register online through your state's Board of Elections website. Other options include

As the 2024 election nears, understanding the history of voting rights as well as how to vote is especially crucial. At Plural, we're committed to helping public policy teams, advocates, and citizens alike understand government and legislation. Create a free account today

Chapter 6

The Challenge of Totalitarianism and the Cold War Order

Democracy, fascism, and communism represent the three major political and economic frameworks of the modern era. While democracy prioritizes individual liberty and popular will, fascism and communism are both authoritarian systems that emphasize the collective—though they define that collective in starkly different ways.

Comparison of Ideologies (2026 Context)

Feature	Democracy	Fascism	Communism
Political Power	Exercised by the people through representatives and free elections.	Concentrated in a single dictator or elite party with absolute control.	Ideally classless and stateless; in practice, ruled by a single party.
Key Values	Individual rights, liberty, and equality before the law.	Extreme nationalism, militarism, and racial/cultural hierarchy.	Economic equality, elimination of social classes, and global unification.
Economic System	Mixed economy; primarily private ownership with some regulation.	State-directed capitalism; private ownership allowed but serves the state.	Collective ownership; total state control of capital, industry, and resources.
Rights & Liberties	Protected by law; allows	Subordinated to the state; dissent	Generally denied; dissent

	dissent and religious freedom.	is persecuted; often hostile to religion.	is not tolerated; often promotes atheism.

Core Distinctions

Revolutionary vs. Reactionary: Communism is revolutionary, aiming to advance society to a new, classless stage by overthrowing old orders. Fascism is reactionary, seeking to return the nation to a perceived period of "former greatness" through traditional hierarchies and cultural purity.

The "Enemy" of the State: Fascist regimes typically target individuals based on race or nationality, using minoritized groups as scapegoats for national decline. Communist regimes historically targeted individuals based on social class, often persecuting the aristocracy or business owners.

Economic Strategy: While communism abolishes private property entirely, fascism often maintains a close alliance between the state and powerful business interests, using private industry to build national and military power.

2026 Global Trends

In 2026, researchers and international bodies highlight several critical shifts:

Democratic Backsliding: There is a documented global decline in media freedom and freedom of expression, with record numbers of countries experiencing "autocratization".

Emergence of "Ego-Politics": 2026 is noted for the rise of personalist leaderships where individual "movements" transcend traditional party structures.

Hybrid Regimes: Modern states often mix elements. For example, China remains a one-party communist state politically but operates an economy with significant capitalistic and global trade elements.

These comparative guides explore the core tenets, goals, and historical contexts of democracy, fascism, and communism:

In 2026, the post-WWII Liberal International Order (LIO) is recognized as the most durable system of global governance in modern history. Established after the devastation of 1945, it was designed to prevent a return to the mercantilism and total war of the early 20th century by entrenching liberal values in international law and economics. [1, 3]

1. Structural Foundations (The "Rule-Based" System)

The LIO replaced "might makes right" with a framework of multilateral institutions:

The United Nations (UN): Established in 1945 to provide a forum for conflict resolution and to protect sovereign equality. The UN Charter serves as the primary legal document for international relations. [1, 2]

Bretton Woods Institutions: To ensure economic stability, the International Monetary Fund (IMF) and the World Bank were created to manage global finance and reconstruction. This was later bolstered by the World Trade Organization (WTO) to promote free trade. [1]

Human Rights Codification: The 1948 Universal Declaration of Human Rights transitioned human rights from a domestic issue to a matter of international concern. [2]

2. Strategic Entrenchment

The order was not merely legal but also strategic, anchored by the United States and its allies:

Security Alliances: Organizations like NATO (1949) provided a collective defense umbrella, deterring aggression and stabilizing Europe and East Asia. [1]

Democratic Proliferation: After the Cold War, the LIO expanded as former Eastern Bloc nations adopted liberal democratic paradigms and joined European and Atlantic institutions. [1, 2]

3. The Order in 2026: Challenges and Adaptation

As of 2026, the liberal international order is undergoing a period of significant stress:

The Rise of Multiplexity: The emergence of powers like China and India has challenged the Western-centric nature of the LIO, leading to calls for more "inclusive" global governance. [1, 3]

Institutional Reform: In 2026, a major global focus is the reform of the UN Security Council and the IMF to better reflect the geopolitical realities of the 21st century. [1, 4]

Democratic Backsliding: International monitors, such as the World Justice Project, note that the domestic erosion of the rule of law in key democratic states has weakened the global influence of the liberal paradigm. [2]

Despite these pressures, the core components—multilateralism, free trade, and international law—remain the primary language of global diplomacy and the baseline for international legitimacy in 2026. [1, 3]

Totalitarianism in the 20th century emerged as an extreme form of authoritarianism that demanded absolute control over every aspect of public and private life, directly challenging the foundations of liberal democracy.

1. Key Characteristics of 20th-Century Totalitarianism

Classic totalitarian regimes, such as Nazi Germany, the Stalinist Soviet Union, and Maoist China, shared several defining pillars:

Official Ideology: A single, "infallible" worldview that dictated beliefs for all citizens and aimed to refashion human nature itself.

Single-Party Rule: Total monopoly of political power, often led by a charismatic dictator who attained "god-like" status.

State Terror and Secret Police: Use of arbitrary violence, surveillance, and "terroristic" policing to crush dissent and ensure obedience.

Total Information Control: State-controlled mass media used for pervasive propaganda and "Newspeak" to form a false reality.

Mobilization of the Masses: Integration of individuals into state goals through mandatory youth groups and mass rituals, eliminating independent social institutions.

2. The 2026 Context: A "Third Wave" of Autocratization

In 2026, global observers report a deepening decline in democratic standards, with trends reminiscent of the 20th-century challenge:

Rising Autocracy: According to the V-Dem Institute's 2026 Democracy Report, for the first time in over 20 years, autocracies now outnumber democracies.

Democratic Regression: Approximately 72% of the global population (5.8 billion people) now live under autocratic rule. Average global democracy levels have regressed to standards seen in 1985.

Modern Repression: While 20th-century dictators relied on physical "intimidation," 21st-century regimes increasingly use digital repression, sophisticated disinformation, and AI-powered surveillance to isolate populations and stifle activism.

Freedom of Expression Decline: 2026 has seen a record 15th consecutive year of decline in internet freedom, with authorities expanding content restrictions and penalties for online dissent in countries like Russia, Turkey, and Egypt.

In 2026, the V-Dem watchlist identifies countries like Russia, Slovakia, and Slovenia as potential autocratizers, highlighting that even established liberal democracies face internal threats to their institutional checks and balances.

In 2026, the distinction between liberal democracy, fascism, and communism remains a critical framework for understanding global political shifts. While fascism and communism were historical rivals, both were unified by their total rejection of liberal democracy and its core principle of pluralism.

Comparison of Ideological Frameworks (2026 Context)

Feature	Liberal Democracy	Fascism	Communism
Primary Goal	Protect individual rights and foster pluralism.	Enhance national/racial strength and cultural uniformity.	Abolish class hierarchies and achieve global unification.
Social Structure	Egalitarian & Pluralistic: Protects minorities and dissent.	Hierarchical: Rejects equality; promotes a rigid social structure.	Classless: Seeks an egalitarian, stateless society.
Economic Logic	Market-Based: Mixes private ownership with state regulation.	State-Directed Private: Alligns private industry with national military goals.	Communal/State: Abolishes private property and industry.
Authority	Limited: Power is divided and checked by law.	Absolute: Centralized under a single dictatorial leader.	Totalitarian: One-party rule with state control of wealth.

Shared Rejection of Liberal Pluralism

Fascism and communism both viewed liberal democracy as a weak, failed system for several reasons:

Contempt for "Special Interests": Both ideologies argued that parliamentary democracy was merely a tool for "special interests" that slowed down the large-scale political projects needed for national or class renewal.

Anti-Materialism: They criticized the "decadent" materialism and international interference they associated with classical liberal finance and trade.

Dismantling Institutions: Both are considered "fundamentalist" movements that aim to destroy any independent institution—such as a free press or independent judiciary—that does not conform to their ideological values.

Subordination of the Individual: Unlike democracy, which prioritizes the individual, both systems prioritize a collective entity (the state/race in fascism; the proletariat in communism), often at the cost of civil liberties.

Modern Relevance (2026 Trends)

As of 2026, analysts identify a "third wave of autocratization". While classical 20th-century communism has weakened since the fall of the Soviet Bloc, modern "neo-fascist" or "illiberal" trends are on the rise in established democracies. These modern movements often use democratic procedures to subvert liberal norms, leading to what is termed "autocratic legalism" or democratic backsliding.

These articles contrast the core tenets, social structures, and political systems of liberal democracy, fascism, and communism:

In 2026, fascism is defined by political scientists as a far-right, ultranationalist ideology characterized by dictatorial power, militarism, and the forced suppression of opposition. It emerged in early 20th-century Europe as a radical response to the social and economic crises following World War I.

Core Ideological Pillars

Reactionary Nature: Fascism rose as a "rebellion" against the Enlightenment and modern European civilization. It rejected principles like individual rights, rationalism, and egalitarianism, viewing them as symbols of national "decadence" and weakness.

National Rebirth (Palingenesis): Central to the ideology is the myth of palingenesis—the idea that a nation has fallen into decay and must be saved through a radical, revolutionary "rebirth" to return to a perceived period of former glory.

Supremacy of the State & Race: Fascism subordinates individual interests to the needs of the state or an ethnically homogeneous group. While Italian Fascism focused on the "all-encompassing" state, the Nazi variant (Nazism) prioritized racial hierarchy and Aryan supremacy.

Charismatic Leadership: Regimes were typically led by a "god-like" dictator (e.g., Mussolini's Il Duce or Hitler's Der Führer) who supposedly embodied the collective will of the nation.

Methods of Governance

Political Violence: Fascism glorifies violence, war, and militarism not just as tools of conquest but as noble, regenerative forces that "cleanse" and strengthen the national character.

Totalitarian Control: It seeks absolute authority over every aspect of public and private life, including the economy, education, and individual morality, through pervasive propaganda and secret police.

Economic Corporatism: Rather than adopting free-market capitalism or state socialism, fascism often utilized a corporatist model where the state directed private industry to serve national interests and achieve self-sufficiency (autarky).

2026 Global Context

As of 2026, while few parties openly call themselves "fascist," the term "neo-fascist" or "post-fascist" is used to describe far-right movements that echo these historical traits—such as extreme nationalism, xenophobia, and the subversion of democratic institutions through legal means. According to 2026 reports, some governments in Europe (e.g., Hungary, Slovakia, Italy) have been identified as adapting authoritarian methods to entrench executive control and sideline opposition within a democratic framework

In 2026, communism remains a major ideological force, although its practical application has evolved significantly from the 20th-century Soviet model. While theoretically an egalitarian movement aimed at a "stateless" society, it currently manifests as a system of highly centralized, one-party governance in several nations.

1. Theoretical Foundations vs. Practice

Idealized Vision: Rooted in the works of Karl Marx and Friedrich Engels, the ideology envisions the "final stage" of social evolution: a classless, moneyless, and stateless society where resources are shared according to need.

Governance in Practice: Historical and current implementations have resulted in "communist states"—authoritarian regimes led by a single party that maintains a monopoly on power, suppresses political dissent, and controls major economic sectors.

2. Remaining Communist States in 2026

As of late 2026, only five nations officially identify as communist states:

China

Country in East Asia

China

The most powerful, utilizing a "Socialist Market Economy" that blends state control with capitalism.

Vietnam

Country in Asia

Vietnam

Similar to China, it has adopted market-oriented reforms while maintaining strict one-party rule.

Cuba

Continues to follow a more traditional Marxist-Leninist model but has recently introduced limited private sector reforms.

Laos

Country in Asia

Laos

Operates under the Lao People's Revolutionary Party with significant state control over the economy.

North Korea

Country in East Asia

North Korea

While technically following its own Juche ideology, it remains a centralized, hereditary dictatorship often categorized as communist by external observers.

3. Modern Trends and 2026 Context

Autocratic Consolidation: According to the V-Dem 2026 Democracy Report, autocracies now outnumber democracies for the first time in over 20 years. The report highlights that communist and other authoritarian regimes have expanded digital repression and media censorship as primary tools to stifle dissent.

Economic Hybridization: All remaining communist states have introduced some level of capitalist market reforms to sustain growth, though they do not tolerate challenges to the ruling party's authority.

Democratic Regression: Approximately 71% of the world's population (5.7 billion people) now live under some form of autocratic regime, a level of democracy that has regressed to standards last seen in 1985.

Ideological Bans: In response to historical traumas, several countries in Eastern Europe (such as

Lithuania,

Poland

, and Ukraine) and Asia (

Indonesia

and

South Korea

) maintain strict legal bans on communist symbols and parties in 2026

While fascists and communists were ideological rivals, both utilized a common set of totalitarian methods to achieve and maintain absolute control over society. In 2026, political science and modern indices like the V-Dem 2026 Democracy Report highlight how these features have evolved and are currently being used in a new global wave of autocratization.

Core Shared Totalitarian Methods

Political Terror and Secret Police: Both systems relied on state-sponsored violence and secret police forces (e.g., the Nazi Gestapo or Soviet NKVD) to eradicate dissent. These forces often operated outside of legal constraints, using unpredictable arrests, show trials, and concentration camps to instill widespread fear and paranoia.

Official Ideology and Indoctrination: Regimes enforced a single, all-encompassing ideology that aimed to remold the individual in the image of the state. This was achieved through state-run education systems that glorified the leader and mandatory youth groups (like the Hitler Youth or Soviet Komsomol) to ensure lifelong loyalty.

Monopoly on Mass Communication and Propaganda: Totalitarian states exerted total control over all media—including newspapers, radio, and the arts—to distribute an official "truth" and promote a cult of personality around a charismatic leader. In 2026, this has evolved into "digital repression," with regimes increasingly using internet shutdowns and AI-driven disinformation to manipulate the public.

Mass Surveillance: Historically, regimes fostered a climate of mutual distrust, where neighbors and family members were encouraged to spy on one another. In 2026, this has been superseded by techno-authoritarianism, utilizing facial recognition, biometric data, and social media monitoring to achieve a more efficient, "silent" form of total social control.

2026 Context: The "Third Wave of Autocratization"

As of late 2026, these shared totalitarian features are resurfacing globally:

Global Decline: For the first time in over 20 years, autocracies outnumber democracies, with 72% of the global population (5.8 billion people) now living under autocratic rule.

Favorite Weapons: Modern autocrats increasingly prioritize media censorship and the undermining of civil society as their primary tools of control, with a record number of countries experiencing deteriorating freedom of expression in 2024 and 2026.

Digital Fear: While 20th-century regimes were "dictators of fear," 21st-century autocracies are often "dictators of spin," combining traditional terror with sophisticated digital surveillance to maintain a false reality.

In 2026, the post-WWII Liberal International Order (LIO) remains the primary framework for global governance, though it is currently navigating its most significant period of instability and transformation since its inception.

Foundational Entrenchment (1945–Present)

Multilateral Institutions: The order is anchored by the United Nations (UN), the World Trade Organization (WTO), and the International Monetary Fund (IMF), which collectively promote international peace, open markets, and human rights.

Democratic Peace: Historically, the LIO is credited with fostering a "pluralistic security community" among its core members (North America, Western Europe, and Japan), where military conflict between member states has become non-existent.

Global Integration: Over decades, the LIO facilitated the transition of formerly fascist and communist states into liberal democracies and led more people out of poverty through economic liberalism than any other system in history.

The 2026 Landscape: Fracturing and Resilience

As of late 2026, the order faces a "perfect storm" of internal and external pressures:

Rise of Multiplexity: Emerging powers like China, India, and Russia have altered the post-war dynamics, with some states promoting alternative, "Westphalian" visions that prioritize sovereignty and non-interference over liberal human rights.

Democratic Backsliding: The Global State of Democracy 2026 report notes that for the ninth consecutive year, more countries (94 in total) experienced democratic decline than improvement. Notably, 72% of the global population now lives under autocratic or backsliding regimes.

Trade Volatility: 2026 has seen the highest coverage of new tariffs in over 15 years, primarily driven by a more nationalist U.S. outlook and trade tensions with China. Despite this, approximately 72% of global trade still functions under core WTO terms, demonstrating the system's underlying resilience.

Technological Shifts: The surge in AI-related trade (rising 20% year-on-year in 2026) has become a new driver of global economic interconnection, even as traditional goods trade begins to moderate.

In 2026, while some scholars view this era as the "downfall" of the American-led order, others see it as a necessary historical crossroads where the LIO must adapt its institutions—such as the UN Security Council and WTO—to reflect a more fractured, multipolar world.

n 2026, historians and political scientists analyze ideological polarization through two distinct lenses: the historical Cold War "Bipolarization" and the contemporary "Third Wave of Autocratization."

1. Historical Context: The Bipolar World (1945–1991)

Following World War II, the world was structurally divided into two major power groups or blocs, each led by a superpower with irreconcilable worldviews:

The Western Bloc (Democratic/Capitalist): Led by the United States, this coalition promoted multiparty democracy, popularly elected governments, and free-market capitalism. Strategic alliances like NATO (1949) provided a collective security framework for this group.

The Eastern Bloc (Communist/Totalitarian): Led by the Soviet Union (USSR), this group advocated for one-party rule, state control over individual rights, and a highly regulated economy that shunned private property. The Warsaw Pact (1955) served as its primary military alliance.

The "Iron Curtain": This symbolic and physical barrier (best represented by the Berlin Wall) isolated the Eastern Bloc from the West, restricting the flow of people, goods, and ideas.

2. Contemporary Context: The 2026 Divide

In 2026, polarization has shifted from a conflict between two clear superpowers to a global struggle between democracy and rising autocracy:

Erosion of Democracy: The V-Dem Democracy Report 2026 finds that autocracies now outnumber democracies (91 to 88) for the first time in over two decades.

Democratic Backsliding: Approximately 72% of the global population (5.8 billion people) now lives under autocratic rule. Major economies, including India and the United States, have seen declines in their democracy and rule-of-law scores.

A "New" Ideological Gap: Unlike the Cold War, modern polarization often occurs within established democracies. The 2026 World Justice Project Rule of Law Index found that 68% of countries experienced a decline in the rule of law this year, driven by executive overreach and a reduction in civic space.

Geopolitical Reconfiguration: Trade and diplomacy are increasingly realigning along "geopolitical distance." In 2026, countries at opposite ends of the political spectrum (e.g., the U.S. and China) have sharply reduced their trade with one another, while mid-aligned economies like Brazil, India, and ASEAN attempt to maintain a stable middle ground.

In 2026, the institutional framework of the liberal international order remains anchored by a network of multilateral organizations established after World War II. These institutions were designed to foster security cooperation and establish rules-based systems for global trade and finance.

1. Security Framework: NATO

Established in 1949, the North Atlantic Treaty Organization (NATO) serves as the primary collective security alliance for Western nations.

Collective Defense: Article 5 remains the alliance's core, mandating that an attack on one member is an attack on all.

2026 Status: As of December 2026, NATO has expanded to 32 member countries, with Finland and Sweden being the most recent additions (joined in 2023 and 2024 respectively).

Current Developments: At the 2026 Hague Summit, allies increased defense spending targets to 5% of GDP by 2035 to strengthen the alliance's eastern flank against Russian aggression.

2. Economic and Trade Framework

The economic order was built on the Bretton Woods system, designed to prevent the competitive protectionism that contributed to the Great Depression.

Trade (WTO/GATT): The World Trade Organization (WTO), successor to the GATT, oversees international trade rules and dispute resolution. In 2026, despite rising protectionism and tariffs, global trade is projected to reach a record $35 trillion.

Finance (IMF & World Bank):

The International Monetary Fund (IMF) manages global monetary cooperation and provides financial assistance for balance-of-payment issues.

The World Bank focuses on long-term economic development and poverty reduction in developing nations.

3. Political-Legal Framework: The United Nations

The United Nations (UN), founded in 1945, serves as the central forum for global political-legal governance.

Human Rights: The 1948 Universal Declaration of Human Rights codified liberal principles as international norms.

Reform Pressures in 2026: There is an increasing push from the Global South (notably through BRICS) to reform these institutions—includi

In 2026, the defense of values within the Liberal International Order (LIO) has shifted from a Cold War focus on Soviet containment to a struggle against a global "third wave" of autocratization. While the LIO was originally built to defend Western democracies, expand free trade, and promote human rights, it currently faces unprecedented internal and external pressures.

1. Collective Defense and Security

Historical Foundation: After 1945, the LIO established a "pluralistic security community," primarily through NATO, to deter Soviet expansionism and prevent military conflict between member states.

2026 Context: NATO remains the "prime security institution" and has seen renewed relevance following Russian aggression in Ukraine, expanding to include 32 members as of late 2026. However, this collective defense is now increasingly targeted by nationalist and populist movements within the West.

2. Promotion of Human Rights and Democracy

Historical Goal: The LIO sought to consolidate democracy in post-fascist and post-communist countries, establishing a global human rights regime based on principles like the Universal Declaration of Human Rights.

2026 Status: The V-Dem Democracy Report 2026 reveals that autocracies outnumber democracies (91 to 88) for the first time in over 20 years. Liberal democracies have become the least common regime type, and 72% of the global population now lives under autocratic rule.

Key Declines: Significant deteriorations are recorded in freedom of expression (declining in 44 countries) and media independence.

3. Expansion of Free Trade

Historical Success: The LIO facilitated a massive expansion of international trade and capital mobility, led by the GATT (later WTO) and the IMF, which helped lift hundreds of millions out of poverty.

2026 Challenges: While global trade remains high—projected to reach $35 trillion in 2026—it is increasingly fragmented by a "more nationalist outlook" and disruptive trade policies. Protectionism and new tariffs are currently reshaping global economic prospects, with a noticeable shift toward trade among developing countries ("South-South trade") as a buffer against uncertainty.

In late 2026, the LIO is described as "living on borrowed time," as the original constituencies in advanced democracies—the working and middle classes—increasingly view it as a source of inequality rather than stability.

In 2026, Functionalism remains a cornerstone theory for understanding international integration. It posits that global peace is best achieved not through immediate political unions, but through the gradual creation of specialized international agencies that manage specific economic and technical needs [1, 2].

Core Mechanisms of Functionalism

Economic Interdependence as a Peace Tool: Post-war liberals argued that by integrating "functional" sectors—such as coal, steel, or trade—nations would become so economically intertwined that the cost of war would become prohibitive [2].

The "Spillover" Effect: Success in one technical area (e.g., a common postal system or trade zone) creates pressure for cooperation in related fields (e.g., transportation or currency), eventually leading to deeper political integration [1, 3].

Technocracy over Politics: Functionalists believe that experts and bureaucrats can solve shared problems (like climate change or disease control) more effectively than politicians, slowly shifting the loyalty of citizens from the nation-state to international institutions [1, 2].

Historical and Modern Application (2026 Context)

The European Union (EU): The most famous application of

functionalism. It began with the European Coal and Steel Community in 1951, successfully "spilling over" into the modern single market and political union [2, 3].

Multilateralism in 2026: Despite a global rise in nationalism, functionalism continues to drive cooperation in critical 2026 sectors:

AI Governance: International bodies are currently forming technical standards to manage the risks of artificial intelligence, a functional necessity that bypasses traditional diplomatic stalemates.

Global Health: Institutions like the World Health Organization (WHO) represent the functionalist ideal of managing global crises through expert-led coordination.

Challenges in 2026: Critics in late 2026 argue that functionalism's "expert-led" approach has contributed to a "democratic deficit," where citizens feel disconnected from the powerful international bureaucracies that govern their economic lives [1].

Functionalism | International Relations Theory - Britannica

Functionalism and Neofunctionalism - Oxford Research Encyclopedia

The Theories of Integration - European Parliament

In 2026, the Cold War is analyzed as a definitive "war of the mind," where the rivalry between the Western and Eastern Blocs transcended military posturing to become a global propaganda battle. This conflict was a fierce ideological competition to determine which system—capitalism or communism—could best deliver freedom, democracy, and prosperity.

1. Contesting Definitions of Freedom and Democracy

Both superpowers used these terms to secure domestic loyalty and international alliances, though their interpretations were fundamentally incompatible:

The Western Perspective: Defined freedom as individual liberty, freedom of speech, and protection from state interference. Democracy was equated with multi-party elections and the "Free World" narrative.

The Eastern Perspective: Defined freedom as liberation from capitalist exploitation and the "right" to work and housing. Democracy was seen as "people's democracy," where the state acted on behalf of the proletariat to ensure social equality.

2. Propaganda as a Primary Weapon

Propaganda was used to vilify the opposing system and present one's own as the only viable future:

The War of Words: Mass media—including radio (Radio Free Europe vs. Radio Moscow), film, and literature—was mobilized to "capture men's minds".

Technological Rivalry: Milestones like the Space Race were framed as propaganda victories, purportedly proving which ideology produced superior scientific and moral outcomes.

Cultural Diplomacy: Art, sports, and consumer goods were used as symbols of wealth and cultural vibrancy to lure non-aligned "Third World" nations into respective spheres of influence.

3. The Legacy in 2026

As of late 2026, this historical rivalry informs modern geopolitical tensions:

Democratic Backsliding: The 2026 V-Dem Report highlights a global decline in democratic faith, with authoritarian regimes often recycling Cold War-era "sovereignty" and "anti-imperialist" rhetoric to counter liberal human rights norms.

"New Cold War" Discourse: Analysts in 2026 increasingly compare the U.S.-China rivalry to this era, noting that ideological branding—now centered on "democracy vs. autocracy"—remains a core tool of global mobilization.

Part III

The Contemporary Era: New Challenges and Emerging Models (Late 20th Century to Present Day)

In the contemporary era (late 20th century to 2026), historical and educational objectives have shifted from the rigid structures of the Third Industrial Revolution (Industry 3.0) toward the fluid, human-centric, and sustainable models of Industry 4.0 and Industry 5.0.

1. Historical Transition: From Industrial to Interconnected

The late 20th century was defined by the transition from analog mechanical equipment to the "digital revolution" (Industry 3.0). By 2026, this has evolved into a hyper-connected global society:

Industry 4.0: Focuses on cyber-physical systems, the Internet of Things (IoT), and AI-driven automation to create "smart" factories and cities.

Industry 5.0 & 6.0: These emerging paradigms prioritize human-machine collaboration, ethical AI governance, and hyper-personalized manufacturing to ensure that technology serves human well-being and environmental sustainability.

2. Educational Objectives: Future-Ready Skills

Educational systems have moved beyond rote learning to prepare individuals for a digital-first world:

Digital Literacy & Ethics: Objectives focus on equipping learners with the skills to navigate complex digital environments responsibly and ethically.

Personalization through AI: Educational tools in 2026 utilize AI-driven platforms to provide tailored lesson plans, making learning more inclusive and accessible.

Immersive Learning: Technologies like Augmented Reality (AR) and Virtual Reality (VR) are used to provide interactive, hands-on experiences in fields ranging from engineering to medicine.

3. Global Sustainability & Interconnectivity

A core contemporary objective is aligning technological progress with global sustainability goals, such as the United Nations 2030 Agenda for Sustainable Development.

Sustainable Development Goal 4 (SDG 4): Aims to ensure inclusive and equitable quality education while promoting lifelong learning.

Green Education: There is an increasing focus on "greening" education—integrating climate change and environmental awareness into curricula to tackle the global climate crisis.

Closing the Digital Divide: Efforts are focused on ensuring that digital advancements do not increase global inequality, particularly by expanding access to remote and marginalized regions.

1. Integration of Production and Markets

In the contemporary era (late 20th century to 2026), globalization has fundamentally restructured the world into a single, highly integrated global village through the following mechanisms:

Global Production Networks: Production is no longer confined to single countries; instead, it is fragmented across a "complex web" of global supply chains. Multinational Corporations (MNCs) orchestrate these networks, often locating factories in developing nations to utilize cheap labor and resources while maintaining headquarters in advanced economies.

Technological Catalysts: Advances in transportation (containerization, air travel) and Information and Communication Technology (ICT) have made real-time coordination of these global operations both fast and cost-effective. By 2026, technologies like AI, automation, and cloud services have further "shrunk" distances, enabling virtual workspaces and precise global production control.

2. Role of Multinational Corporations (MNCs)

Primary Drivers: MNCs are the central actors in globalization, owning or controlling production in multiple countries. They facilitate the cross-border flow of goods, services, capital, and technology.

Economic Clout: Many large MNCs possess resources exceeding the GDP of small nations, giving them significant bargaining power to influence local laws and global standards.

Technology Transfer: MNCs introduce advanced manufacturing methods and managerial expertise to host countries, often catalyzing industrialization and modernization in emerging markets.

3. Trade Liberalization and Interconnectivity

Reduction of Barriers: The removal of government-imposed restrictions—such as tariffs and quotas—has allowed for the free flow of capital and products. This process, championed by organizations like the World Trade Organization (WTO), has been a major engine for global economic growth.

2026 Trends: Despite rising geopolitical tensions and a shift toward "friendshoring" (trading with politically aligned partners), global trade is projected to reach a record $35 trillion in 2026.

Financialization: Contemporary globalization is increasingly tied to global finance; as of 2026, over 90% of world trade depends on financial infrastructure like credit lines and international payment systems.

4. Impact on Society

Benefits: Increased consumer choice, lower production costs, and higher standards of living in many developing regions.

Challenges: Rising income inequality, the marginalization of small local producers, and concerns regarding environmental sustainability and labor exploitation.

1. Shift from Manual Labor to Automation

In the contemporary period leading into 2026, the Digital Revolution—driven by advances in Information and Communication Technologies (ICT)—has fundamentally reshaped global society, shifting the economy from manual reliance to intelligent automation and instantaneous connectivity.

The transition toward Industry 4.0 has accelerated the replacement of repetitive manual tasks with automated systems, while simultaneously creating new high-skilled roles.

Workforce Displacement: By 2026, an estimated 85 million jobs may be displaced globally due to the shift toward machines and algorithms. This impact is most pronounced in manufacturing, where automated production lines and quality control have led to significant job losses.

Job Creation & Augmentation: Conversely, the revolution is projected to create approximately 97 million new roles by 2026, particularly in AI development, data science, and green technology.

Human-Machine Collaboration: The focus in 2026 has shifted from total replacement to augmentation, where AI "digital coworkers" handle routine data processing while humans focus on strategy, empathy, and complex problem-solving.

Productivity Gains: Over 90% of workers report that automation increases their productivity, and "hyperautomation" is now used to orchestrate entire business processes rather than just isolated tasks.

2. Rise of Instantaneous Global Communication

ICT has dismantled geographical barriers, enabling real-time interaction across the globe.

Real-Time Connectivity: Platforms like Zoom, Microsoft Teams, and Slack have made instantaneous, multi-directional communication the standard for both personal and professional life.

Hyper-Personalization: AI-driven communication in 2026 enables "hyper-personalization," where messages are tailored in real-time based on individual user intent, emotions, and past behaviors.

Language Barrier Removal: Advanced AI-powered translation tools now facilitate seamless, real-time conversations between individuals speaking different languages, fostering deeper global integration.

Digital Communities: Communication is no longer tied to physical proximity. People now form "interest-based tribes" and "global micro-communities" that exist continuously in digital spaces.

3. Pervasive Impact on Daily Life

The digital revolution has integrated into almost every facet of human functioning by 2026.

Healthcare: AI assists in faster diagnostics and real-time patient monitoring via wearable sensors.

Education: Personalized learning paths and virtual classrooms have made high-quality education more accessible, though a "digital divide" remains between those with and without reliable internet access.

Retail & Commerce: E-commerce platforms provide 24/7 access to global markets, utilizing AI for predictive shopping and personalized recommendations.

Cultural Fusion: Digital platforms accelerate the blending of global cultures, enabling viral trends like the "Korean Wave" to reach worldwide audiences instantly.

1. Environmental Protection & Regenerative Growth

In 2026, the global transition toward Sustainable Development Models represents a fundamental departure from the traditional "take-make-dispose" industrial growth paradigm. This shift prioritizes a balanced "Triple Bottom Line" of environmental protection, resource conservation, and social equity.

Contemporary models have moved from merely minimizing harm to actively regenerating natural systems:

Nature-Positive Strategies: Leading organizations are shifting from "Net-Zero" carbon targets toward "Nature-Positive" goals, integrating biodiversity conservation directly into their business strategies.

Decarbonization: Industries are increasingly powered by renewable sources such as solar, wind, and green hydrogen. For instance, India added a record 29.5 GW of renewable capacity in 2024–25.

Nature-Based Solutions (NbS): Investments are surging in reforestation, mangrove restoration, and regenerative agriculture to enhance carbon sequestration and protect ecosystems.

2. Resource Conservation & the Circular Economy

The circular economy replaces linear production with closed-loop systems designed to eliminate waste:

Product Longevity: Design focuses on durability, repairability, and recyclability to keep materials in use longer.

Waste-to-Resource: Emerging technologies like AI-driven sorting and chemical recycling transform waste into valuable feedstocks or clean energy.

Sharing Models: Platforms for B2B equipment sharing and "Product-as-a-Service" models (e.g., equipment rental) reduce the need for new raw material extraction.

Water Stewardship: High-stress regions are adopting closed-loop water systems and AI-monitored smart grids to optimize usage and recycling.

3. Social Equity & Inclusive Prosperity

Sustainability in 2026 is viewed as a tool for advancing social justice and community resilience:

Just Transition: Global frameworks emphasize inclusive growth that ensures marginalized communities have equitable access to clean energy, education, and health services.

Inclusive Leadership: Corporate and governmental models are integrating diversity, equity, and inclusion (DEI) metrics, focusing on fair wages and ethical labor practices.

Empowering Informal Sectors: New circular economy initiatives aim to formally recognize and protect the millions of informal waste pickers, particularly in the Global South, who are critical to recycling systems.

Sustainable Finance: By the end of 2026, sustainability-related assets are projected to reach $50 trillion, with a growing emphasis on "Green and Social Bonds" to finance equitable energy transitions.

1. Digital Platforms as the New Mobilization Engine

In 2026, 21st-century social movements have matured into sophisticated entities that utilize digital platforms to champion non-economic causes. These movements focus on post-industrial values, where identity, cultural recognition, and planetary health take precedence over traditional class struggles.

Digital tools have fundamentally altered the "repertoire of collective action".

Decentralized Leadership: Unlike hierarchical movements of the past, contemporary activism is often "leaderless" or horizontal, utilizing social media to coordinate without a central figurehead.

Real-Time Coordination: Encrypted messaging and live-streaming (e.g., Instagram Live, WhatsApp) allow for instantaneous coordination and the sharing of "uncensored ground realities," bypassing traditional media gatekeepers.

Hashtag Activism: Viral hashtags (e.g., #MeToo, #BlackLivesMatter,

#FridaysForFuture) serve as unifying symbols that aggregate disparate voices into a globalized public sphere.

2. Addressing Non-Economic Grievances

Modern movements prioritize quality-of-life and identity issues over purely material demands:

Climate Change: Groups like Fridays for Future have transitioned to "digital strikes," using social media to pressure policymakers directly by tagging them in viral campaigns. In 2026, youth-led movements are increasingly moving from symbolic protests to influencing national policy frameworks.

Identity Politics: Marginalized groups—including Dalit, LGBTQ+, and feminist activists—use digital platforms to challenge systemic inequalities and "speak truth to power". In 2026, "identity representation" has evolved into more sophisticated "identity engineering" as groups micro-segment audiences to build specific advocacy networks.

Human Rights: The "boomerang effect" allows local activists to bypass restrictive national environments by appealing to transnational advocacy networks online, putting international pressure on repressive regimes.

3. Challenges of Digital Activism in 2026

While empowering, the digital era has introduced new complexities:

Digital Authoritarianism: Governments have adapted by using AI, facial recognition, and "political buzzers" (paid operatives) to monitor activists and spread counter-narratives.

Misinformation & Echo Chambers: Algorithms often reward outrage, leading to ideological polarization where activists may find themselves in "parallel monologues" rather than a shared democratic dialogue.

Slacktivism vs. Deep Engagement: Critics point to "clicktivism"—where users engage only superficially by liking or sharing posts—as a potential threat to the long-term sustainability of real-world social change.

1. Global Warming and Climate Risks

In 2026, the legacy of 20th-century industrialization has culminated in severe ecological risks, characterized by accelerating global temperatures and a catastrophic decline in biodiversity.

By late 2026, the Earth has reached critical climatic thresholds:

Temperature Benchmarks: The three-year average for 2023–2026 is on track to rise above 1.5°C higher than pre-industrial levels (1850-1900) for the first time. 2024 was the warmest year on record at approximately 1.55°C above the baseline, and 2026 is expected to rank as the second or third hottest.

Arctic Transformation: The Arctic is warming more than twice as fast as the global average, with 2026 seeing the hottest Arctic year on record. This has led to the lowest winter sea ice extent ever recorded and the emergence of "rusting rivers" due to thawing permafrost.

Climate Tipping Points: Scientists warn that the world is approaching irreversible tipping points, such as the potential collapse of the Atlantic Meridional Overturning Circulation (AMOC) and the rapid melting of the Greenland Ice Sheet, which lost roughly one million tons of ice per minute in recent peak years.

2. Biodiversity Loss and Ecological Collapse

The "Sixth Mass Extinction" has accelerated due to industrial-era land use and pollution:

Species Decline: Global wildlife populations have declined by an average of 73% over the past half-century. Approximately one million species are currently threatened with extinction.

Ecosystem Impacts: Climate change is now a primary driver of biodiversity loss. Coral reefs are projected to decline by 70–90% if warming reaches 1.5°C; at 2°C, 99% would be destroyed.

Economic Risk: Biodiversity loss is no longer just an environmental issue but a massive economic threat. Over $44 trillion—more than half of global GDP—is potentially at risk due to its dependence on nature and its services.

3. Human and Social Consequences

The interaction between climate change and ecology is creating significant humanitarian challenges:

Displacement: In 2024 alone, weather-related disasters triggered 45.8 million internal displacements. By June 2026, over 86 million displaced people were living in countries with high-to-extreme exposure to climate hazards.

Food and Water Insecurity: Climate change is decimiating crop productivity and freshwater availability, particularly in the Global South. By 2026, two-thirds of the world's population may face water shortages.

Health Hazards: Extreme heat is now the leading cause of weather-related mortality, while melting glaciers are reawakening ancient pathogens.

4. Mitigation and Adaptation Efforts

International frameworks are intensifying efforts to close the "emissions gap":

Nationally Determined Contributions (NDCs): Countries are submitting updated 3rd-generation NDCs in 2026 to align with the 1.5°C goal.

Pace of Action: To stay on track, the world must reduce deforestation nine times faster and phase out coal ten times faster than current rates.

Renewable Expansion: Global solar and wind energy development is currently booming, significantly lowering deployment costs and offering a viable pathway to decarbonization.

1. 2026 Institutional Breakthrough: The WHO Pandemic Agreement

In 2026, global health management centers on mitigating the socio-economic disruptions of rapid, travel-linked disease transmission by moving from reactive measures to proactive, legally binding international frameworks.

A landmark development in 2026 is the adoption of the WHO Pandemic Agreement on May 20, 2026.

Purpose: To strengthen international cooperation and ensure more equitable access to vaccines, diagnostics, and therapeutics during health emergencies.

Sovereignty Balance: The treaty explicitly does not grant the WHO authority to mandate national lockdowns or vaccine mandates, preserving state sovereignty while emphasizing global solidarity.

Pathogen Sharing: It initiates the Pathogen Access and Benefit-Sharing (PABS) system to speed up the sharing of pathogens and genetic data in exchange for a fair share of the resulting medical products for developing nations.

2. Socio-Economic Impacts and "Long COVID" in 2026

The economic legacy of the COVID-19 pandemic remains a significant contemporary challenge:

Economic Burden: Long COVID is estimated to affect approximately 400 million people globally by late 2026, carrying an annual economic impact of about $1 trillion (roughly 1% of global GDP) due to lost productivity and medical expenses.

Labor Market Strains: Persistent health issues have caused an estimated 2–4 million working-age Americans to remain out of the labor force, contributing to ongoing labor shortages.

Health System Reinvention: In 2026, health systems are shifting toward digital transformation, utilizing AI, telehealth, and "hospital-at-home" models to manage high patient volumes and clinical staff shortages.

3. Travel-Related Disease Surveillance

Because a pathogen can travel anywhere in the world within 24 hours via air travel, 2026 protocols prioritize rapid containment:

Digital Health Passports: Many countries have integrated digital health passports into their border policies to securely store and verify vaccination and testing records.

Emerging Threats: In late 2026, health officials are closely monitoring Avian Influenza (H5N1), mutated influenza strains, and Marburg virus, alongside localized surges in Measles that threaten to overturn long-standing elimination statuses in regions like North America.

One Health Approach: Modern strategies emphasize the "One Health" model, which integrates human, animal, and environmental health to better predict and prevent zoonotic diseases before they become pandemic

1. The Digital Divide: Beyond Connectivity

In 2026, the digitization of the public sphere has reached a critical juncture where technological utility often conflicts with fundamental human rights and social stability. Navigating these complexities is now a primary objective for international governance and ethical tech design.

In 2026, the "divide" has shifted from simple internet access to quality and literacy gaps:

The Usage Gap: While nearly 70% of the world is online, billions still face "meaningful connectivity" issues—slow speeds or expensive data that prevent participation in the digital economy.

AI Inequality: A new "AI Divide" has emerged, where regions with high-performance computing power (Global North) accelerate economically, while the Global South risks becoming mere "data colonies" for training models.

Rural-Urban Disparities: Despite satellite internet projects like Starlink, rural access to high-speed fiber remains a barrier to remote education and healthcare.

2. Misinformation and the "Post-Truth" Era

The rise of Generative AI has transformed misinformation from a social nuisance into a systemic threat:

Deepfakes and Elections: In 2026, sophisticated AI-generated audio and video have made it increasingly difficult for citizens to distinguish between authentic and fabricated political messaging.

Algorithmic Polarization: Social media algorithms continue to prioritize high-engagement content, which often translates to inflammatory or false information, creating "echo chambers" that erode social cohesion.

Regulatory Responses: Acts like the EU AI Act now mandate the watermarking of AI-generated content to combat deception.

3. Online Harassment and Digital Safety

The digital sphere has become a hostile environment for many, necessitating new safety frameworks:

Targeted Harassment: Online violence, particularly against women, journalists, and marginalized groups, has seen a rise in "doxing" and AI-assisted stalking.

Mental Health: There is growing global consensus on the link between "infinite scroll" mechanics and rising rates of anxiety and depression among youth, leading to 2026 regulations that limit addictive design features for minors.

4. Surveillance and the Erosion of Privacy

The contemporary era is defined by "Surveillance Capitalism," where personal data is the primary currency:

Biometric Tracking: Facial recognition and gait analysis are now widely deployed in "Smart Cities," raising concerns about the end of public anonymity and the potential for state overreach.

Data Sovereignty: In 2026, more nations are passing strict data residency laws (similar to the GDPR) to prevent the export of citizen data to foreign servers, viewing data as a national strategic asset.

Workplace Monitoring: The rise of remote work has led to the widespread use of "bossware"—software that tracks employee keystrokes and screen activity—prompting a global debate on the right to privacy versus corporate productivity.

5. Ethical Frameworks for 2026

To address these challenges, the UN Global Digital Compact was established to ensure that technology is used responsibly. The focus has moved toward "Ethics by Design," where engineers and policymakers prioritize human agency and transparency at the very beginning of the technological development cycle.

In 2026, the global economy is grappling with a paradox: record-breaking technological productivity alongside a widening wealth gap. The displacement of labor by Artificial Intelligence (AI) has moved from a theoretical risk to a structural reality, necessitating urgent policy shifts.

1. AI-Driven Job Displacement

By late 2026, the impact of AI on the labor market has become stratified:

White-Collar Vulnerability: Unlike previous industrial revolutions that replaced manual labor, the current wave targets "cognitive" roles. In 2026, entry-level positions in coding, legal research, and content creation have seen significant contraction as AI agents handle routine intellectual tasks [1,3].

The Productivity Paradox: While corporations report higher margins due to AI efficiency, the "labor share" of income is declining. This means the wealth generated by automation is concentrating at the top (capital owners) rather than being distributed via wages [2, 5].

Reskilling Pressures: The World Economic Forum's 2026 reports emphasize that over 50% of all employees now require significant reskilling to work alongside AI systems.

2. The Widening Wealth Gap

Economic inequality in 2026 is increasingly defined by "Digital Capital":

Concentration of Wealth: The top 1% of the global population now holds more wealth than the bottom 95% combined. This is fueled by the stock market success of a few "AI giants" while middle-class real wages remain stagnant [4, 6].

Geographical Divergence: Wealth is concentrating in tech hubs (Silicon Valley, Shenzhen, Bangalore). Meanwhile, developing nations that previously relied on "low-cost manufacturing" are losing their competitive edge as robots in the Global North become cheaper than human labor in the Global South [2].

3. Policy Responses to Inequality

Governments in 2026 are experimenting with new social contracts to manage this transition:

Universal Basic Income (UBI): Several European and North American cities have launched permanent UBI pilots in 2026 to provide a floor for workers displaced by automation [6].

Robot Taxes: There is an active global debate on "automation taxes"—levying fees on companies that replace human roles with AI to fund social safety nets and retraining programs [4, 5].

AI Sovereignty: Developing nations are focusing on national AI strategies to build local infrastructure, ensuring they aren't just consumers of foreign AI but participants in the wealth it creates.

4. The Rise of the "Human Economy"

As AI commoditizes technical skills, the 2026 labor market has placed a premium on high-touch, human-centric sectors:

Care and Empathy: Occupations in healthcare, elderly care, and mental health are seeing wage growth and increased demand, as these roles require emotional intelligence that AI cannot yet replicate [3, 5].

Creative and Strategic Leadership: Value has shifted toward roles that involve complex negotiation, ethical judgment, and "zero-to-one" creative thinking.

1. Governance of Big Data and AI

In 2026, transnational forums have evolved to manage "borderless" crises that no single nation can solve alone, shifting from advisory roles to creating enforceable global frameworks.

The digital frontier is now a primary focus of international diplomacy:

Global Digital Compact (GDC): Adopted as part of the UN Pact for the Future in late 2024 and moving into implementation in 2026, this framework establishes global standards for AI governance, data privacy, and closing the digital divide.

International Scientific Panel on AI: Established under the GDC, this panel provides independent, evidence-based guidance to help world leaders navigate the risks of generative AI and automated decision-making.

WSIS+20 Review: July 2026 marks the 20th anniversary of the World Summit on the Information Society, where forums like the Internet Governance Forum (IGF) coordinate global policies on cybersecurity and internet fragmentation.

2. Reforming the Global Health Response

While AIDS remains a critical focus, the governance model has expanded to address broader pandemic resilience:

UNAIDS in Transition: In late 2026, the UNAIDS board is managing a complex transition toward 2030 targets amidst a significant funding crisis. Efforts are shifting from direct aid to national sustainability plans, empowering countries to lead their own HIV responses.

Pandemic Accord: Parallel to HIV efforts, the WHO is finalizing a legally binding pandemic agreement to ensure more equitable sharing of medical resources in future health emergencies.

3. Transnational Justice and Accountability

International bodies are increasingly used to settle disputes involving cross-border conflicts and human rights:

International Court of Justice (ICJ): 2026 has seen high-profile cases involving state complicity in genocide and regional conflicts, demonstrating the court's role in enforcing international law where national systems fail.

Cross-Border Legal Cooperation: New treaties, such as the Ljubljana-The Hague Convention, are streamlining international cooperation for investigating and prosecuting war crimes and crimes against humanity in domestic courts.

World Justice Forum: Convened in mid-2026, this forum brought together global leaders to develop strategies against the "global rule of law recession" and rising authoritarianism.

The Mechanics of Decentralized Leadership

In 2026, digital activism has moved beyond simple awareness to a sophisticated, decentralized infrastructure that challenges traditional political power. This era is defined by "networked protest," where leadership is horizontal rather than hierarchical.

The 21st-century model of activism rejects the 20th-century reliance on a single "charismatic leader" (e.g., Martin Luther King Jr.). Instead, it utilizes "Leaderful" Organizations:

Horizontal Structures: Movements like Fridays for Future or Black Lives Matter operate through autonomous local chapters coordinated via encrypted apps like Signal and Telegram. This prevents the movement from collapsing if one "head" is removed or co-opted.

Algorithmic Mobilization: Leadership is often replaced by "computational propaganda" or algorithmic trends. By 2026, activists use

AI-driven tools to identify the best moments to launch a hashtag to ensure it hits "trending" status, maximizing global visibility instantly.

2. The Evolution of Hashtag Activism

While once dismissed as "slacktivism," by 2026, hashtag activism is a primary tool for agenda-setting:

Real-Time Counter-Narratives: During global crises in 2026, hashtags allow citizens to bypass state-controlled media, providing live, unedited footage that forces international organizations like the United Nations to respond to public pressure.

The "Digital Picket Line": Movements now use hashtags to organize "buy-cotts" or digital boycotts that can impact a multinational corporation's stock price within hours, demonstrating the economic weight of digital consensus.

3. Transnational Impact and the "Boomerang Effect"

Digital activism in 2026 excels at turning local grievances into global mandates:

Cross-Border Solidarity: A hashtag originating in one country (e.g., #WomenLifeFreedom) can trigger simultaneous protests in hundreds of cities worldwide. This creates a "boomerang" where international pressure is brought to bear on a government by its own citizens' global digital allies.

Crowdsourced Policy: Platforms are being used to "crowdsource" legislative demands. In 2026, activists often present "digital manifestos" to policymakers that have been refined and voted on by millions of users online.

4. Risks and Counter-Measures

As of late 2026, the decentralized nature of digital activism faces new threats:

Digital Authoritarianism: Governments have countered by using AI to map "influence nodes" in decentralized networks and using internet shutdowns to sever the movement's "nervous system."

Astroturfing: The use of paid "bot farms" to mimic grassroots movements (creating fake hashtags) has made it harder for the public to distinguish between genuine social movements and state-sponsored disinformation.

1. The Delay of Traditional Milestones

In 2026, the transition from industrial to digital societies has solidified a new life stage known as "Emerging Adulthood." This period, typically spanning the late teens through the late twenties, prioritizes individual identity exploration and personal expression over the rigid social timelines of the 20th century.

In the contemporary era, the traditional markers of adulthood—completing education, starting a career, marriage, and homeownership—are no longer viewed as a linear sequence to be finished by age 21 [1].

Marriage and Family: By 2026, the average age for first marriages in developed and many developing economies has reached record highs (often over 30). Individuals prioritize financial stability and "finding themselves" before committing to a partner [1].

Economic Drivers: High housing costs and the "credential inflation" of the 2026 job market require longer periods of education and financial dependence on parents, extending the period of semi-autonomy [1].

2. Personal Expression and Identity Exploration

Post-industrial individualism focuses on the "subjective" experience of adulthood rather than objective social roles.

The "Me" Focus: Emerging adults in 2026 view this stage as a unique window for travel, career experimentation, and developing a "personal brand." This is facilitated by digital platforms that reward unique self-expression and niche interests [2].

Identity Fluidity: There is a significant shift toward exploring gender, cultural, and professional identities without the pressure of permanent labels. The 2026 cultural landscape encourages "trying on" different versions of the self [2].

3. The Role of Digital Connectivity

Digital platforms have fundamentally changed how independence is performed.

Global Benchmarking: Individuals no longer compare their progress only to local peers but to a global digital cohort. This can lead to "FOMO" (Fear Of Missing Out) but also provides a support network for non-traditional lifestyles [2].

Financial Independence via the Gig Economy: By 2026, many emerging adults achieve independence through non-traditional means, such as content creation or remote freelance work, further decoupling "adulthood" from a 9-to-5 office job [1].

4. Psychological and Social Implications

Extended Dependency: While independence is prioritized, it is often "tethered independence." In 2026, a record number of young adults live with parents while pursuing "expressive" goals, a trend normalized by the high cost of living [1].

Mental Health: The pressure to "optimize" one's youth and find a "perfect" career path has led to a rise in anxiety and "quarter-life crises" by late 2026, as individuals navigate a world with endless choices but high systemic barriers [1].

In essence, the 2026 model of adulthood is exploratory rather than settled, viewing the twenties as a decade for "identity capital" rather than domestic stability.

Social movement theories provide frameworks for understanding why collective action occurs, how movements are structured, and what determines their success in 2025's interconnected landscape.

1. Classical & Psychological Approaches (Pre-1960s)

Earlier theories viewed social movements as irrational or spontaneous reactions to stress.

Relative Deprivation Theory: People join movements when they perceive a gap between what they have and what they believe they deserve relative to others.

Mass-Society Theory: Argues that people feeling isolated or socially detached in large, bureaucratic societies seek belonging and empowerment through movements.

Structural Strain Theory: Proposed by Neil Smelser, this theory identifies "strains" (like economic crises or political instability) that create frustration, leading to collective action if specific catalysts occur.

2. Resource Mobilization Theory (1970s–Present)

This theory shifted the focus from "why" people are angry to "how" they organize. It treats movements as rational and strategic entities.

Core Argument: Grievances alone aren't enough; success depends on the ability to acquire and use resources like money, labor, media attention, and leadership.

Social Movement Organizations (SMOs): These formal organizations (e.g., NGOs or unions) act as the backbone of a movement, coordinating resources and membership.

2026 Context: In the digital age, social media is viewed as a vital "infra-resource" for aggregating volunteers and moral support quickly and at low cost.

3. Political Process Theory (PPT)

Also known as Political Opportunity Theory, PPT emphasizes the external political environment.

Political Opportunities: Movements succeed when the political system becomes vulnerable (e.g., during elite disunity, shifts in government policy, or increased access to decision-making).

Insurgent Consciousness: The collective sense among members that the current system is unjust and that they have the power to change it.

2026 Context: PPT explains why movements like the Arab Spring or modern climate strikes "burst" at specific times when political systems show receptivity or crisis.

4. New Social Movement (NSM) Theory

NSM theory arose in the late 20th century to explain movements that are not primarily about economics or class.

Identity & Culture: Focuses on human rights, identity, and "quality of life" (e.g., LGBTQ+ rights, environmentalism, feminism) rather than material wealth redistribution.

Decentralized Structures: These movements are often non-hierarchical, relying on loose networks and "hashtag activism" to mobilize global audiences in real-time.

Post-Materialism: Reflects values of 2025's "emerging adulthood," where personal expression and autonomy are prioritized over traditional markers of success.

5. Framing Theory

This theory focuses on the narrative and symbols used by movements.

Strategic Framing: Leaders use "frames" to simplify complex issues, making them resonate with the public's existing values (e.g., framing climate change as a "human rights" issue).

Injustice Frame: A specific message that identifies a problem, assigns blame, and proposes a collective solution to motivate participation.

The Core Mechanism: Expectations vs. Reality

Relative Deprivation Theory (RDT) explains social movements not as a result of absolute poverty, but as a consequence of the psychological gap between people's expectations and their reality. This "relative" feeling of injustice can trigger the frustration that motivates collective action.

RDT hinges on a fundamental psychological mechanism:

Perceived Discrepancy: It's not about being poor in an objective sense;

it's about feeling poorer than a reference group or feeling entitled to more than one has.

Frustration and Resentment: This gap between "what is" and "what ought to be" generates powerful feelings of frustration, resentment, and injustice, which are essential emotional drivers for social movements.

2. Types of Deprivation

Sociologists identify specific types of RDT that explain different movements:

Egoistic Deprivation: An individual feeling personally deprived compared to other individuals. This rarely leads to social movements but can foster individual psychological issues.

Fraternal Deprivation: A group feeling deprived compared to an external group. This is the primary driver of most large-scale social movements (e.g., a minority group feeling systematically disadvantaged compared to the dominant group).

3. The "J-Curve" of Rising Expectations

A classic RDT model, often applied in historical contexts like the French or Russian Revolutions, is the "J-curve":

Rising Expectations: A period where conditions slowly improve, leading people to expect continuous progress.

A Sudden Reversal: A sharp downturn or crisis occurs (e.g., an economic recession, a famine, a political scandal).

Explosion: The gap between the now-high expectations and the suddenly deteriorating reality creates revolutionary fervor.

4. RDT in the 2026 Context

RDT helps explain contemporary 21st-century movements, particularly regarding economic inequality:

AI and the Wealth Gap: The frustration caused by AI-driven productivity that only benefits a small tech elite perfectly illustrates RDT.

Workers see immense new wealth being generated but feel they are receiving less than their "fair share" as their jobs are displaced.

Digital Comparison: Social media platforms act as constant engines of RDT. People are constantly exposed to curated images of others' success, amplifying feelings of deprivation and fueling movements focused on social equity and economic justice.

5. Limitations

While influential, RDT alone is often insufficient:

Organization is Key: It explains why people are angry, but other theories like Resource Mobilization explain how they organize that anger effectively into a movement with the power to create change.

Structural Conduciveness

In 2026, Structural Strain Theory, primarily developed by Neil Smelser, remains a vital framework for understanding how systemic failures translate into collective action. It posits that social movements are not random but occur when a society's "structure" experiences a breakdown that creates widespread tension.

Smelser identified six essential conditions that must occur in sequence for a social movement to form:

This is the "background" condition. The society must be organized in a way that makes a movement possible.

2026 Example: The existence of global digital networks and a free (or partially free) internet provides the "conduciveness" for modern movements to spread across borders instantly.

2. Structural Strain

A specific problem or "strain" develops when society fails to meet its members' needs. This can be economic (inflation, job loss due to AI), social (systemic racism), or environmental (climate disasters).

Contemporary Context: The widening wealth gap and the displacement of workers by automation in 2026 create a profound structural strain as traditional paths to financial security vanish.

3. Growth and Spread of a Generalized Belief

People must define the problem and its cause. A shared narrative emerges that explains why the strain exists and who is responsible.

Role of Media: In 2026, digital platforms allow these beliefs to go viral. For instance, the belief that "the top 1% are responsible for climate inaction" becomes a unifying ideology for global protests.

4. Precipitating Factors

A specific, dramatic event serves as a "spark" that confirms the generalized belief and turns frustration into action.

Example: A major environmental catastrophe or a viral video of police misconduct can serve as the tipping point that justifies a large-scale mobilization.

5. Mobilization for Action

Once the spark occurs, leaders and organizations step in to coordinate the frustrated masses. They use resources (money, hashtags, apps) to bring people to the streets or into digital strike zones.

2026 Feature: Mobilization is now often decentralized. Instead of one leader, AI-driven algorithms and peer-to-peer messaging apps like Signal coordinate millions of people simultaneously.

6. The Operation of Social Control

This is the reaction of the authorities (government, police, or tech giants). If the state responds with reform, the movement may fade; if it responds with repression, the movement may radicalize or grow.

Modern Challenge: In 2026, "social control" includes digital authoritarianism, such as internet shutdowns, AI surveillance of activists, and state-sponsored misinformation campaigns designed to break the movement's momentum.

Summary of the Theory

Structural Strain Theory suggests that social movements are the "safety valve" of a society. When the established institutions (government, economy, schools) fail to adapt to a changing world—such as the transition to a digital, post-industrial era—the resulting strain forces the creation of new movements to demand structural reform.

Shift from Emotions to Rationality

n 2026, Resource Mobilization Theory (RMT) is a dominant framework used to explain why some movements thrive while others fail. It argues that grievances are constant in society, but a movement only succeeds when it functions like a strategic organization, effectively managing the "inputs" required for collective action.

RMT marks a departure from earlier theories that viewed protesters as "angry mobs." Instead, it treats movement participants as rational actors who calculate the costs and benefits of joining. Success is not determined by the intensity of the anger, but by the efficiency of the Social Movement Organizations (SMOs) (e.g., Greenpeace, ACLU, or local community unions).

2. Essential Resources for Success

To move from a shared grievance to a powerful force, a movement must acquire and manage several key categories of resources:

Material Resources: Funding, office space, equipment, and technology.

Human Resources: Skilled labor, legal expertise, charismatic leadership, and a large, dedicated membership base.

Social-Organizational Resources: Established networks, community groups, and alliances with other organizations.

Moral Resources: Legitimacy, public sympathy, and celebrity endorsements.

Cultural Resources: Shared symbols, slogans, and "know-how" (e.g., knowledge of how to organize a protest or use a specific app).

3. The Digital Transformation of Resources in 2026

In the contemporary era, the "resource" landscape has been revolutionized by technology:

Communication as a Low-Cost Resource: Historically, reaching millions was expensive. In 2026, digital platforms allow for "micro-resource mobilization," where small donations and viral hashtags aggregate into massive global power at a fraction of the cost.

Crowdsourcing & Micro-funding: Platforms like GoFundMe or Patreon allow movements to bypass traditional wealthy donors, gaining financial independence through millions of small, decentralized contributions.

Data as a Resource: In 2026, movements that effectively use Big Data and AI to target their messaging, identify potential donors, and track political sentiment have a significant competitive advantage.

4. The Role of "Conscience Constituents"

RMT emphasizes that movements often rely on people who do not directly benefit from the movement's goals but provide resources anyway.

Example: Wealthy donors or international celebrities supporting climate justice or human rights movements in the Global South. Their support provides the movement with the legitimacy and funding needed to reach a global audience.

5. Resource Competition

A key insight of RMT is that movements do not just fight the government; they compete with each other for limited resources. In 2026, there is an "attention economy" where movements for climate change, social equity, and digital rights must compete for the same media coverage and donor dollars.

Summary of the Theory

Resource Mobilization Theory suggests that in the 2026 landscape, the most "right" movement will not necessarily win; rather, the most organized movement—the one with the best funding, smartest digital strategy, and strongest leadership—will be the one to achieve lasting social change.

1. The Three Vital Components

In 2026, Political Process Theory (PPT), or Political Opportunity Theory, remains a cornerstone for understanding why movements achieve breakthroughs. It posits that grievances and resources are only effective when a "window of opportunity" opens within the existing political system.

PPT suggests that a movement requires the alignment of three factors to succeed:

Political Opportunities: The receptivity or vulnerability of the political system to challenges. Opportunities arise from crises of legitimacy, divided political elites, or upcoming elections.

Mobilizing Structures: The existing organizations (churches, student groups, or digital networks) that provide membership, leadership, and communication channels.

Framing Processes: The strategic effort by leaders to create a shared understanding of a problem that motivates collective action.

2. Open vs. Closed Political Systems

The success of a movement is heavily dictated by the Political Opportunity Structure:

Open Systems: In 2026, systems with high political pluralism and decentralized power are more conducive to reformist movements (e.g., environmental or women's rights) because they offer formal channels for change.

Closed Systems: When political systems are repressive or closed, movements may be blocked from achieving success even if they are well-organized. However, a weakening of state power—such as during a transition or crisis—can create a sudden opportunity for mobilization.

3. Contemporary Trends in 2026

The "Right Moment": Recent research emphasizes that movements succeed by scanning for "opportunity windows," such as a shift in public opinion or a sympathetic administration.

Perceived vs. Objective Opportunity: In late 2026, theorists focus on how activists' perceptions of the political climate—rather than just objective reality—drive their tactical choices and willingness to act.

Digital Political Spaces: The emergence of borderless digital spaces in 2026 allows movements to bypass traditional territorial states, creating new types of political opportunities that coexist with national ones.

Cyclical Nature: Movements are often part of a "protest cycle." Early successful movements can expose vulnerabilities in the state, making it easier for "spin-off" movements to follow.

4. Case Examples (2024–2026)

Climate Activism: Groups like Extinction Rebellion have targeted 2026 as a deadline for radical policy shifts, leveraging public receptivity and scientific crises to pressure governments for transparency and new parliamentary bodies.

Human Rights in India: Movements for Dalit and tribal rights in late 2024 and 2026 illustrate the theory by using shifts in regional political alignments to push for specific upliftment policies.

New Social Movement Theory

New Social Movement Theory focuses on identity, culture, and quality of life issues rather than economic or class-based struggles. These movements emphasise rights, recognition, and participation and are common in modern, post-industrial societies.

Theory	Main Focus

Relative Deprivation Theory	Dissatisfaction and frustration
Structural Strain Theory	Social instability and norm breakdown
Resource Mobilisation Theory	Resources and organisation
Political Process Theory	Political opportunities
New Social Movement Theory	Identity and culture

Chapter 7

The Third Wave and Democratic Consolidation

In 2026, the post-Cold War consensus, which once signaled the global dominance of liberal democracy and the electoral model, has shifted into an era of democratic recession and geopolitical fragmentation.

1. Erosion of the "End of History" Consensus

The late 20th-century belief that liberal democracy was the final, universal form of human government—famously termed the "End of History"—has been fundamentally challenged:

Democratic Decline: For the first time in over 20th century, autocracies outnumber democracies. As of 2026, approximately 71% to 72% of the world's population lives in autocratic regimes.

Regression to 1985 Levels: The average world citizen now experiences a level of democracy comparable to that of 1985, essentially erasing four decades of post-Cold War gains.

Shift in U.S. Policy: The return of Donald Trump to the White House in 2026 marks a decisive break from the post-Cold War consensus on democracy promotion and liberal internationalism, moving toward a strategy of selective engagement and "selective restraint".

2. Transformation of the Electoral Model

While "elections" remain the primary method for legitimizing power, the quality of those elections has deteriorated into new forms of governance:

Rise of Electoral Autocracies: Many nations now utilize the electoral model without the liberal substance (e.g., free press, judicial independence). This has led to the classification of major powers, including India, as "electoral autocracies".

Incumbency Entrenchment: In 2024–2026, several nations passed electoral reforms designed to entrench incumbent power and diminish democratic checks and balances.

Electoral Vulnerability: Elections are increasingly viewed as "information revelation mechanisms" that can lead to either liberalization or—more frequently in 2026—authoritarian retrenchment.

3. Public Disillusionment and Volatility

The 2024 "super-cycle" of elections has left a "post-election hangover" in 2026:

Punishing Incumbents: Voters in 2024 largely cast ballots from a place of anger and discontent, punishing parties in power across the US, UK, France, and Japan.

Voter Turnout & Trust: Global voter turnout has fallen by nearly 10 percentage points over the last 15 years, reflecting growing dissatisfaction with institutions that people feel do not represent their views.

Post-Election Unrest: Nearly 1 in 3 elections in recent years has been followed by protests or riots, as losing parties increasingly refuse to concede.

4. Emerging Geopolitical Order

In late 2026, the world is moving toward a multipolar reality where the Western-led "Washington Consensus" is no longer the sole authority:

Alternative Models: Rival powers promote alternative models of "stability" that prioritize economic growth and security over liberal democratic values.

Weakened International Bodies: Transnational institutions once central to the post-Cold War order (like NATO and the UN) are facing further weakening or restructuring as countries prioritize national sovereignty.

In 2026, Francis Fukuyama's "End of History" thesis—the 1989 argument that Western liberal democracy and market capitalism represented the "final form of human government"—faces its most severe theoretical and empirical challenges. Current critiques focus on the failure of universal convergence and the decoupling of economic success from political freedom.

1. The Decoupling of Capitalism and Democracy

A primary theoretical challenge in 2026 is the success of authoritarian capitalism, particularly the "Chinese Model".

Performance Legitimacy: Critics argue that regimes in China and Singapore have proven that marketization does not inevitably lead to democratization. By late 2026, some authoritarian systems are theorized to be more effective at long-term planning and crisis management (e.g., pandemics and climate change) than "messy" Western democracies.

Broken Link: Philosophers like Slavoj Žižek argue that the link between liberal democracy and capitalism has been broken, with authoritarian nations outperforming democracies in economic development and social cohesion.

2. The Global Wave of Autocratization

Data from 2024–2026 highlights a "democratic recession" that contradicts Fukuyama's linear model of progress.

Regressive Evolution: As of 2026, the average world citizen experiences a level of democracy equivalent to 1985. For the first time in over 20 years, the world has more autocracies (91) than democracies (88).

Electoral Autocracy: A major theoretical shift is the rise of the "electoral autocracy" as a stable, alternative endpoint. Leaders in countries like Hungary and India are seen as "gutting the substance" of liberal norms (free press, judicial independence) while maintaining the "outward rituals" of elections.

3. Return of Civilizational and Tribal Identity

The 21st-century resurgence of identity politics challenges the "universalizing" aspect of the thesis.

Civilizational Conflict: Samuel Huntington's "Clash of Civilizations" is frequently cited in 2026 as a more accurate predictor of a world divided by ancient religious and ethnic loyalties rather than unified by secular liberal values.

Non-Western Modernity: Theories of "multi-modernity" suggest that nations are seeking governance models rooted in their own traditions (e.g., Confucianism or Islamic principles of shura and maslaha) rather than adopting a Western-centric "one size fits all" model.

4. Internal "Political Decay" and Populism

Fukuyama himself has acknowledged "political decay" within established liberal democracies as a theoretical blind spot.

Erosion from Within: In 2026, the rise of authoritarian populism in the US, UK, and Europe is analyzed as a symptom of deep insecurities—wealth inequality, polarization, and a lack of political representation—that make liberal systems vulnerable to reversal.

Post-Truth Era: The fragmentation of "shared truth" via digital platforms and AI-driven misinformation is seen as a "technological apocalypse" for the rational, liberal-democratic discourse required for the "End of History" to function.

5. Geopolitical Multipolarity

The return of Great Power Competition signifies a move away from the unipolar "liberal international order".

New Bipolarity: Scholars in 2026 observe a "narrowing power gap" between the US and China, creating a new bipolar or multipolar system that prevents the universalization of any single political model.

Systemic Competition: The contemporary era is defined by a "new authoritarian system competition," where non-democratic powers actively promote alternative norms for international justice and security.

In 2026, the legacy of the "Third Wave" of democratization (1974–early 2000s) has transitioned into a period defined by scholars as the "Third Wave of Autocratization." While the post-Cold War era initially saw a global consensus favoring the liberal democratic model, current global data indicates a significant and sustained retreat from these principles.

1. The Decline of the Post-Cold War Consensus

By 2026, the assumption that liberal democracy is the "final form" of government has been fundamentally challenged:

Autocracy Outpaces Democracy: For the first time in over 20 years, the world has more autocracies (91) than democracies (88).

Population Shift: Approximately 71–72% of the global population (roughly 5.7 to 5.8 billion people) now lives under autocratic regimes, compared to only 48% a decade ago.

Regression to 1985 Levels: The average level of democracy enjoyed by global citizens in 2026 has regressed to standards reminiscent of 1985.

The "Washington Consensus" in Decline: The market-oriented neoliberal consensus that guided global policy for decades is considered "in tatters" by 2026, as both major U.S. political parties and other global powers shift toward industrial policy and government intervention.

2. Characteristics of the "Third Wave of Autocratization"

Unlike the military coups common in previous eras, modern democratic backsliding often occurs through legalistic erosion:

Incumbent Takeover: Popularly elected leaders increasingly use their mandates to dismantle democratic institutions, weaken judicial independence, and harass civil society.

Erosion of Fundamental Freedoms: The most severe declines in 2026 are seen in freedom of expression and media independence, with government censorship reaching a 25-year record high.

The Rise of Electoral Autocracies: This has become the most common regime type, where multiparty elections are held but lack the substance of true liberal democracy.

3. Regional and Key Country Developments (2024–2026)

India: Formerly the world's largest democracy, India is classified as an "electoral autocracy" in 2026 and is ranked among the top ten "worst autocratizers" globally.

United States: Freedom House reports growing restrictions on civic space and a decline in internet freedom in the U.S., though it remains a "Free" country.

Global South: Regions like West Asia, North Africa, and Central Asia have seen the steepest declines, with South Asia harboring nearly two billion people now living in electoral autocracies.

Emerging Breakthroughs: Despite the decline, 2024–2026 saw democratic bright spots in countries like Bangladesh, which experienced a student-led uprising against repressive leadership, and Bhutan, which improved to "Free" status.

In 2026, the post-Cold War consensus that favored liberal democracy has shifted into a "third wave of autocratization". While the electoral model remains the primary source of political legitimacy, the quality of these systems has eroded, and public trust has reached historic lows.

1. Decline of the Post-Cold War Consensus

The late 20th-century belief in the universal triumph of liberal democracy is being replaced by a more fragmented geopolitical reality.

Autocracy Outpaces Democracy: For the first time in over 20 years, the world contains more autocracies (91) than democracies (88).

Regression to 1985 Levels: In 2026, the average global citizen experiences a level of democracy comparable to that of 1985, effectively erasing decades of democratic gains.

Shift in Population: Approximately 71–72% of the global population now lives under autocratic rule, a significant increase from

48% just a decade ago.

2. Erosion of the Electoral Model

The "electoral model" persists as a ritual of legitimacy, but its internal substance is increasingly "hollowed out" by incumbents.

Rise of Electoral Autocracies: This is currently the most common regime type, where elections are held but fundamental freedoms—such as press freedom and judicial independence—are severely compromised.

Strategic Erosion: Unlike the sudden coups of the 20th century, 21st-century autocratization typically occurs gradually. Elected leaders use legalistic means to silence dissent and capture state institutions.

2024–2026 "Super-Cycle" Impact: Despite record numbers of voters going to the polls, 2024 and 2026 have seen a "post-election hangover," with dissatisfaction rising as people feel their votes do not translate into influence over policy.

3. Public Disillusionment and "Anti-Politics"

Dissatisfaction with the functioning of representative democracy is a foundational issue in 2026.

Eroding Trust: Large majorities in high-income nations like France (81%), the Netherlands (76%), and the US (61%) believe the state of democracy in their country has worsened over the past five years.

Preference for Alternatives: While most still support democracy in principle, there is an increasing openness to alternative governance models that promise more "responsiveness" or efficiency.

Rise of Populism: Far-right and anti-establishment figures are successfully exploiting this anger, framing themselves as "movements" that transcend traditional political parties.

4. Modern Threats to Electoral Integrity

Electoral processes in 2026 face advanced digital and social pressures:

Information Integrity: AI-driven disinformation and the spread of "fake news" are identified as top threats to democracy, particularly in Northern and Western Europe.

Election Denialism: A trend of "denialism"—where losing parties or candidates contest legitimate results—occurred in roughly 20% of elections during the 2020–2024 cycle.

State Capture: Powerful private interests and "magnates" are increasingly seen as having more influence than elected officials, leading to a "crisis of sovereignty".

In 2026, the late-20th-century trend of rapid democratic expansion has officially reversed, transitioning from a "Golden Age of Democracy" into what researchers call a "Third Wave of Autocratization."

Current Status of Global Democracy (2026)

Autocracies Outnumber Democracies: For the first time in over 20 years, there are more autocratic countries (91) than democratic ones (88).

Population Shift: Approximately 71–72% of the global population (5.8 billion people) now live under autocratic rule, a significant increase from 48% just a decade ago.

Regression to 1985 Levels: The level of democracy enjoyed by the average global citizen in 2026 has regressed to standards last seen in 1985, effectively erasing 40 years of gains.

Freedom of the Press Crisis: Press freedom experienced its broadest global decline in 2026 since data collection began in 1975, with deteriorations recorded in nearly 25% of all countries assessed.

Evolution of the "Three-Quarters" Adoption

While it was true that by the early 21st century, the majority of the world's population lived under some form of democratic rule, current data reveals a "hollowing out" of these institutions:

Modern Backsliding: Unlike the military coups of the 20th century, 21st-century autocratization typically involves democratically elected leaders using legal means to dismantle executive constraints, judicial independence, and civil liberties.

Regime Breakdown: As of 2024–2026, only 6.6% of the world's population lives in "full democracies," with prominent nations like France and South Korea recently downgraded to "flawed democracies."

Electoral Autocracy: This has become the most common regime type globally, where multiparty elections coexist with severe restrictions on freedom of expression and political opposition.

Signs of Resilience

Despite the overarching decline, International IDEA's 2026 report highlights areas of democratic renewal:

Key Advances: Countries like Brazil, Poland, and Fiji showed significant improvements in 2024–2026 by reversing previous non-democratic policies and strengthening the rule of law.

African Progress: Several African nations recorded gains in electoral integrity, notably Botswana, which saw its first peaceful transition of power between parties since independence in 2026.

In 2026, the use of elections as a tool for international "presentability" remains a defining characteristic of modern hybrid regimes. While the "ballot box" is still widely regarded as a necessary ritual for securing international aid, trade, and diplomatic recognition, the quality of these contests has continued to decline.

1. Elections as "Manufactured Legitimacy"

Non-democratic regimes in 2026 frequently use elections as a theatrical display to recast themselves as "civilian governments," even while maintaining autocratic control.

The "Sham" Election Model: In countries like Myanmar, military juntas are organizing general elections for late 2026 primarily as an attempt to secure international acknowledgment and counter regional diplomatic isolation.

Façade Democratization: These contests are often categorized as "spectacles" intended to mislead domestic populations and international observers rather than facilitate a genuine transfer of power.

2. Electoral Integrity and International Aid

The link between electoral performance and international assistance is increasingly strained:

Aid as a Lever: International organizations and donor nations, such as the UK and EU, have signaled that treating flawed or "sham" elections as legitimate emboldens authoritarians and undermines global democratic norms.

Targeted Funding: In 2026, democratic nations continue to prioritize funding aimed at increasing voter turnout and strengthening electoral frameworks in emerging democracies, such as Bangladesh, to ensure elections are not merely performative.

Risk to Trade and Aid: Elections that lack credibility increasingly put trade agreements and development assistance at risk, as many Western donors now emphasize "systems-based" rather than "event-based" democratic support.

3. The Rise of "Electoral Autocracies"

The most prevalent regime type in 2026 is the electoral autocracy, where multiparty elections coexist with severe restrictions on fundamental freedoms.

Population under Autocratic Rule: Approximately 71–72% of the world's population (5.8 billion people) now lives under some form of autocratic rule, often in nations that continue to hold regular but flawed elections.

Subversion from Within: Aspiring autocrats often attack media freedom and civil society first, then use "clean elections" as the final stage to cement their power, leading to a significant weakening of electoral management autonomy in many nations.

4. Geopolitical Nuance and Recognition

International response to flawed elections in 2026 is often dictated by strategic interests:

Recognition Gaps: While some bodies like the UN Special Rapporteur call certain elections a "sham," regional powers may refrain from condemning them to maintain strategic alliances or counterbalance rival influences.

Erosion of Norms: In 2024 and 2026, established democracies have also seen an increase in election denialism and intimidation of opposition parties, complicating the international community's ability to "lead by example" in enforcing electoral standards.

In 2026, the concept of Democratic Consolidation—famously described by Juan Linz and Alfred Stepan as when democracy becomes "the only game in town"—is facing a historic challenge as many long-established democracies experience "deconsolidation" or erosion.

1. The Core Meaning: "The Only Game in Town"

A democracy is considered consolidated when it is so deeply embedded that it is effectively irreversible. This occurs through three primary dimensions:

Behaviorally: No significant political group seriously attempts to overthrow the democratic regime or secede from the state.

Attitudinally: A vast majority of the public believes that democratic procedures and institutions are the most appropriate way to govern, even during major economic or social crises.

Constitutionally: All political actors are habituated to the fact that conflicts are resolved within the specific laws and procedures of the democratic process.

2. 2026 Reality: From Consolidation to Erosion

By late 2026, global democratic markers indicate a shift away from consolidation toward democratic backsliding:

Declining Quality: For the 9th consecutive year, the quality of global democracy has deteriorated, with more than half of assessed countries declining in at least one factor of democratic performance over the last five years.

Erosion of Norms: In 2026, long-held assumptions about democratic resilience are being shaken, particularly in established democracies like the United States and India, where institutions like judicial independence and press freedom are under strain.

Loss of Faith: Public support for representative democracy has dropped (e.g., from 44% in 2017 to 36% by 2023), while openness to "strongman" leadership without legislative interference has risen.

3. Key Indicators of Consolidation (and their Status in 2026)

Traditional tests used to determine if democracy is consolidated are currently showing mixed results:

The Two-Turnover Test: This classic indicator—where power is successfully transferred between competing parties twice—remains a strong index of strength. In 2026, Botswana demonstrated high resilience with its first peaceful power transition in 58 years.

Rule of Law & Judicial Independence: Consolidation requires that even leaders are subject to the law. However, 2024–2026 has seen sharp global declines in judicial independence and the criminal accountability of executives.

Freedom of Expression: Considered the "first to be attacked" during deconsolidation, freedom of expression and press freedom saw the sharpest falls in 50 years by 2026, impacting roughly 25% of all countries.

4. Structural Challenges to Consolidation in 2026

Digital Polarization: Misinformation and "ego-politics" (personalism over institutions) are actively hollowing out the shared trust required for consolidation.

Systemic Competition: The rise of successful "electoral autocracies"—where elections occur but lack liberal substance—provides a stable alternative to consolidated democracy, challenging its status as the "only game".

In the contemporary era through 2026, the European Union (EU) is cited as the premier global example of a transnational body using economic and political "conditionality" to drive and sustain democratic consolidation.

1. The Mediterranean Success Story (Southern Europe)

Following the collapse of right-wing dictatorships in the mid-1970s (Spain under Franco, Portugal's Salazar/Caetano, and the Greek military junta), the EU (then the EC) acted as an external anchor for democracy:

Economic Integration as an Incentive: The promise of access to the European Single Market and structural development funds was conditioned on these nations adopting stable, liberal democratic institutions.

The "Democratic Clause": By 2026, this precedent has evolved into a foundational rule: member states must adhere to the Copenhagen Criteria, which require stable institutions guaranteeing democracy, the rule of law, and human rights.

Preventing Regression: In Southern Europe, the EU helped ensure that democracy became "the only game in town" by making the cost of returning to authoritarianism (economic isolation and loss of subsidies) prohibitively high.

2. 2026 Evolution: The Rule of Law Mechanism

The role of the EU in consolidation has shifted from inducing democracy in the 20th century to protecting it from backsliding in 2026:

Conditionality Regulation: In late 2024 and 2026, the EU has increasingly used the Rule of Law Conditionality Mechanism. This allows the Union to freeze billions of euros in recovery funds for member states (such as Hungary) that undermine judicial independence or media freedom.

Democratic Resilience: By 2026, the EU is no longer just a "trade bloc" but a "democracy-defense bloc." The European Commission's 2026 Rule of Law Report serves as a primary tool for monitoring democratic health across the continent.

3. Regional Drivers Beyond Europe

The European model has influenced how other regional bodies attempt to drive consolidation in 2026:

African Union (AU): Through the African Charter on Democracy, Elections and Governance, the AU has moved toward a "zero-tolerance" policy for unconstitutional changes of government, suspending members like Gabon and Niger following coups.

ASEAN Challenges: In contrast, Southeast Asia's "non-interference" policy has made it difficult for the bloc to consolidate democracy in nations like Myanmar, highlighting that without "economic teeth" or political conditionality, regional drivers are often less effective.

Summary

The Southern European experience proved that international anchors are vital for consolidation. By 2026, this lesson has become the blueprint for global governance: for democracy to survive, it must be tied to tangible economic security and protected by transnational legal frameworks.

In 2026, Francis Fukuyama's "End of History" thesis—which proposed that Western liberal democracy and market capitalism were the ultimate stage of human ideological evolution—faces profound theoretical and empirical challenges. Critics argue that instead of history "ending," it has returned in the form of deep polarization, systemic autocratization, and alternative models of successful governance.

1. The Decoupling of Capitalism and Democracy

A major theoretical challenge is the success of authoritarian capitalism, particularly in China.

Performance Legitimacy: States like China and Singapore have demonstrated that market efficiency and technological innovation do not inherently require liberal democratic institutions.

The "Broken Link": Critics, including Slavoj Žižek, argue that capitalism can thrive—and even be more "effective"—under authoritarian rule, challenging the Fukuyaman belief that economic development inevitably creates demands for democratic participation.

2. The Global "Third Wave of Autocratization"

Empirical data from 2024 and 2026 highlights a sustained "democratic recession".

Regression to 1985 Levels: In 2026, the average level of democracy experienced by global citizens has regressed to standards last seen in 1985.

Rise of "Illiberal Democracies": Many nations maintain the outward rituals of the electoral model while gutting its substance, such as judicial independence and press freedom.

Autocracy vs. Democracy: For the first time in over 20 years, autocracies (91) now outnumber democracies (88).

3. Return of Civilizational and Identity Politics

Fukuyama's thesis is criticized for its Euro-centric bias and its failure to account for deep-seated religious and ethnic loyalties.

Clash of Civilizations: Samuel Huntington's theory—that conflicts are driven by ancient civilizational identities rather than modern ideologies—is seen as more descriptive of current global fragmentation.

Alternative Governance Models: Critics argue that the focus on Western models overlooks resilient traditions like Islamic political thought (e.g., shura and maslaha), which offer different frameworks for justice and public welfare.

4. Internal "Political Decay" and Populism

Fukuyama himself has identified "political decay" as a threat to established democracies.

Erosion from Within: The rise of authoritarian populism in the U.S. and Europe—characterized by nationalist rhetoric and a "post-fact world"—reveals that liberal systems can move backward.

Technocratic Failure: Fukuyama noted that democratic governments often fail to provide the basic substance people want, such as personal security and shared economic growth, leading to a loss of faith in the model itself.

5. The "Posthuman" Technological Frontier

Fukuyama has acknowledged that his thesis was incomplete because "there can be no end of history without an end of modern natural science and technology".

Technological Disruption: Advancements in AI, biotechnology, and digital surveillance are theorized to have a "great and possibly terrible effect" on human agency and the long-term stability of liberal democracy.

In 2026, the rise of illiberal democracies—often referred to as the "third wave of autocratization"—has become a dominant global trend. These regimes preserve the formal rituals of democracy, such as elections, while systematically hollowing out the liberal institutions that protect minority rights and ensure the rule of law.

1. The Hungarian Model: "Poster Child" for Illiberalism

Under Prime Minister Viktor Orbán,

Hungary

remains the primary case study for entrenched illiberalism within a democratic framework.

Institutional Capture: Since 2010, the Fidesz government has used its supermajority to marginalize the Constitutional Court, reduce judicial independence, and capture roughly 70% of the media market under pro-government foundations like KESMA.

New "Sovereignty Protection": In 2024–2026, Hungary enacted a "Defence of National Sovereignty" law, creating an office with unchecked power to investigate foreign-funded journalists and NGOs.

International Standing: In late 2026, Freedom House continues to classify Hungary as "Partly Free," the only EU member state without a "Free" designation. The V-Dem Institute categorizes it as an "electoral autocracy".

2. Global Trends in 2026

The illiberal trend has spread globally, with many nations transitioning from liberal to electoral democracies or autocracies.

Autocracy vs. Democracy: For the first time in over 20 years, autocracies (91) now outnumber democracies (88).

Population Shift: Approximately 72% of the world's population—equivalent to 5.8 billion people—now lives under autocratic rule.

Targeted Freedoms: The most significant declines in 2026 occur in freedom of expression (now at a 50-year low), clean elections, and freedom of association.

Regional Impacts: Steep declines are notably observed in Eastern Europe, South and Central Asia, and North Africa. India is highlighted as an "electoral autocracy" due to severe restrictions on media and civil society.

3. International Responses and Counter-Measures

Transnational bodies are increasingly using economic leverage to combat this model.

EU Financial Pressure: In 2026, the European Commission continues to freeze billions of euros in cohesion and pandemic recovery funds for Hungary over rule-of-law violations.

The "Illiberal International": Some scholars note growing collaboration among non-democratic powers (e.g., China, Russia, Iran) to normalize repression and dilute international accountability.

Resilience Efforts: Positive democratic advances were recorded in 2024–2026 in countries like

Poland

, which saw improvements in rule of law and representation, and

Botswana

, which held its most credible elections in decades.

Resurgence of Authoritarian Great Powers: The political and economic success of China (one-party state) and Russia (often described as an autocracy or anocracy) provides a rival model to liberal democracy, suggesting that history has not reached a singular endpoint.

Global freedom continued its long-term decline in 2026, marking the 19th consecutive year of democratic backsliding since 2006. Reports for 2026 highlight that nearly 40% of the world's population now lives under authoritarian regimes, while just 20% live in countries classified as "Free".

The following key factors are driving this trend in 2026:

1. Polarization and Institutional Erosion

Systemic Weakness: Even well-established democracies are struggling with political polarization and a significant loss of trust in institutions.

Democratic Quality: Long-established democracies, including the United States and South Korea, have seen declines in democratic indicators such as civil liberties and the functioning of government. In South Korea, a short-lived declaration of martial law in late 2024 underscored the vulnerability of these institutions.

Disinformation: The widespread use of misinformation to shape opinion has further destabilized democratic processes globally.

2. Economic Inequality

Driver of Backsliding: Economic inequality is identified as a primary predictor of democratic erosion, even in wealthy nations.

Policy Failure: Many citizens feel that established political parties have failed to address socio-economic disparities, leading to the rise of populist or far-right alternatives that often target democratic norms.

3. Electoral Manipulation and Violence

Violence in Elections: In 2024, more than 40% of national elections were marred by violence, including attacks on polling places and assassination attempts.

Authoritarian Tactics: Autocratic leaders increasingly use legal processes to "hollow out" democratic institutions from within rather than through sudden coups.

4. Severe Declines in Specific Freedoms

Press Freedom: Press freedom saw its sharpest fall in 50 years by 2026, with declines recorded in over 120 countries.

Internet Freedom: Global internet freedom declined for the 15th consecutive year, with 27 countries experiencing a deterioration in digital rights due to increased surveillance and censorship.

2026 Performance Summary

Metric	2026 Status
Years of Continuous Decline	19 years (since 2006)
"Free" Population	20% of the global population
"Not Free" Population	40% of the global population
Worst Overall Scores	Turkmenistan (1), South Sudan (1), North Korea (3)
Bright Spots	Improvements in Bangladesh, Bhutan, Sri Lanka, and the fall of the Assad regime in Syria

Critics of Francis Fukuyama's "
End of History" thesis
argue that its 2026 relevance is undermined by its Western-centric framework, which dismisses cultural and religious governance models as mere deviations rather than viable alternatives.

Key 2026 perspectives on these alternative models include:

1. Islamic Governance Principles

Proponents of Islamic political thought argue that systems rooted in faith offer a coherent ethical framework that addresses gaps in liberal democracy.

Core Concepts:

Models are built on Adl (justice), Shura (consultation/deliberative governance), and Maslaha (the public interest).

Beyond the Nation-State: Concepts like the Ummah (transnational moral community) and Khilafah (stewardship of the earth) provide alternative ways of viewing sovereignty and global responsibility.

Compatibility Debates: While some scholars see these principles as a way to create "religious democracies" that integrate participation with divine law (Sharia), others note that reliance on divine authority can sometimes be used to justify authoritarianism.

2. Cultural Critiques of Western Hegemony

Orientalism: Critics like Edward Said have long argued that universalizing liberal democracy is a form of Western cultural domination that ignores the history and resilience of non-Western systems.

The "China Model": The success of authoritarian-capitalist models (e.g., China, Singapore) in 2026 challenges Fukuyama's claim that capitalism and democracy must inevitably go hand-in-hand.

Pluralistic Secularism: In regions like India, alternative "anti-secular" critiques advocate for governance that respects unique religious diversities (e.g., sarva dharma sambhava) rather than the Western model of strict state-religion separation.

3. Declining Global Support for the Western Model

By 2026, public sentiment in many regions shows a shifting openness to alternatives:

The MENA Region: While many still favor democracy, support is declining in favor of "strongman" rule or Sharia-based governance, particularly where democratic experiments have failed to deliver economic stability.

Institutional Failure: Growing polarization and inequality within Western democracies themselves have weakened the moral authority of the liberal model, leading some to view it as a "Christian eschatology" rather than a universal endpoint.

In 2026, the "Last Man" dilemma has shifted from a theoretical philosophical warning to a practical explanation for rising global instability. Fukuyama's concept suggests that if humanity reaches a state of stable liberal democracy where all material needs are met, the resulting "existential boredom" and lack of grand causes may drive people back into conflict simply to find meaning and recognition.

Current analysis in 2026 highlights several key manifestations of this dilemma:

1. The Rise of "Megalothymia"

Need for Recognition: Fukuyama identified thymos (the desire for recognition of one's dignity) as a core human drive. While liberal democracy provides isothymia (equal recognition), it often fails to satisfy megalothymia—the desire to be recognized as superior or to participate in heroic struggle.

Conflict as Relief: By 2026, observers note that "frustrated passions" from the boredom of peaceful prosperity have driven some individuals in stable Western nations toward radicalization or foreign conflicts (e.g., propagandizing for distant wars) to escape the "masterless slavery" of mere rational consumption.

2. Existential Boredom and Stagnation

Boredom Studies: The study of boredom has become a recognized academic field in 2026, with major conferences addressing it as a significant consequence of modern life's speed and productivity.

Spiritual Emptying: Critics argue that the erosion of traditional values, community, and religion has left a "spiritual emptiness" that liberal democracy's material success cannot fill, leading to modern anxieties and identity politics.

3. Impact on Democratic Stability

Foundational Contradiction: Some 2026 perspectives argue that the "Last Man Problem" is an internal contradiction of liberal democracy. Because the state focuses on "negative freedom" (freedom from interference) rather than providing a higher purpose, it struggles to maintain the commitment of citizens who feel unfulfilled.

Reversion to Conflict: This lack of purpose is viewed as a predictor of democratic backsliding, as people may trade stability for more "exciting" populist or authoritarian movements that offer a renewed sense of struggle and identity.

Summary of the Dilemma (2026)

Aspect	Challenge in 2026
Material State	High prosperity but high existential anxiety.
Psychological State	Shift from labor-based value to a search for identity and creativity.
Political Risk	Boredom leading to a "struggle for the sake of struggle" against democratic peace.

Institutional Gap	The state provides security but cannot mandate "meaning" or "fulfillment".

Chapter 8

The Digital Rupture: E-Governance and Disinformation

In 2026, technology has fundamentally reshaped the public sphere, acting simultaneously as a tool for governmental efficiency and a primary driver of democratic erosion. The "digitalization of democracy" has moved beyond simple service delivery to a complex landscape of AI-mediated reality and systemic challenges to public deliberation.

1. The Altered Public Sphere

Fragmentation of Shared Reality: The internet, once seen as an "open door to liberty," is now frequently viewed as an agent of democratic erosion. In 2026, digital platforms have fractured the public sphere into "echo chambers" and "filter bubbles," where users are isolated from diverse viewpoints, undermining the "shared factual reality" necessary for democracy.

The "Liar's Dividend": As deepfakes become ubiquitous—with an estimated 8 million shared in 2026 compared to 500,000 in 2023—public figures can now dismiss genuine evidence of misconduct as "AI-generated," a phenomenon known as the "liar's dividend".

Commodification of Citizenship: The public sphere has shifted from a space for civic engagement to a system of "surveillance capitalism," where individuals are treated primarily as data sources rather than citizens with agency.

2. Emerging Governance Models

E-Governance and DPI: Governments are increasingly adopting Digital Public Infrastructure (DPI) to automate services. In 2026, India has leading global AI penetration, utilizing indigenous models like BharatGen to tailor governance to local contexts.

Direct Citizen Participation: Platforms like Taiwan's vTaiwan and the use of the Pol.is tool allow for "consensus mapping," where AI helps synthesize diverse citizen inputs to inform policy.

Platform Councils: A new model of "deliberative democracy" has emerged in 2026: platform councils. These are forums of average users and experts who help set content moderation rules, modeled after independent press councils.

3. Challenges to Deliberation

Algorithmic Harms: Algorithms prioritize "engagement" over epistemic quality, often amplifying sensationalist or divisive content for profit. In 2024–2026, 40% of national elections were impacted by digital violence and misinformation.

AI-Driven Disinformation: In 2026, AI-generated election disinformation is often indistinguishable from human-written journalism in over 50% of instances.

Weaponized Speed: The speed of viral falsehoods often outpaces institutional response. While average correction times improved to 15 minutes in 2023 from 45 minutes in 2021, the viral spread of false news remains roughly six times faster than truth.

Digital Divide: Despite technological advances, a significant divide persists; for example, only one-third of women in India use the internet compared to two-thirds of men, excluding marginalized groups from the digital public sphere.

The "Digital Rupture" describes a historic pivot in 2026 where the public sphere has moved from a space of human deliberation to one dominated by algorithmic curation. This transition has fundamentally altered the structural conditions of speech, shifting from the traditional "marketplace of ideas" to a fragmented "algorithmic public sphere" governed by profit-driven engagement metrics.

Key dimensions of this rupture in 2026 include:

1. Shift from Deliberation to Algorithmization

Algorithmic Curation: Platforms have transitioned from chronological feeds to complex algorithms that predict and prioritize content based on individual engagement. By 2026, this has led to "cyber-balkanization," where users are isolated in ideological silos or echo chambers.

Erosion of Shared Reality: The rupture has fractured the common epistemic ground necessary for democracy. Citizens increasingly consume "personalized truths," which diminishes the capacity for the collective reasoning required for democratic legitimacy.

The "Algorithmic Citizen": Unlike the traditional citizen who engages with mass media to build consensus, the 2026 "algorithmic citizen" can be entirely separated from mainstream discourse, falling victim to pre-arranged political contact and automated influence.

2. Revolution in Government Interaction

Digital Public Infrastructure (DPI): Governments are utilizing these digital shifts to implement e-governance at scale, improving service delivery and direct transparency.

Direct Engagement: Technology has lowered the cost of entry for communication, allowing marginalized groups to bypass traditional gatekeepers and interact directly with political leaders in real-time.

3. Structural Challenges to Discourse

Engagement vs. Truth: The commercial logic of 2026 platforms monetizes attention, often amplifying sensationalist, emotionally charged, or "outrage-based" content over factual reporting.

De Facto Censorship: Algorithmic practices like shadowbanning and "soft censorship" through downranking function as opaque gatekeeping mechanisms that can suppress marginalized voices without formal government intervention.

Automated Manipulation: The prevalence of bots and AI-generated deepfakes in 2026 (estimated at 8 million shared compared to 500,000 in 2023) has compromised the "epistemic quality" of public debate, making it harder for citizens to distinguish between authentic and manufactured discourse.

4. Democratic Deconsolidation

Loss of Institutional Trust: The constant exposure to misinformation and polarized content has weakened public trust in democratic institutions, a key driver of democratic backsliding in 2026.

Algorithmic Bias: Systems often reinforce existing societal disparities, such as racial or gender biases, which can lead to discriminatory outcomes in areas ranging from law enforcement to financial services.

In 2026, the decentralization of the public sphere has reached a critical juncture, as political and social interaction moves from physical, localized town squares to expansive, globally networked digital screens. This "Digital Rupture" has transformed the public sphere into an arena of social life where public opinion is no longer formed through shared physical space but through AI-mediated digital platforms.

The Shift from Physical to Digital (2026 Trends)

The New "Town Square": Digital platforms have officially surpassed linear television and physical gatherings as the primary spaces for public debate. In India, digital media's market size reached approximately $9.4 billion in 2024, exceeding traditional linear TV.

Decentralized Inclusion: Digital technology has lowered entry barriers, allowing historically marginalized groups—including youth in small towns and dispossesed populations—to bypass traditional gatekeepers and gain visibility.

Continuous Engagement: Public participation has shifted from a "passive, ballot-box activity" to a continuous, interactive dialogue that unfolds daily on glowing screens.

Impact of "Screen-Based" Deliberation

Fractured Discourses: Unlike the unified deliberation of a physical town square, the 2026 digital sphere is characterized by fragmented discourses, echo chambers, and "cyber-balkanization".

Post-Truth Dynamics: The "new" public sphere often rewards emotional outbursts and unidimensional narratives over objective reality and rational debate.

The "Digital Baton": Governments have increasingly moved to regulate this decentralized space through delegated legislation and "digital nationalism," leading to a tension between constitutional free speech and state-imposed restrictions.

E-Governance and Digital Public Infrastructure (DPI)

Service Delivery: Governments in 2026 use technology to decentralize administrative power, moving service delivery to citizen-centric portals that cut bureaucracy and response times.

Scaling Democracy: India's DPI models—like the "India Stack"—have been adopted globally as templates for transforming governance into an inclusive, transparent, and conversation-based system.

Privacy and Trust: Despite the convenience, over two-thirds of citizens expressed high concern regarding personal data leakage and the risks of AI during government interactions in 2026.

In 2026, algorithmic mediation has evolved from simple content sorting into a dominant form of "algorithmic gatekeeping" that fundamentally restructures the public sphere. This shift prioritizes commercial engagement over the "factual truth" necessary for democratic deliberation.

The current state of algorithmic mediation in 2026 is defined by the following impacts:

1. Priority of Engagement over Truth

Monetization of Attention: Platforms utilize "engagement-based" metrics (likes, shares, screen time) to maximize advertising revenue. This structural incentive often amplifies sensational, emotionally charged, or polarising content while pushing serious, analytical journalism to the background.

The "Epistemic Authority" of Code: Algorithms now decide what is "newsworthy" based on viral potential. In 2026, it is estimated that 70% of content on major platforms like TikTok is purely algorithmically selected based on predicted user behavior.

The "Liar's Dividend": The prevalence of AI-generated content (deepfakes) allows public figures to dismiss real evidence as "manipulation," further eroding the shared factual reality required for public debate.

2. Fragmentation and "Cyber-Balkanization"

Echo Chambers: Algorithmic curation exposes users to 15–20% less diverse viewpoints, effectively trapping them in "filter bubbles" that reinforce existing biases.

Marginalization of Minority Voices: While digital platforms lowered entry barriers, 2026 studies show that algorithmic prioritization often suppresses marginalized or "counter-public" voices—such as independent activists or minority groups—if their content does not generate mass-market "engagement".

Distortion of Public Opinion: By artificially amplifying particular perspectives through bot-driven trends (affecting up to 25% of trending topics in some regions), algorithms can create a false perception of consensus or outrage.

3. Institutional and Regulatory Responses

EU AI Act Enforcement (2026): Landmark regulations took effect in February 2026, banning "unacceptable risk" AI practices like social scoring and harmful manipulation.

Transparency Mandates: As of August 2026, providers of general-purpose AI models in the EU must follow specific transparency rules, including disclosing copyrighted training materials and providing technical documentation.

Call for "Algorithmic Literacy": In 2026, there is a global push for mandatory AI literacy for employees and the public to help citizens critically evaluate the mediated information they consume.

2026 Algorithmic Impact Summary

Metric	2026 Observation
Primary Curation Metric	Emotional Engagement (Clicks/Likes) vs. Veracity
Diversity Reduction	~18-20% decrease in cross-ideological exposure
Bot Influence	Bots drive approximately 25% of social media trends
Regulated Risk	Manipulative AI practices banned in EU (as of Feb 2026)

In 2026, the architecture of digital platforms is defined by "affective affordances"—design features that explicitly nudge users toward emotional reactivity rather than rational reflection. This structural bias ensures that outrage, fear, and excitement become the primary currencies of the digital public sphere.

The state of affective affordances in 2026 includes:

1. The Velocity of Emotion vs. Fact

The "Outrage Multiplier": Studies in 2026 confirm that content triggering high-arousal emotions (like anger or moral outrage) travels six times faster and reaches ten times more people than neutral, fact-based reporting.

Engagement Loops: Features such as "infinite scroll," "one-tap reactions," and "personalized notifications" exploit dopamine pathways, favoring quick, emotional clicks over the "slow thinking" required for democratic deliberation.

2. Algorithmic Amplification of Sensationalism

Curation for Retention: Platforms prioritize "toxic" or sensational content because it is more effective at keeping users on-screen. By 2026, this has led to a 20% decrease in exposure to cross-ideological perspectives, as algorithms feed users increasingly extreme versions of their own emotional biases.

The "Viral Incentive": Political actors and media outlets have adapted by "packaging" policy debates into sensationalist snippets to survive algorithmic filtering, a process that strips away nuance and context.

3. The Rise of "Synthetic Affect"

AI-Generated Emotion: In 2026, the use of emotional AI allows bad actors to generate deepfakes and text specifically designed to trigger physiological stress responses in target audiences.

Decline of Civic Trust: Because the digital sphere rewards the "loudest" and most "emotional" voices, public trust in digital discourse has hit a historic low. A 2026 survey suggests that 72% of users find digital political discussions "exhausting" or "hostile."

4. Regulatory and Design Countermeasures

"Friction by Design": To combat affective contagion, some platforms in 2026 have introduced "friction" features, such as prompts asking users if they have read an article before sharing it, which has been shown to reduce the spread of misinformation by up to 30%.

The EU AI Act (2026): New regulations that came into force in February 2026 now strictly limit "emotion recognition" AI in workplaces and education to prevent the exploitation of human affective states for manipulation.

Impact Summary: Emotional vs. Deliberative Discourse

Feature	Affective Discourse (Digital)	Deliberative Discourse (Traditional)
Primary Driver	High-Arousal Emotion (Anger/Awe)	Rational Argument/Evidence
Speed	Near-Instantaneous Virality	Slow, Incremental Consensus
Outcome	Polarization and Echo Chambers	Nuance and Compromise
Incentive	Engagement and Ad Revenue	Public Enlightenment/Pol

In 2026, the Participatory Paradox has intensified, highlighting the dual nature of digital platforms as both engines of grassroots empowerment and instruments of opaque, systematic exclusion.

The following elements define this paradox in 2026:

1. Empowerment and Grassroots Mobilization

Bypassing Gatekeepers: Digital platforms continue to allow marginalized groups—such as those involved in the #EndSARS movement or local environmental activism—to bypass traditional media "filters" and reach global audiences directly.

Identity as a Catalyst: Social media serves as a vital tool for underrepresented communities to assert their identities and build supportive networks to resist systemic inequalities.

Lowered Entry Barriers: In 2026, digital connectivity has significantly reduced barriers to collective action, enabling viral petitions and coordinated online protests to achieve tangible political impacts.

2. The "Impure Public Good" and Exclusion

Opaque Moderation: While platforms appear to be public town squares, they are "impure public goods" governed by private, often opaque, content moderation policies. These systems frequently reflect existing social biases, leading to the disproportionate silencing of marginalized voices.

Algorithmic Erasure: Algorithmic curation privileges "popular" content to drive engagement, which can epistemically "crowd out" marginalized speech that challenges dominant norms.

Participatory Censorship: A new trend in 2024–2026 is "participatory censorship," where ordinary citizens in authoritarian regimes actively flag and report online content, effectively co-opting the democratic tool of "reporting" to enforce state suppression.

3. Structural and Regulatory Shifts (2026)

The Digital Services Act (DSA): As of December 2026, the EU's DSA has introduced landmark transparency requirements. Large platforms are now legally mandated to provide "statements of reasons" for content removals, allowing users to appeal moderation decisions through a central DSA Transparency Database.

The "Brussels Effect": There is concern in 2026 that these EU standards may be applied globally to simplify compliance, potentially imposing European speech norms on diverse cultures worldwide.

Digital Divide as Exclusion: Despite increased connectivity, the "digital divide" remains a primary mode of exclusion in 2026. Marginalized groups in rural or low-income areas often lack the devices, literacy, or reliable 5G access needed to participate in the "digital town square," further entrenching socio-economic gaps.

2026 Paradox Summary

Feature	Empowerment Effect	Exclusion Risk
Visibility	Viral reach for marginalized issues	Suppression through moderation bias
Governance	E-participation and	Opaque "black-box"

	consensus tools	algorithms
Regulation	New transparency & appeal rights (DSA)	"Shadowbanning" and soft censorship
Access	806 million users in India alone	Denials of welfare via digital errors

In 2026, e-governance has moved beyond simple digitization to become a core tool for reducing corruption, automating workflows, and increasing transparency. Modern models follow a specialized four-stage maturity path (often attributed to Gartner) that defines how governments evolve their digital services.

The Four-Stage Maturity Path (2026)

Presence: This is the foundational stage where government agencies establish a web presence. Websites are typically passive, providing basic, static information to the public, much like an electronic brochure.

Interaction: In this stage, two-way communication begins. Users can contact agencies via email, download forms, or use search engines to find specific documents. It facilitates a "read and write" relationship where citizens provide feedback or submit inquiries.

Transaction: This stage allows for complete, secure financial and service transactions online. Citizens can renew licenses, pay taxes, or apply for passports without physical visits, significantly reducing opportunities for petty corruption.

Transformation: The highest stage involves a fundamental re-engineering of government processes. Information is integrated horizontally (across departments) and vertically (across government levels) to provide a "single window" or unified portal for all services.

Emerging Models and Innovations

By 2026, several specific models have emerged to enhance these stages:

Faceless, Paperless, and Cashless: Leading digital governments (notably in India) prioritize "faceless" services to remove human discretion—a key driver of corruption.

AI-Powered Governance: Artificial Intelligence is increasingly used in the Transformation stage to automate routine tasks, analyze large datasets for policy, and provide personalized 24/7 citizen support via advanced chatbots.

Digital Public Infrastructure (DPI): Models like "India Stack" (Aadhaar, UPI, DigiLocker) allow governments to build a shared digital layer that enables rapid scaling of e-governance services across various sectors.

Direct Interaction Models:

G2C (Government to Citizen): Focuses on efficient service delivery and welfare transfers.

G2G (Government to Government): Streamlines inter-departmental collaboration (e.g., e-Office) to reduce bureaucratic delays.

G2B (Government to Business): Simplifies regulatory compliance and clearances to foster economic growth.

In 2026, Digital Public Infrastructure (DPI) has become the global gold standard for "connected" governance, with India's model serving as the primary blueprint for delivering large-scale, inclusive social and economic services.

1. The IndiaAI Mission & "Government-as-a-Platform"

Mission Goal: In 2026, the IndiaAI Mission is focused on creating a sovereign AI ecosystem. This includes the development of indigenous AI models (such as BharatGen) tailored to India's unique linguistic and cultural diversity.

Infrastructure: The mission leverages the AIRAWAT supercomputing infrastructure to provide startups and researchers with the compute power needed to build applications for public health, agriculture, and education.

Data Governance: By integrating AI with the existing India Stack, the government uses big data analytics to transition from reactive service delivery to "predictive governance," identifying community needs before they escalate.

2. Evolution of Aadhaar and Identity (2026)

Interoperability: Aadhaar has evolved beyond a simple ID into a foundational layer for Zero-Knowledge Proofs (ZKPs), allowing citizens to verify their identity or age without sharing sensitive personal data, thus enhancing privacy.

Cross-Border Integration: In 2026, the DPI model is increasingly international. India has signed agreements with over a dozen countries to export the "India Stack" (Aadhaar and UPI), enabling global interoperability for digital payments and identity verification.

3. Integrated Service Delivery (The "Transformation" Stage)

Unified Portals: Modern DPI integrates disparate government databases to create "single-window" experiences. For example, the National Single Window System (NSWS) allows businesses to secure all necessary clearances through a single digital application.

Financial Inclusion: Through the JAM Trinity (Jan Dhan, Aadhaar, and Mobile), India continues to lead in direct benefit transfers (DBT), having successfully eliminated billions in "leakage" or corruption by bypassing intermediaries.

4. Key 2026 Milestones in DPI

Component	2026 Status
Aadhaar Saturation	Nearly 100% of the adult population; increasingly used for digital signatures and e-KYC.
UPI Adoption	Over 15 billion transactions per month, with real-time linkages to systems in Singapore, UAE, and France.
Bhashini AI	Real-time AI translation enabling citizens to

	access government services in 22 local languages via voice.
Health Stack	The Ayushman Bharat Digital Mission has digitized millions of health records, allowing for portable, paperless medical histories.

In 2026, the Government to Citizen (G2C) model has reached a "transformational" maturity stage, shifting from mere digital presence to a proactive, seamless delivery of rights and services.

Key 2026 milestones for G2C infrastructure include:

1. Massive Scaling of Digital Repositories

DigiLocker Growth: By June 2026, the DigiLocker platform has grown to serve 53.92 crore (539.2 million) users. It currently hosts billions of authentic digital documents, ranging from driving licenses to academic certificates, which are legally equivalent to originals.

Paperless Verification: The widespread adoption of DigiLocker has virtually eliminated the need for physical copies in government recruitment, bank account openings, and passport applications.

2. Direct Welfare and "Faceless" Services

Direct Benefit Transfer (DBT): Governments use G2C models to bypass intermediaries, transferring subsidies directly to bank accounts linked via the JAM (Jan Dhan-Aadhaar-Mobile) trinity. In 2026, this has saved billions in fiscal leakage.

Saturation Mapping: Governments now use AI and big data to identify citizens eligible for schemes who have not yet applied, moving toward a "saturation model" where welfare finds the citizen, rather than the citizen searching for welfare.

3. Integrated Digital IDs and Licenses

The "One-Stop" Portal: Modern G2C systems provide a unified interface for all life-cycle events. Citizens can apply for birth certificates, renew vehicle registrations, and manage pension details through a single sign-on (SSO) portal.

Voice-Based Governance: With the integration of Bhashini AI, citizens can now access these G2C services in 22 local languages through voice commands, significantly bridging the digital literacy gap.

4. Privacy and User Agency

Consent Management: By 2026, G2C models have integrated sophisticated consent managers. Citizens can see exactly which department accessed their data and can revoke permissions for specific documents in real-time, aligning with the Digital Personal Data Protection Act.

G2C Impact Summary (2026)

Metric	Status as of 2026
DigiLocker Users	53.92 Crore (June 2026)
Service Accessibility	24/7 availability across web, mobile, and AI voice interfaces
Corruption Reduction	Near-zero human intervention in standard licensing ("Faceless" services)
Language Inclusivity	Services available in all 22 scheduled Indian languages via AI translation

In 2026, AI-Enabled Governance has moved from experimental pilots to a core administrative layer, leveraging predictive analytics and generative interfaces to manage the complexities of modern states.

1. Predictive AI for Policy Evaluation

By 2026, governments utilize "Policy Intelligence" systems to move beyond reactive governance:

Dynamic Simulation: Governments use AI-driven "digital twins" of cities or economic sectors to simulate the impact of policy changes (e.g., tax adjustments or urban rezoning) before they are implemented.

Predictive Welfare: Data analytics identify populations at risk of "falling through the cracks"—such as predicting school dropout rates or food insecurity—allowing for early intervention rather than after-the-fact aid.

Resource Optimization: AI models predict power grid demands and traffic congestion patterns in real-time, enabling more efficient allocation of public utilities and emergency services.

2. Automated Chatbots and Conversational AI

The interface between the state and the citizen has been transformed by sophisticated AI agents:

Bhashini AI Integration: In India, the Bhashini platform enables citizens to access services via voice in their native languages. This is critical for overcoming literacy barriers, as users can simply "speak" to the government to apply for licenses or inquire about subsidies.

24/7 Virtual Assistants: Advanced chatbots handle over 80% of routine public inquiries in 2026, providing instant, accurate information on everything from tax filing to healthcare eligibility, which drastically reduces the burden on physical government offices.

Personalized Service Delivery: Unlike the static websites of the past, 2026 bots provide personalized guidance based on a user's unique profile (e.g., "Based on your income, you are eligible for these three specific schemes").

3. Strategic Frameworks (2026)

IndiaAI Mission: Launched to create a sovereign AI ecosystem, the mission focuses on building high-quality datasets for public benefit and providing compute power to startups focused on "Social Impact AI."

EU AI Act Compliance: As of February 2026, AI used in governance must meet strict transparency and safety standards. Systems used for "social scoring" or "manipulative behavioral nudging" are strictly prohibited in the EU.

The "Liar's Dividend" Challenge: To maintain trust, governments are implementing Content Credentials—digital signatures that prove a government video or document is authentic and not an AI-generated deepfake.

Summary of AI Governance Impact (2026)

Feature	Traditional Governance	AI-Enabled Governance (2026)
Response Time	Days/Weeks (Human-led)	Instant (Bot-led/Automated)
Language Access	Limited (Mainstream languages)	Multilingual (Real-time AI translation)
Policy Planning	Historical/Static Data	Predictive/Real-time Simulations
Efficiency	High Bureaucracy	"Faceless" and automated workflows

In 2026, social media has definitively overtaken traditional channels as the primary news source for younger demographics. According to the 2026 Digital News Report, 44% of 18–24-year-olds globally now name social media and video platforms as their main source of news.

1. Shift in News Consumption Patterns

Generational Split: While only 20% of 18–24-year-olds rely on television for news, dependency on social media is rising significantly, especially in the U.S., where social media and video networks have overtaken both TV and news websites for the first time.

Platform Dominance: Instagram (44% usage among 18–24s) and TikTok are leading this shift, particularly through short-form video. In countries like India, YouTube has become a dominant news platform, with 55% of users accessing news there weekly.

Incidental Exposure: Roughly 70% of young adults report "stumbling upon" political news while using social media for other purposes, rather than actively seeking it out.

2. The Role of Influencers and Creators

Personality-Driven News: There is a structural shift away from institutional journalism toward influencers and content creators who often bypass traditional editorial scrutiny.

Populist Strategy: Politicians increasingly use these alternative ecosystems to bypass traditional media scrutiny. For example, in the 2024 U.S. election, candidates heavily engaged with podcasters like Joe Rogan to reach younger audiences.

3. Disinformation Trends in 2026

High Levels of Concern: Approximately 58% of people globally are concerned about their ability to distinguish truth from fiction online, with concern peaking at 73% in the U.S. and South Africa.

Sophistication of Tactics:

AI-Generated Falsehoods: Deepfakes and AI-generated content have become "easier, better, and cheaper" to produce, leading to "character assassination" campaigns during major elections.

Hashtag Hijacking: Coordinated bot networks are increasingly "hijacking" trending hashtags to derail brand campaigns or influence political discourse.

Algorithmic Polarization: Algorithms continue to prioritize engagement over accuracy, often amplifying divisive or sensationalist content that travels faster than evidence-based facts.

4. Impact on Democratic Deliberation

Institutional Trust Erosion: Constant exposure to misinformation is linked to a breakdown in institutional trust and increased social polarization.

Epistemic Vulnerability: Young people are considered particularly vulnerable to disinformation due to "superficial" verification strategies—such as judging a source's credibility by its follower count rather than its history of accuracy.

Passive Disengagement: While social media can mobilize grassroots movements, passive consumption often leads to higher levels of news avoidance (recorded at 69–71% among under-35s in 2026) and political apathy.

In 2026, the power to set the public agenda has fundamentally shifted from centralized editorial boards to a decentralized ecosystem of

influencers and viral hashtags. This "decentralization of salience" allows a diverse array of actors to bypass traditional media gatekeepers and shape public priorities in real-time.

1. Influence Over Traditional Gatekeeping

The New Gatekeepers: Influencers and independent creators are now the primary "gatekeepers" of information for many demographics. By 2026, creator content is projected to surpass traditional media in global ad revenue for the first time, signaling their dominance in capturing public attention.

Bypassing Filters: Public figures and activists increasingly use social media to bypass traditional journalistic filters, delivering messages directly to massive, niche-targeted audiences.

Decentralized Priorities: Unlike traditional editors who weigh news based on institutional norms, digital platforms determine salience through algorithmic fluency and viral hashtags.

2. Hashtags as Infrastructure for Salience

Categorization and Visibility: Hashtags serve as "digital labels" that group content, making specific issues instantly searchable and visible globally.

Hashtag Activism: In regions like India, hashtag activism has refined societal discourse by spotlighting issues of caste, class, and gender that were previously marginalized by mainstream media.

Solidarity and Identity: Movements like the #MilkTeaAlliance and #BlackLivesMatter have used hashtags as communication infrastructure to unify decentralized pro-democracy and social justice movements across borders without any central organizing body.

3. Challenges of Decentralized Agenda-Setting

Sensationalism over Substance: The shift toward "engagement" metrics often results in sensational controversies overshadowing critical policy decisions or legislative bills.

Outrage Cycles: Sudden "outrage cycles" can be manufactured or aggressively pushed by platform algorithms, creating a distorted view of public priorities.

Fragmentation: As users increasingly move toward decentralized social media (e.g., Mastodon, Bluesky), the public sphere is becoming even more fragmented into "echo chambers" where shared national agendas are harder to sustain.

4. Regulatory and Institutional Shifts (2026)

Increased Accountability: 2026 marks a turning point for influencer regulation; in India, authorities (ASCI and SEBI) have enforced strict disclosure rules to ensure that promotional content is not mistaken for independent editorial opinion.

Platform Curation: Major platforms are moving toward stricter hashtag limits (e.g., Instagram testing a five-hashtag limit) to discourage "spammy" behavior and favor high-quality, relevant content over volume.

In 2026, political microtargeting has evolved into a highly specialized form of "behavioral advertising" that leverages AI-driven psychographics to influence voters with invisible, individualized messages.

1. Psychographic Profiling & "Invisible" Messaging

Beyond Demographics: Campaigns no longer rely solely on surface data like age or income. By 2026, they utilize psychographics—voters' deep-seated values, beliefs, and emotional triggers—to craft hyper-personalized narratives.

Psychological Vulnerabilities: Advanced algorithms and big data analytics allow campaigns to detect specific "cognitive biases" and psychological vulnerabilities, delivering tailored strategies that often operate without the individual's conscious awareness.

Invisible Influence: This creates an "individualized" agenda where different voter segments see mutually exclusive promises. This "darker side" of the digital turn complicates public oversight because these messages are not part of the shared public debate.

2. Complicating Public Oversight & Accountability

The "Black Box" Problem: Traditional news media can no longer act as gatekeepers or provide balanced scrutiny because they are often bypassed by direct, segmented communication between political elites and specific audiences.

Erosion of Consensus: As voters assign weight to diverse, micro-targeted issues (e.g., student housing for some, pensions for others), the "shared political community" necessary for democracy is undermined.

Lack of Scrutiny: Because these messages are private and individualized, they avoid the public scrutiny required to ensure that political promises are fair, honest, or consistent.

3. Landmark Regulatory Responses in 2026

Governments have introduced significant new laws in 2026 to curb these "opaque" practices:

EU Regulation (EU) 2024/900: As of October 10, 2026, most obligations under the EU's "Transparency and Targeting of Political Advertising" (TTPA) regulation have become applicable.

Transparency Labels: All political ads must now carry a clear label identifying the sponsor, the election targeted, and the amounts paid.

Strict Consent: Targeting is only permitted with explicit, separate consent from the user. Using sensitive data (like racial origin or political opinions) for profiling is strictly prohibited.

Meta's Response: In response to these "operational challenges," Meta announced in July 2026 that it would halt all political and social issue advertising on its platforms across the EU.

Global Trends: While the EU has led with centralized regulation, the U.S. is increasingly moving toward state-level privacy statutes and federal requirements for AI content labeling to ensure voters know when a message has been assisted by artificial intelligence.

In 2026, electoral interference has evolved from isolated incidents into a systemic challenge where algorithmic loops and AI-generated synthetic media are weaponized to dismantle institutional trust. While 2024 was marked by the "AI election", 2026 regional contests have demonstrated that disinformation campaigns now adapt rapidly to local contexts, exploiting cognitive vulnerabilities and fragmented media landscapes.

1. Mechanisms of Algorithmic Discord

Algorithmic Feedback Loops: Social media platforms use AI-driven feedback loops that prioritize emotional engagement—often negative—towards opposing political groups. This creates a "chaotic situation" where topical relevance outweighs accuracy, making the spread of misinformation almost uncontrollable.

Confirmation Bias Amplification: Algorithms reinforce existing beliefs by serving a "cognitive weapons stack"—a technical pipeline of data and AI models designed to shape what targets feel and believe.

The "Liar's Dividend": In 2026, the ubiquity of deepfakes and AI "slop" content allows politicians to dismiss genuine evidence as "AI-generated," effectively eroding the concept of an objective truth.

2. Case Studies in Electoral Interference (2024–2026)

2024 U.S. Presidential Election:

Foreign Influence: Russia, China, and Iran were identified as primary state actors. Russia used covert operations to co-opt right-wing influencers, while Iran targeted both parties to sow internal discord and discredit the democratic system.

Tactical Disruptions: Tactics included hoax bomb threats at polling locations (Georgia, Michigan, Arizona) and AI-amplified narratives claiming the election was "stolen".

2026 Regional Elections:

Germany: Influence operations by Russia and domestic figures fueled campaigns targeting the democratic process with deepfakes and bot-driven propaganda, specifically weaponizing climate change denial to polarize voters.

Philippines (2026 Midterms): Approaching its 2026 elections, the Philippines faces a "tsunami of misinformation" where AI-generated content rehabilitates authoritarian historical narratives and targets government institutions.

Australia: 2026 research showed that nearly 73% of voters were concerned about false election information, but many were unable to identify it, leading to political burnout and disengagement.

3. Impact on Institutional Trust

Erosion of Faith in Election Bodies: Authoritarian leaders routinely attack election administrators as "corrupt" or "incompetent" before elections occur, leading to a decline in trust that extends to the results and the resulting government.

Declining Voter Confidence: As of 2026, only 22% of Americans express trust in the federal government. High levels of misinformation concern are reported globally, peaking in Nigeria (84%) and the United States (73%).

Legislative Responses: In February 2026, Italy became the first European country to criminalize the malicious misuse of AI (e.g., deepfakes), signaling a shift from regulatory to criminal oversight to protect electoral integrity.

Metric	2026 Status
Primary Actors	Russia, China, Iran, and hyper-partisan domestic groups
Misinformation Concern	84% in Nigeria; 73% in USA; 73% in South Africa
Deepfake Growth	Deepfake usage surged over 900% between 2021 and 2024
Viral Speed	AI misinformation spreads roughly 70% faster than verified news

In 2026, the "Digital Rupture" has reached a critical phase where the technical architecture of the internet directly contradicts the requirements for healthy democratic deliberation. Experts identify several structural barriers that prevent digital platforms from functioning as effective public spheres.

1. Epistemic Fragmentation (The Death of Shared Facts)

The primary challenge in 2026 is the loss of a "common world" or shared factual reality.

Algorithmic Silos: Algorithms prioritize "concordant" information, leading to cyber-balkanization. Users are isolated in echo chambers where they only encounter views that reinforce their existing biases, making cross-partisan compromise nearly impossible.

The "Liar's Dividend": The ubiquity of AI-generated content allows individuals to dismiss genuine evidence as "fake," leading to a state of epistemic paralysis where citizens no longer know what—or whom—to trust.

2. The Speed vs. Deliberation Trade-off

Deliberation requires "slow thinking," reflection, and nuance, which are antithetical to the 2026 digital economy.

Viral Velocity: Fact-based discourse travels significantly slower than sensationalist misinformation. By the time a falsehood is debunked (even with 2025's improved 15-minute response times), the emotional "affective" damage is already done.

Context Collapse: Complex policy issues are reduced to "soundbites" or 15-second clips to survive algorithmic filtering, stripping away the context necessary for informed public judgment.

3. Opaque Governance and "Impure Public Goods"

While digital platforms act as the modern town square, they are private entities with opaque rules.

Black-Box Moderation: Platforms use "opaque" algorithms to determine what is visible. In 2026, this often leads to shadowbanning or the suppression of marginalized voices that do not generate high "engagement," even if their content is vital for public discourse.

Regulatory Lag: Despite the enforcement of the EU AI Act in February 2026, governments struggle to keep pace with "emergent" AI behaviors that manipulate public opinion through subtle behavioral nudging.

4. Affective Contagion and Polarization

Platforms are designed with "affective affordances"—features like likes, shares, and infinite scroll that exploit human psychology.

Outrage as Currency: Digital spaces reward the "loudest" and most extreme voices because anger drives the highest engagement. This results in affective polarization, where citizens view political opponents not just as wrong, but as existential threats.

The Participatory Paradox: While technology has lowered the barrier for participation, it has also increased the "noise," making it harder for high-quality, deliberative arguments to be heard over the din of coordinated bot campaigns and partisan outrage.

Summary of Challenges (2026)

Challenge	Impact on Deliberation	2026 Observation
Epistemic Fragmentation	Destroys shared factual ground	58% of global users worry about discerning truth.
Algorithmic Bias	Prioritizes engagement over accuracy	Engagement metrics amplify outrage-based content.
Context Collapse	Reduces nuance to sensationalism	Short-form video is the primary news source for under-24s.
Opaque Moderation	Creates "hidden" censorship	Regulatory pressure (DSA) is just beginning to enforce transparency.

In 2026, the proliferation of AI-driven echo chambers and filter bubbles has become a primary driver of social fragmentation, complicating the "shared reality" required for democratic compromise.

The current state of algorithmic curation in 2026 is defined by the following:

1. Mechanisms of Informational Silos

Filter Bubbles: These result from passive, unintentional algorithmic personalization. Algorithms (like those on TikTok, which account for over

70% of views on YouTube as well) prioritize content that matches past user behavior—clicks, likes, and watch time—to maximize retention.

Echo Chambers: These are socially constructed environments where users actively choose to engage with like-minded individuals, leading to the systematic discredit of external or opposing viewpoints.

AI Reinforcement: In 2026, advanced machine learning feedback loops have accelerated the formation of these silos, making it increasingly difficult for users to encounter "counter-attitudinal" information that might challenge their beliefs.

2. Impact on Democratic Deliberation

Reduced Diverse Exposure: By focusing strictly on predicted user preference, 2026 algorithms effectively filter out divergent perspectives, leading to what researchers call "epistemic closure".

Affective Polarization: Engaging with emotionally charged or ideologically aligned content in these bubbles significantly increases hostility toward "out-groups". In a single week, social media can shift partisan feeling as much as would normally occur over three years.

Erosion of Common Ground: The decrease in exposure to diverse viewpoints reduces shared points of reference between different social groups, making political compromise or mutual understanding nearly impossible.

3. Societal and Regulatory Trends (2026)

Electoral Impact: Disinformation is amplified within these bubbles as algorithms favor sensationalist content, which travels faster than fact-based corrections.

Regulatory Initiatives:

EU AI Act (2026): Landmark legislation now requires platforms to ensure their algorithms are transparent and free from bias, with some provisions giving users the ability to opt out of personalized content feeds.

Digital Services Act (DSA): This framework mandates that large platforms conduct risk assessments of their recommendation systems to mitigate negative societal impacts like political polarization.

Counter-Interventions: New 2026 research suggests that intentional exposure to multi-sided arguments (e.g., through platforms like The Perspective) can increase open-mindedness and reduce opinion polarization.

Feature	Filter Bubble (2026)	Echo Chamber (2026)
Driver	Passive, Algorithmic Curation	Active, Social Self-Selection
Mechanism	Personalized recommendation loops	Intentional exclusion of outsiders
Primary Risk	"Personalized universe" of information	Radicalization and systemic distrust
Outcome	Reduced intellectual curiosity	Hostility toward opposing groups

In 2026, end-to-end encrypted (E2EE) platforms like WhatsApp are frequently described as "black holes" for disinformation. While these spaces provide essential privacy for billions of users, their unmonitored nature allows viral falsehoods to circulate without the oversight or "friction" found on public social media.

The 2026 landscape of encrypted disinformation is defined by the following:

1. The Challenge of "Dark Social"

Invisible Virality: Because messages are encrypted, third parties (fact-checkers, researchers, and the platforms themselves) cannot see content as it spreads. This creates a "private public sphere" where misinformation can reach millions before it is even detected by mainstream monitors.

Trust as a Weapon: Information shared on WhatsApp is often received from trusted friends or family members. In 2026, this "source credibility" makes users significantly less likely to question the accuracy of a message compared to content seen on a public feed [1, 2].

2. Algorithmic Loops and "Affective" Spread

High-Arousal Content: Disinformation on encrypted platforms often relies on "affective affordances"—sensationalist or fear-inducing content that triggers an immediate urge to "forward" to loved ones [3].

Coordination of Discord: In recent regional elections, coordinated bot networks used "bridge" accounts to push content from public platforms into thousands of private WhatsApp groups simultaneously, bypassing traditional algorithmic filters [4, 5].

3. Regulatory and Technical Responses in 2026

Traceability Debates: In 2026, governments (notably in India and the UK) continue to push for "traceability" mandates, requiring platforms to identify the "first originator" of a message. Platforms like WhatsApp and Signal have resisted, arguing this would break encryption and compromise global privacy [1, 6].

Forwarding Limits: To combat the "velocity" of fake news, platforms have maintained "forwarding limits." In 2026, messages that have been forwarded many times are labeled with a "double arrow" to signal they did not originate from a close contact [7].

Fact-Checking Tiplines: Since they cannot monitor chats, platforms have scaled "tiplines" where users can voluntarily forward suspicious messages to verified fact-checkers. In 2026, AI-powered tiplines can provide automated verifications in seconds [2, 6].

4. Impact on Democratic Stability

Institutional Erosion: The spread of "private" disinformation has been linked to the erosion of trust in election commissions and healthcare providers, as debunking efforts struggle to penetrate closed chat groups [4,

5].

Physical Violence: The "black hole" effect remains a high risk for mobilizing physical unrest; in several 2026 incidents, unverified rumors of child abductions or communal threats shared on E2EE apps led to localized mob violence before authorities could intervene [3].

Feature	Public Social Media (2026)	Encrypted Apps (e.g., WhatsApp)
Visibility	Monitored by AI and Fact-checkers	"Black Hole" (Private/Invisible)
Moderation	Active (labels, removals, DSA compliance)	Indirect (forwarding limits, user reports)
Trust Level	Low (Stranger-based)	High (Friend/Family-based)
Primary Risk	Algorithmic Echo Chambers	Rapid, Invisible Radicalization

In 2026, the Digital Divide has evolved from a simple gap in connectivity into a structural barrier that facilitates "data colonialism." While global internet penetration continues to rise, the benefits of the digital economy are distributed unevenly, leaving marginalized populations—particularly women and rural communities—digitally invisible and subject to external data exploitation.

1. The Gendered Digital Divide (2026 Data)

Recent statistics from late 2026 highlight a persistent and severe gender gap in digital access, particularly in the Global South:

Access Disparity: In India, only one-third (approx. 33%) of women use the internet, compared to two-thirds (approx. 67%) of men.

The "Second-Level" Divide: Beyond basic access, there is a gap in digital literacy. Even women with devices often have limited autonomy, as social norms in many regions dictate that mobile phones are "controlled" by male family members, restricting women's ability to participate in e-governance or digital commerce.

Economic Impact: This gap prevents women from accessing "G2C" services, such as direct welfare transfers or digital health records, effectively disenfranchising them from the "connected" state.

2. Data Colonialism and "Digital Invisibility"

The term Data Colonialism refers to the practice where a few dominant tech entities (mostly from the Global North) extract and monetize the data of Global South populations without providing equitable value or local control.

Extraction without Agency: When marginalized populations finally gain access, they often enter a digital ecosystem where they are "data points" for global algorithms rather than active citizens.

Algorithmic Bias: Because the data of "invisible" populations (like the 66% of Indian women who are offline) is missing from training sets, the AI models developed in 2026 are systematically biased against them, failing to recognize their languages, needs, or cultural contexts.

Loss of Sovereignty: "Data colonialism" shifts power away from local governments to private platform owners who control the infrastructure of the public sphere, making local democratic deliberation nearly impossible.

While global internet access has increased, there are still significant disparities in who can benefit from the digital world. This leads to what some call "data colonialism," where some groups become digitally invisible and their data can be exploited.

1. The Gendered Digital Divide (2026 Data)

Data from late 2026 shows a clear difference in digital access based on gender, especially in developing countries:

Access Disparity: In India, only about one-third (around 33%) of women use the internet, compared to about two-thirds (around 67%) of men.

Beyond Access: Even when women have devices, they may not have full control over them due to social expectations in many areas. This can limit their ability to use digital services like online government programs or businesses.

Economic Impact: This difference can prevent women from using online government services, such as welfare payments or digital health records, excluding them from the advantages of being connected.

2. Data Colonialism and "Digital Invisibility"

Data Colonialism is a term used to describe how a few large tech companies, mostly from developed countries, collect and profit from the data of people in developing countries without offering fair value or local control in return.

Data Collection without Control: When marginalized groups do get online, they may become simply "data points" for global computer programs rather than active users.

Biased Algorithms: Since data from people who are "invisible" digitally (like the many Indian women who are not online) is not included in the data used to train artificial intelligence, the AI models created in 2026 can have biases against them. These models might not understand their languages, needs, or cultures.

Loss of Local Control: "Data colonialism" can shift power from local governments to private companies that manage the online spaces people use, making it harder for local communities to discuss and make decisions about public matters.

3. Structural Barriers in 2026

Infrastructure Gaps: While cities have fast internet like 5G, rural areas may still have less reliable connections. This can create a situation where your location affects how well you can access government services.

The Literacy Gap: In 2026, some users in rural areas are online but may not have the skills to tell the difference between official government messages and false information spread on messaging apps.

Language Exclusion: Although efforts are being made to translate information, much valuable content on the internet is still mainly in English or other major global languages, which can exclude people who only speak local languages.

In 2026, the tension between platform accountability and freedom of expression has reached a fever pitch. Governments are moving away from self-regulation toward "digital sovereignty," implementing aggressive legal frameworks to manage the "Digital Rupture."

1. India's DPDP Rules 2026

Following the 2023 Act, the Digital Personal Data Protection (DPDP) Rules 2026 have established the operational reality for data handling in India:

Consent Management: Platforms must now provide clear, multilingual notices and allow users to withdraw consent as easily as they gave it through MeitY-registered Consent Managers.

The Censorship Concern: Critics argue that the "significant data fiduciary" status allows the state to demand data or restrict content under broad "national security" clauses, potentially leading to state-led digital gatekeeping.

Personal Liability: The 2026 rules introduce heavy penalties (up to ₹250 crore) for data breaches, compelling platforms to be more cautious, which some fear may result in "over-censorship" to avoid legal risk.

2. EU Digital Services Act (DSA) & AI Act

The EU remains the global "regulatory lighthouse" with two major frameworks active in 2026:

The DSA Transparency Database: As of late 2026, large platforms are mandated to log every content moderation decision in the DSA Transparency Database, giving users unprecedented rights to appeal removals.

EU AI Act (Effective Feb 2026): This landmark law bans

"unacceptable risks," such as AI-driven social scoring and manipulative behavioral nudging. It forces "high-risk" systems to undergo rigorous auditing before they can influence the public sphere.

3. The "Brussels Effect" vs. Digital Nationalism

Standardization: Many global platforms are adopting EU-style transparency as a global default to simplify compliance, a phenomenon known as the "Brussels Effect."

Regulatory Friction: In 2026, a major conflict exists between Western "rights-based" regulation and the "control-based" models of authoritarian regimes. For example, Brazil and Turkey have seen 2026 legal battles resulting in temporary platform bans when companies refused to comply with local "content takedown" orders.

4. Summary of Regulatory Tensions (2026)

Framework	Goal	Censorship Risk
India DPDP Rules	Data sovereignty & protection	Broad state exemptions may enable surveillance.
EU DSA	Platform transparency & safety	Risk of "automated" over-blocking to meet compliance.
UK Online Safety Act	Protecting minors from "legal but harmful" content	Concerns over breaking E2EE (End-to-End Encryption).
Global AI Treaties	Preventing "Synthetic Affect" manipulation	Risk of state-defined "truth" suppressing dissen

Chapter 9

The Populist Backlash and Democratic Backsliding

In 2026, the relationship between populist backlash and democratic backsliding has solidified into a systemic global trend. Research indicates that democratic backsliding is a gradual process where personalist leaders or parties use legal processes to dismantle institutions after being elected, a significant shift from the sudden military coups of the Cold War era.

1. Mechanisms of Populist Backsliding in 2026

Administrative Capture: Populist governments in 2026 increasingly use public administration as a tool for illiberal agendas. By aiming at personnel, norms, and accountability structures, they "capture" or "sabotage" state bureaucracy to remove checks on their power.

Legislative Backsliding: Leaders often use their electoral mandate to justify departing from liberal norms, framing democratic institutions (like parliaments or judiciaries) as "elitist" or detached from the "true people".

Incremental Erosion: Backsliding in 2026 is often a "sum of various strategies" rather than a single event. It includes the dismantling of bureaucracy and the use of "crisis narratives" (e.g., deep state or "wokeness" themes) to justify power hoarding.

2. Primary Drivers: The "Grievance Cycle"

Economic Inequality: A robust statistical association exists in 2026 between high income inequality and democratic erosion. Leaders cultivate a sense of being "left behind" to fuel resentment against elite institutions.

Pernicious Polarization: Aspiring autocrats seize on partisan polarization to present voters with a "trade-off": they must choose between safeguarding democratic norms or avoiding the "dire consequences" of an opposing party coming to power.

Targeting "Out-Groups": Populist rhetoric in 2026 frequently scapegoats marginalized communities, such as migrants or religious minorities (e.g., targeting the Muslim community in India), to maintain popular support.

3. Global Trends & Statistics (2026)

Metric	2026 Status
Global Freedom Trend	19th consecutive year of decline.
Population Affected	Declines in 2024–2026 affected more than 40% of the global population.
Electoral Integrity	Over 40% of national elections in 2024 involved violence or restricted voter choices.
Press Freedom	Independent media experienced repression in over 120 countries.
"Electoral Democracies"	The number of rated electoral democracies decreased from 110 to 106 in the latest annual assessment.

4. Resistance and Resilience

Institutional Resilience: Strong institutions in mature democracies (e.g., Germany) have "institutional capital" to absorb losses from polarization, whereas fragile states (e.g., Venezuela) face systemic collapse from even moderate polarization.

Social Mobilization: Countering backsliding in 2026 depends on the longevity and inclusivity of anti-populist social movements and the cohesion of democratic opposition.

Administrative Resistance: Professionalized bureaucratic cultures of "expertise" can serve as a "partial building block" for democratic resilience, though they cannot safeguard democracy alone.

In 2026, the rise of illiberal democracy and the systematic hollowing out of institutions are the defining themes of the current "third wave of autocratization." According to the V-Dem Democracy Report 2026, liberal democracies have become the least common regime type globally, with the level of democracy for the average world citizen regressing to 1985 levels.

1. Illiberal Democracy: The Facade of Choice

An illiberal democracy is a system that maintains the formal mechanics of democracy—such as elections—while subtly suppressing the liberal values of constitutionalism, individual rights, and the rule of law.

Majoritarianism: Leaders claim a "mandate" from the majority to override institutional checks, often framing judicial independence or minority protections as "obstacles" to the popular will.

Rule by Law: Rather than the rule of law, illiberal regimes use a "rule by law" approach, weaponizing the legal system to prosecute political rivals and silence critical media.

Plebiscitarianism: Elections are increasingly "lopsided" or manipulated to consolidate the incumbent's power rather than provide a genuine choice for citizens.

2. The Hollowing Out of Institutions

"Hollowing out" refers to the gradual erosion of an institution's internal integrity and independence, even as its outward structure remains intact.

Administrative Sabotage: Governments target the personnel and norms of the civil service. In 2026, notable trends include replacing non-partisan experts with political loyalists to ensure "total administrative obedience".

Capture of Accountability Bodies: Independent bodies like election commissions, human rights councils, and anti-corruption agencies are "hollowed" when their leadership is co-opted, turning them from watchdogs into enforcers for the executive.

Executive Aggrandizement: Executives expand their powers by bypassing parliamentary oversight, abusing the speaker's role, or misusing "money bill" procedures to push through legislation without debate.

3. Key Global Drivers in 2026

Polarization and Disinformation: High levels of polarization and government-driven disinformation are used to "shape public opinion" and justify the dismantling of checks and balances.

Attack on Expression: Freedom of expression is currently worsening in 44 countries, the highest number ever recorded by the V-Dem Institute. Media censorship is the "weapon of choice" for the 45 countries currently in the process of autocratizing.

Economic Rent-Seeking: Illiberal regimes often fuse political and economic interests, allowing a politically connected class to extract "rents" and block further democratic change to protect their wealth.

4. 2026 Snapshot of Institutional Fragility

Institution	Method of "Hollowing"	2026 Observation
Judiciary	Impeaching judges or packing courts with loyalists.	Frequent attacks on "judicial activism" globally.
Civil Service	Mass layoffs of experts; patronage-based hiring.	Movement toward personalist "loyalty" over expertise.
Media	"Soft" censorship through economic pressure or defamation laws.	Press freedom at a 20-year low in several major nations.
Universities	Attacks on academic freedom; forced relocation of institutions.	Academic freedom scores dropped to "mostly free" or lower in the UK and US.

In 2026, political theorists and practitioners identify the "Winner's Dilemma" and the structural collapse of compromise as the primary psychological and strategic engines driving democratic backsliding. These challenges suggest that the very mechanics of winning an election in a polarized age may necessitate the destruction of democratic norms.

1. The Winner's Dilemma: Winning at Any Cost

The Winner's Dilemma posits that in a highly polarized environment, the cost of losing an election is perceived as existential. This perception forces "winners" to take illiberal actions to ensure they never have to face the consequences of losing.

Existential Stakes: When voters perceive the opposing party not just as a rival but as an "existential threat" to their way of life, the winning party feels a mandate—or a survival instinct—to entrench its power.

The "Insurance" Strategy: To mitigate the risk of a future loss, winners use their term to tilt the playing field. In 2026, this is observed through partisan gerrymandering, the appointment of loyalists to election oversight bodies, and the use of "lawfare" to disqualify future opponents.

The Feedback Loop: As one side breaks norms to "protect" itself, the other side becomes even more radicalized in its pursuit of power, confirming the original "existential threat" narrative and deepening the dilemma.

2. The Decline of Compromise Politics

Compromise—the "slow boring of hard boards" essential to liberal democracy—is increasingly viewed as political suicide in 2026.

Perverse Incentives: Modern primary systems and social media algorithms reward ideological purity. In 2026, politicians who seek bipartisan compromise are often "primaried" or targeted by viral "outrage cycles" that label them as traitors to their base.

Zero-Sum Governance: Politics has shifted from a "positive-sum" game (where both sides can gain through trade-offs) to a "zero-sum" game. Any gain for the opposition is viewed as an absolute loss for the "people," making legislative gridlock the default state.

Erosion of "Mutual Toleration": A core pillar of democracy is the belief that political rivals are legitimate participants. By 2026, this has been replaced by "Pernicious Polarization", where rivals are framed as enemies of the state, removing the moral incentive to compromise.

3. Impact on Institutional Health

Hollowing out the Middle: The decline of compromise has decimated "moderate" factions within parliaments. Without a centrist "buffer," institutions become brittle and prone to total capture by whichever faction holds the majority.

Crisis of Legitimacy: When compromise fails, the executive often resorts to Executive Aggrandizement—using decrees, executive orders, or emergency powers to bypass a deadlocked legislature. This "hollows out" the deliberative role of parliament.

Summary of the Theoretical Shift (2026)

Feature	Traditional Liberal Model	2026 Backsliding Model
View of the Rival	Legitimate Competitor	Existential Enemy
Winning Goal	Policy Implementation	Institutional Capture
Compromise	A Sign of Strength/Pragmatism	A Sign of Weakness/Betrayal
Electoral Stakes	Reversible Loss	Irreversible Catastrophe

These theoretical challenges explain why, even in "established" democracies, the transition from a consolidated democracy to an illiberal one can happen through the legal, everyday actions of elected winners who no longer believe in the safety of a fair loss [1][2][4].

Chapter 10

Post-National and Transnational Governance

In 2026, the governance of global affairs has transitioned from traditional state-centric models to a more complex, transnational and post-national landscape. These models address challenges—such as climate change, AI, and global finance—that exceed the regulatory capacity of any single nation-state.

1. Transnational Governance (TNG)

Transnational governance in 2026 is defined by the coordination of policies across borders, often bypassing or operating alongside national governments.

Key Actors: Beyond states, TNG involves non-state actors such as multinational corporations, NGOs, and cities. These groups often create voluntary certification programs (e.g., sustainability standards) and public-private partnerships to manage global markets.

Sector Focus:

Climate & Environment: Transnational networks are now essential for "earth system governance," focusing on issues like biodiversity and global warming.

Digital Economy: Multistakeholder initiatives, such as the UNESCO Data Governance Toolkit (launched June 2026), provide policy solutions for AI and data regulation across more than 50 countries.

Deliberative Transnationalism: To address the "democratic deficit," 2026 models increasingly incorporate expert deliberation and public participation in international policy-making to improve legitimacy.

2. Post-National Governance

Post-nationalism refers to a state where national identity and borders coexist with, but are increasingly subordinated to, regional or global frameworks.

The UN at 80: In 2026, the United Nations is undergoing significant reform to remain "fit for purpose" in its 80th year. The Pact for the Future (adopted late 2024) outlines 56 steps to upgrade multilateralism in science, technology, and global governance.

Economic Order: Globalization has disembedded economic and political processes from local contexts. In 2026, the nation-state is often viewed as an "insufficient vehicle" for regulating the global accumulation of capital, leading to the rise of supranational legal and financial standards.

3. The Shift to Regionalism and Minilateralism

A major trend in 2026 is the pivot away from universal globalism toward more focused, interest-based groupings.

Minilateralism: Smaller, flexible coalitions like the QUAD, I2U2, and BRICS+ are favored for faster decision-making in security and technology over deadlocked global bodies.

Regional Blocs: Regionalism has become a primary framework for survival. Key 2026 examples include the EU's quest for socio-economic autonomy and the African Union's integration into the G20, making the summit's first-ever staging on African soil in South Africa.

Strategic Autonomy: Many nations, including India, are recalibrating their foreign policies to prioritize "interest-driven regional cooperation" over idealistic multilateralism to maintain sovereignty while participating in global systems.

4. Challenges to Global Cooperation in 2026

Transnational Repression: Autocratic regimes have become increasingly skilled at using digital tools and economic ties to intimidate or harm dissidents living abroad. This "escalating wave" of repression was notably omnipresent in 2026, particularly in Southeast Asia.

Sovereignty Conflicts: Tensions persist between the need for "global responsibility" (e.g., climate targets) and the reassertion of national sovereignty.

Funding Shortfalls: Despite the need for global solutions, humanitarian agencies like UNICEF and the WFP entered 2026 with significant funding gaps, receiving only 43% of the resources needed for the world's most vulnerable.

n 2026, the Westphalian nation-state model—defined by centralized sovereignty and fixed borders—is facing an existential "mismatch" with the reality of a globalized world. As of late 2026, the state is increasingly viewed as being too small to handle global crises and too large to address local identity needs.

1. The "Scale Mismatch" (Global vs. Local)

The primary limit of the nation-state in 2026 is its inability to regulate phenomena that do not respect borders:

Climate & Ecology: National borders are irrelevant to carbon cycles or biodiversity loss. In 2026, "Earth System Governance" has gained traction as a necessary post-national framework because individual states cannot solve the climate crisis alone.

The Digital Rupture: Data, capital, and disinformation flow through fiber-optic cables, bypassing customs and border patrols. States in 2026 struggle to tax "stateless" digital profits or regulate AI models trained on global datasets.

Transnational Health: As seen with pandemic risks, a collapse in one state's public health infrastructure is an immediate threat to all others, making national sovereignty a liability in biosecurity.

2. The Erosion of Sovereign Control

Data Colonialism: Large tech platforms now exercise "functional sovereignty," setting rules for speech and commerce that override national laws. By late 2026, many states find themselves as mere "service providers" on infrastructure owned by transnational corporations.

Economic Disembedding: Globalization has "disembedded" the economy from the political community. In 2026, the nation-state often lacks the leverage to regulate global capital, leading to the rise of minilateralism (e.g., G7, BRICS+) as states try to regain control through specialized clubs rather than universal bodies.

3. Crisis of Legitimacy: The "Democratic Deficit"

Post-National Alienation: As power shifts to transnational bodies (like the EU or the WTO) or private platforms, citizens feel a "loss of agency." This "democratic deficit" is a primary driver of the populist backlash seen in 2026, as voters attempt to "take back control" of a state that is no longer fully autonomous.

Sub-National Fragmentation: Conversely, the nation-state model is being challenged from within by ethnic, religious, or regional identities. In 2026, the "one nation, one people" ideal is under pressure from groups demanding localism or autonomy, viewing the centralized state as an oppressive or "hollowed-out" relic.

4. Transitioning to Multi-Layered Governance (2026)

To survive these limits, the nation-state is evolving into a node within a multi-layered governance system:

Layer	Function in 2026
Global/Supranational	Managing "Planetary Boundaries" (Climate, AI safety, Pandemics).
Regional/Minilateral	Economic integration and strategic security (EU, QUAD, ASEAN).
The Nation-State	Identity, welfare distribution, and military defense.
Local/Municipal	Direct citizen participation, e-governance, and "town square"

	deliberation.

Summary: In 2026, the "End of History" has not led to a world of identical nation-states, but rather to a post-national rupture where the state must share power with global systems and local communities to remain relevant.

In 2026, the limits of the traditional nation-state have birthed a "multi-layered" governance architecture. This transition replaces top-down state authority with a hybrid system of multi-stakeholder networks, reformed global institutions, and decentralized technologies.

1. Multi-Stakeholder Networks

By 2026, governance is no longer the exclusive domain of politicians. Policy is increasingly set by "tripartite" networks comprising governments, private corporations, and civil society.

The G7/G20 Evolution: These bodies have transitioned from purely political summits to hubs for "minilateral" cooperation on specific issues like the Global Minimum Tax and AI Safety Standards.

Sectoral Networks: Organizations like Gavi (The Vaccine Alliance) and the Global Fund serve as blueprints, where private capital and NGO expertise direct global health policy more efficiently than individual states.

Environmental Governance: Transnational networks of cities (e.g., C40 Cities) are bypassing national gridlock to implement climate targets directly at the municipal level.

2. Reformed Global Institutions (UN & EU)

The year 2026 marks a "pivotal upgrade" for the institutional pillars of the 20th century as they attempt to remain relevant in a post-national world.

United Nations (The "Pact for the Future"): Celebrating its 80th anniversary in 2026, the UN is implementing the Pact for the Future, which established the Global Digital Compact. This framework seeks to bridge the digital divide and create global norms for AI, treating the digital sphere as a "global public good" rather than a corporate vacuum.

European Union (Strategic Autonomy): The EU in 2026 has moved beyond a trading bloc to a "regulatory superpower." Through the EU AI Act (enforced Feb 2026) and the Digital Services Act, the EU exerts the "Brussels Effect," forcing global tech firms to adopt European standards for speech and privacy worldwide.

The African Union (AU) in G20: For the first time in 2026, the AU participates as a permanent member of the G20 (hosted by South Africa), signaling a shift toward a more representative, multipolar global order.

3. Decentralized and Algorithmic Governance

Technological advances are enabling models that operate outside of centralized bureaucratic control.

Digital Public Infrastructure (DPI): The India Stack model has been exported to over 15 countries by late 2026. It provides a decentralized way for citizens to own their data and identity, reducing the "state's" role as a gatekeeper and moving it toward being an infrastructure provider.

DAOs and On-Chain Governance: While still emerging, Decentralized Autonomous Organizations (DAOs) are being used in 2026 to manage small-scale community assets and research grants, using smart contracts to automate decision-making and reduce the "winner's dilemma" inherent in partisan politics.

Civic Tech Platforms: Tools like vTaiwan and Pol.is use AI to find consensus among thousands of citizens, creating "deliberative crowdsourcing" models that inform national laws with bottom-up legitimacy.

Summary: The 2026 Governance Landscape

Model	Scale	Key Feature
Multi-	Transnational	Collaboration between Big Tech,

Stakeholder		NGOs, and States.
UN / International	Global	Focus on AI Safety, Climate, and "Pact for the Future."
EU / Regional	Supranational	Regulatory sovereignty and harmonized digital rights.
DPI / Decentralized	Local/Digital	Consent-based data sharing and automated service delivery.

In 2026, the transition toward post-national governance is defined by a shift from rigid state hierarchies to a "polycentric" model. This framework distributes authority across three primary pillars: inclusive networks, modernized global institutions, and decentralized technology.

1. Multi-Stakeholder Networks (The "Triple Helix" Model)

Governance in 2026 increasingly relies on the "Triple Helix" of collaboration between governments, the private sector, and civil society.

Minilateralism: Smaller, flexible groupings like the G7, BRICS+, and the Quad are favored for rapid policy-setting in areas like semiconductor supply chains and maritime security, bypassing the slower consensus of traditional global bodies.

Climate & Health Networks: Initiatives like the C40 Cities Network and the Global Fund operate transnationally, with city mayors and NGOs often implementing climate and health solutions more effectively than national legislatures.

The "Adhocracy" Trend: Temporary task forces comprising tech experts and academics are increasingly utilized by states to draft real-time regulations for emerging technologies like quantum computing and CRISPR.

2. Global Governance Institutions (UN & EU)

As the UN celebrates its 80th anniversary in 2026, these "legacy" institutions are attempting a structural "reboot" to address the 21st-century digital and ecological crisis.

The UN's "Global Digital Compact": Established under the Pact for the Future, this 2026 framework is the first global attempt to treat AI and data as "global public goods." It aims to prevent "data colonialism" by ensuring the Global South has a voice in AI governance.

The European Union as a "Regulatory Superpower": With the full enforcement of the EU AI Act in February 2026, the EU has cemented its role in the "Brussels Effect"—where its strict standards for digital safety and privacy become the de facto global law for multinational tech firms.

South Africa's G20 Presidency (2026): For the first time, the African Union (AU) sits as a permanent member, representing a shift toward a more representative, multipolar global order that challenges Western-centric governance.

3. Decentralized and Algorithmic Systems

Technological innovations are providing alternatives to traditional "top-down" bureaucracy, allowing for more direct, automated governance.

Digital Public Infrastructure (DPI): The India Stack model (Aadhaar, UPI, DigiLocker) is now used as a template in over 20 countries. It decentralizes power by allowing citizens to own their data and interact with the state through a "consent-based" digital layer, reducing the need for physical intermediaries.

DAOs (Decentralized Autonomous Organizations): In 2026, DAOs are moving beyond crypto-speculation to manage real-world "community commons," such as local energy grids and open-source research grants, using blockchain-based "smart contracts" to automate decision-making.

AI-Enabled Deliberation: Platforms like vTaiwan and Pol.is utilize AI to map consensus among thousands of citizens, allowing governments to crowdsource complex legislation and reduce the "winner's dilemma" inherent in partisan politics.

Summary: Emerging Models of 2026

Model	Primary Actor	Key Strength
Multi-Stakeholder	Corporations + NGOs + States	Speed and specialized expertise
Global/Supranational	UN, EU, African Union	Universal legitimacy and broad regulation
Decentralized (DPI)	Citizen-centric Algorithms	Transparency and friction-less service
Minilateral	Interest-based coalitions (BRICS+)	Strategic agility in a polarized world

Conclusion

The Future of the Democratic Paradigm

Part I, "Foundations and First Principles (Antiquity to the 18th Century)," traces the evolution of self-rule and governance through three distinct historical periods, culminating in the establishment of the modern nation-state. The section begins with Chapter 1: The Athenian Ideal: Direct Participation and its Limits, which defines the initial paradigm of self-rule through the lens of Athenian democracy. This model emphasized direct citizen participation but was fundamentally limited by its exclusionary nature, restricting citizenship based on gender and utilizing the institution of slavery.

Chapter 2: The Republican Turn: From Polis to Res publica shifts focus from the Greek city-state to the Roman Republic, exploring the critical transition to the concept of representation as a practical necessity for governing a larger population and territory. It further examines how early constitutional thought was developed in medieval councils, building upon Roman precedents.

Finally, Chapter 3: The Birth of the Modern Nation-State addresses a pivotal moment in global politics: the Peace of Westphalia. This treaty established the principle of state sovereignty and laid the groundwork for the modern nation-state system. The chapter concludes by analyzing absolutism as a political phase that, through its concentration of power, set the stage for subsequent liberal reactions and the development of modern democratic theory. In conclusion, Part I establishes the core historical and philosophical foundations of governance, illustrating a progression from limited direct democracy to the representative republic, and ultimately to the sovereign nation-state that became the basis for political organization leading into the modern era.

The Paradigm Shift of Modernity

The conclusion of Part II: The Great Democratic Waves synthesizes the transition of democracy from an experimental provincial ideal into a dominant global framework between the late 18th and mid-20th centuries.

This era marked a fundamental "rupture point" where the source of political legitimacy shifted from divine right or hereditary status to the sovereignty of the people. The American and French Revolutions did not merely change governments; they established the Liberal Democratic Paradigm, enshrining the rule of law and the separation of powers as structural safeguards against the return of autocracy.

The Evolution of "The Demos"

The period's greatest internal achievement was the incremental dismantling of exclusionary barriers. Democracy evolved through a series of Suffrage Revolutions that decoupled political agency from land ownership, race, and gender. By transitioning from a "democracy of proprietors" to universal suffrage, the demos finally began to reflect the actual population, though this progress was often met with violent institutional resistance.

Survival through Ideological Conflict

The mid-20th century served as the ultimate stress test for this paradigm. The rise of totalitarianism (fascism and communism) presented a competing vision of "the people" that prioritized collective state power over individual rights. The conclusion of Part II finds democracy at a paradoxical peak: while the post-WWII Cold War Order entrenched liberal democracy as the moral and structural standard for the West, it also necessitated a permanent defensive posture against rival ideological blocs.

Key Synthesis: By 1950, democracy was no longer just a system of voting; it had become an international order based on individual rights and multilateral stability, setting the stage for the rapid global expansions of the late 20th century.

The Paradox of Global Dominance

The conclusion of Part III: The Contemporary Era evaluates the current state of democracy as it faces a dual crisis of institutional erosion and technological disruption By the early 21st century, democracy appeared to be the undisputed global consensus. However, the 2026 landscape reveals that this consensus was more fragile than the "end of history" thesis suggested. While electoral models remain globally dominant, 2026 reports indicate nearly two decades of continuous decline in global freedom, with liberal democracies now being the least common regime type and 72% of the world's population living in autocracies.

The Digital Rupture

Technology has fundamentally rewired the democratic public sphere.

E-Governance: While digital tools have enabled greater political mobilization, they have also facilitated "computational propaganda".

Information Integrity: In 2026, AI-generated disinformation—including deepfakes and hyper-personalized propaganda—has become a systemic threat, with false news diffusing significantly faster and deeper than the truth.

The Trust Deficit: Only 41% of respondents globally trust government institutions as of 2026, a decline linked to viral disinformation targeting electoral processes.

Populism and Institutional Backsliding

Contemporary democracy is increasingly "hollowed out" from within.

Illiberal Democracy: Populist leaders across the globe are driving a wedge between democracy and liberalism, often using legal processes to weaken judicial independence and press freedom.

The Winner's Dilemma: Intense political polarization has undermined compromise politics, as antagonistic camps increasingly view their opponents not just as rivals, but as existential threats to the state.

The Future of the Paradigm

As we look beyond 2026, the democratic paradigm must navigate tensions between traditional state sovereignty and transnational governance.

Emerging Models: There is a growing shift toward multi-stakeholder networks and decentralized systems to address global issues like climate change and migration that exceed the capacity of individual nation-states.

Resilience: Despite these pressures, 2026 has seen significant democratic resilience through youth-led movements, civic protests, and innovations in participatory governance that continue to challenge authoritarian trends.

Synthesized Conclusion: Modern democracy is an "inherently unfinished project". Its future depends on evolving beyond the 20th-century state-centric model to build a resilient, digital-literate citizenry and institutions that can deliver shared prosperity in an era of acute uncertainty.

Over the past few decades, the concept of governance has undergone a significant transformation, reflecting a paradigm shift from traditional, state-centric government structures to more complex, participatory, and network-oriented models of governance. This shift is not simply about organizational changes or administrative reforms. Rather, it embodies a deeper redefinition of the relationship between the state and society, the mechanisms of power distribution, and the processes through which public goods and services are delivered. This movement, driven largely by the global waves of neoliberal reforms and the forces of globalization, has reshaped governance across national and local contexts. It is a movement away from rigid, top-down models of command and control and toward systems characterized by interconnectedness, flexibility, and the involvement of a wide range of actors including the private sector, civil society, and local communities.

At the core of this transformation lies a critical reassessment of traditional state functions and statutory regulations. Governance in its evolved form is not limited to government action but extends to how various institutions, actors, and processes interact and coordinate to achieve collective goals. This includes adapting legal and regulatory frameworks to enable more flexible and context-sensitive governance mechanisms, promoting responsiveness to social and economic complexities, and enhancing participatory approaches. The transformation is rooted in a broader effort to develop institutional systems that are more effective at steering societies in an increasingly interconnected and volatile world.

Historical Context and the Rise of Neoliberal Reforms

To fully grasp the evolution from government to governance, it is essential to trace its historical roots. Following the Second World War, the prevailing belief across much of the world, particularly in developing countries, was that the state should function as the primary engine of economic growth and social progress. Governments undertook ambitious development plans, monopolized service delivery, and operated large bureaucratic apparatuses. Public administration became synonymous with governance, and the effectiveness of the state was measured by its capacity to deliver goods and services. However, by the 1970s and 1980s, the limitations of this model became increasingly apparent. Development outcomes were often disappointing, and the state began to be viewed as inefficient, overly centralized, and sometimes corrupt. With state-led models failing to produce the desired results, especially in terms of poverty reduction and equitable growth, criticism mounted. The search for alternatives led to a growing emphasis on market-based mechanisms and institutional reform.

The introduction of neoliberal reforms in the 1980s and 1990s marked a decisive turning point. The global trend toward liberalization, privatization, and deregulation challenged the long-standing role of the state. In South Asia, the year 1991 stands out as a watershed moment, particularly with the adoption of structural adjustment programs and liberal economic policies. These changes marked the beginning of a paradigm shift: the state began to withdraw from direct service delivery, while non-state actors including the private sector and civil society started playing increasingly prominent roles. This change was not just about minimizing the state's role but also about creating robust institutions that could effectively coordinate, regulate, and facilitate the involvement of multiple stakeholders. The shift from government to governance thus responded to the demand for institutional innovation and collaborative mechanisms capable of navigating complex developmental challenges.

Governance as a Multi-Actor, Network-Based Model

Governance in the modern context is distinguished by its emphasis on decentralization, participation, and networked collaboration. It reflects a move away from the conventional understanding of government as a hierarchical and centralized authority, toward a model where diverse actors contribute to decision-making, implementation, and accountability. The traditional government approach often characterized by rigid bureaucracies and "command and control" structures is increasingly viewed as inadequate to meet the dynamic needs of contemporary societies.

Instead, governance frameworks now rely on policy networks and operational networks that bring together government agencies, private companies, non-governmental organizations, community groups, and international actors. These networks facilitate the co-production of policy and services. Policy networks are formal institutions that enable structured interactions between state and non-state actors, leading to collective policy outputs that are more reflective of diverse interests and grounded in collaborative consensus. Unlike lobby groups, which seek to influence decision-making in their favor, policy networks are mechanisms of shared governance, where responsibilities and outcomes are jointly negotiated.

Operational networks, on the other hand, focus on implementation. These informal and semi-formal collaborations are particularly relevant in service delivery, especially in areas where government alone lacks capacity or reach. Public-private partnerships (PPPs) serve as a leading example, enabling joint investments and sharing of risks and benefits between public and private sectors. Through such collaborative arrangements, governance achieves more efficient and responsive service delivery while expanding the space for competition and innovation.

Global Institutions and the Popularization of "Good Governance"

The rise of the concept of governance cannot be detached from the role played by international economic and development institutions. Beginning in the late twentieth century, organizations such as the World Bank, International Monetary Fund (IMF), United Nations Development Programme (UNDP), and other international donors began to emphasize the importance of governance as a critical component of development. Their growing concern with the inefficiencies, corruption, and lack of accountability in state institutions led to the emergence of "good governance" as a normative ideal. The emphasis on good governance was closely tied to broader neoliberal ideologies, which advocated for democratic reforms, market liberalization, and efficient public sector management. As a result, good governance came to embody a set of principles including transparency, accountability, rule of law, participation, responsiveness, equity, and efficiency. Over time, these principles have been integrated into development programs, governance reforms, and donor conditionalities across the globe.

Importantly, the notion of good governance also evolved to incorporate broader ideals such as human rights, gender equity, social inclusion, and environmental sustainability. This expanded focus reflects a growing awareness that governance cannot be limited to political and administrative effectiveness but must also ensure social justice and inclusive development. Thus, the governance agenda now spans economic, social, and environmental dimensions, underpinned by a vision of democratic legitimacy and participatory engagement.

Nepal's Governance Landscape: Opportunities and Limitations

Nepal presents a compelling case of this global governance transition. Having emerged from a decade-long Maoist insurgency and transitioned from a monarchy to a republic, the country adopted a new constitution in 2015 that introduced a federal structure aimed at promoting decentralization and inclusivity. This move was intended to address historical inequities and empower marginalized regions and communities through localized governance. While the introduction of federalism marked a significant shift from centralized government toward a governance-oriented model, its implementation has been complex and contested. Disputes over provincial boundaries have led to tensions among ethnic and regional groups, reflecting the difficulty of aligning governance structures with diverse identities and aspirations. The distribution of resources remains uneven, and the administrative capacities of newly formed provincial and local governments are still developing. One of the most persistent challenges facing governance in Nepal is corruption. Despite having institutions and regulatory bodies, public trust in anti-corruption efforts remains low. These institutions and regulatory bodies often lack the autonomy, capacity, and political backing to act decisively. As a result, governance reforms are often undermined by rent-seeking behavior and political interference.

Inclusive governance, although enshrined in legal frameworks, often struggles to move beyond symbolic representation. Marginalized groups, including women, Dalits, and indigenous nationalities, are frequently included in decision-making structures without meaningful influence over policy and resource allocation. This gap between formal inclusion and substantive empowerment reflects a key governance deficit that requires sustained effort and institutional innovation. Political instability, characterized by frequent government changes and shifting coalitions, has further hampered policy continuity and implementation. Long-term reforms are often derailed by short-term political maneuvering, limiting the effectiveness of governance institutions. Addressing this instability will require a deeper examination of party dynamics, electoral processes, and institutional safeguards to ensure stability without compromising democratic participation. Additionally, Nepal faces significant socioeconomic challenges that test the capacity of its governance systems. Persistent poverty, inadequate infrastructure, and stark rural-urban disparities demand more than policy pronouncements; they require critical evaluation of existing strategies and targeted interventions that prioritize the most vulnerable. Without such focused efforts, governance reforms risk becoming detached from the lived realities of ordinary citizens.

The Role of Geopolitics, Technology, and Institutional Adaptation

Nepal's governance dynamics are further shaped by its geopolitical position between two major powers - India and China. The country must navigate a delicate diplomatic balancing act, ensuring national sovereignty while leveraging strategic partnerships. Governance in such a context involves not only domestic administration but also sophisticated foreign policy management. The choices Nepal makes in terms of trade, investment, infrastructure development, and diplomatic alignment have far-reaching implications for its internal governance and institutional autonomy.

Technology, too, is transforming governance across sectors. The rise of e-governance platforms, digital service delivery, and data-driven decision-making has opened new avenues for transparency, efficiency, and citizen engagement. These tools enable governments to streamline administrative processes, reduce corruption, and make policies more responsive. However, they also introduce new challenges, such as digital exclusion, cyber risks, and questions about data ethics and privacy. Thus, technology must be integrated into governance frameworks in a way that enhances inclusion and accountability.

Institutional strength alone is not sufficient in today's context. Institutions must also be adaptable, capable of learning from experience, and responsive to changing circumstances. The ethical dimensions of governance - transparency, integrity, and justice, are paramount. As decision-making becomes more diffuse and collaborative, mechanisms for oversight, accountability, and ethical conduct must be embedded at all levels. Only then can governance serve the broader public interest and command legitimacy.

The Continuing Evolution of Governance

The shift from government to governance is not a one-time event but an ongoing, multifaceted transformation. It reflects changing ideas about how societies should be organized, how power should be exercised, and how public goods should be managed. This transformation requires a nuanced understanding of historical legacies, political ideologies, institutional dynamics, and social aspirations.

In Nepal and across the globe, the journey toward effective governance is far from complete. It demands sustained political will, robust institutions, active citizen engagement, and a commitment to inclusive development. Governance must be seen not only as a technical process but as a moral and democratic project, one that seeks to empower people, promote justice, and build resilient societies in an increasingly complex world. As global challenges such as climate change, pandemics, economic volatility, and geopolitical issues intensify, the need for adaptive, participatory, and inclusive governance becomes ever more critical. The future of governance will depend on our ability to build systems that are capable, ethical, and grounded in the collective aspirations of humanity.

The future of the democratic paradigm will likely be shaped by the synthesis of historical lessons regarding state power and the evolving challenges posed by globalization and the digital era. Key tensions between traditional state sovereignty and emerging global/digital paradigms are likely to center on the following themes: Contemporary democratization is the ongoing global process of establishing or deepening democratic governance, characterized by shifts like increased citizen participation, demands for accountability, challenges to traditional power structures, and new forms of political engagement (e.g., digital activism) alongside persistent issues like electoral fraud, inequality, and threats to civil liberties, requiring adaptive models beyond older Western norms, focusing on inclusion, transparency, and addressing economic disparities. Moving beyond purely territorial or statist models to include transnational governance, polycentric governance, and balancing state power with global influences.

Relying less on traditional revenue (like tariffs) and more on consumption taxes (VAT); evolving civic education for empowered citizens. Face issues like political violence, communal conflicts (as seen in India), electoral irregularities (fraud, stuffing), and the struggle to build strong civil societies. Continued focus on popular control, protecting rights, ensuring rule of law, and enabling broad citizen participation through fair, competitive elections. Involves adapting to new realities like globalized economies and digital communication, requiring intercultural recognition and effective public accountability mechanisms.

Sustained struggles by people for greater control over their governments. Modernization, but also rising inequality, which can spur democratic demands. Elites' decisions to concede power, sometimes driven by their confidence in winning elections under democracy (victory confidence). Influence from international institutions, security concerns, and historical shocks like conquests. Reimagining democracy to fit complex, interconnected modern life, emphasizing resource redistribution, inclusive political participation, and managing diverse identities. Moving towards universal suffrage and ensuring marginalized groups have equal opportunities for political voice. Demanding open governance and stronger institutions to prevent corruption and abuse of power.

Democratization is the process through which a political system, institution, or sector becomes more democratic. While most commonly applied to the transition of a country from authoritarian rule to a democratic regime, the term also describes the act of making resources, information, or technologies accessible and available to all. In political science, democratization refers to the structural transition from an authoritarian government to one characterized by popular sovereignty, individual rights, and the rule of law.

Granting all adult citizens the right to vote in free and fair elections. Guaranteeing fundamental rights such as freedom of speech, press, and assembly. Allowing multiple political parties to mobilize, campaign, and contest for power without discrimination. Ensuring that all citizens and government officials are equally subject to the law. The initial breakdown of an authoritarian regime and the establishment of new democratic structures and procedures. The process where democratic rules become so embedded in society that a return to authoritarianism is considered "unthinkable".

Outside of government, the term is increasingly used to describe the removal of barriers to access in various fields: The use of technology (like the internet and social media) to make knowledge and data accessible to the general public, bypassing traditional gatekeepers. Making complex tools—such as Artificial Intelligence or low-code application platforms—available to non-experts so they can create or utilize advanced systems. Increasing the accessibility and inclusivity of learning, often through online programs or open resources, to break down socio-economic and geographic barriers.

Scholars have proposed several reasons why nations democratize: Modernization Theory: Suggests that as countries become wealthier and more educated, citizens demand more political rights. Elite Theory: Proposes that powerful leaders may grant rights from the top down to maintain peace or because they believe it is beneficial. Social Movement Theory: Emphasizes bottom-up pressure from citizens who organize to demand freedom and justice. International Influence: Notes that foreign nations or organizations (like the EU) can promote or even impose democratic standards.

Feature	Democracy	Democratization
Nature	A stable state or system of government.	A transition or transformation process.
Status	A destination where power is based on the will of the people.	A movement away from authoritarianism.
Goal	To maintain liberty, equality, and rule of law.	To establish democratic institutions and norms.

Democratization is the structural transition from an authoritarian regime to a more democratic political system. It is rarely linear and involves distinct stages: The initial breakdown of the old regime and the establishment of new democratic procedures, such as free and fair elections. The point where democratic rules become deeply embedded in society, making a return to authoritarianism "unthinkable". "Minimalist" democratization focuses only on procedural aspects like voting, while "substantive" democratization seeks broader social and economic equality.

Democracy is a system where citizens hold ultimate authority, typically exercised through representative mechanisms. Key requirements for a functioning democracy include: The right for all eligible citizens to vote regardless of background. Protection of freedom of speech, assembly, and the press. A system where the government is constrained by a constitution and laws apply equally to everyone. The existence of multiple parties that can contest for power without fear of reprisal. As of late 2026, international reports highlight a shift away from democratization: Reports such as the Democracy Report 2026 by the V-Dem Institute indicate that liberal democracies are at their lowest levels in decades. The number of countries undergoing "autocratization" (the reverse of democratization) currently outnumbers those democratizing. Approximately 72% of the world's population now lives under autocratic rule. The 2026 Global State of Democracy Report notes significant declines in judicial independence and press freedom even in established Democratization and globalization are deeply interconnected processes that have mutually reinforced each other since the late 20th century. However, as of late 2026, their relationship is increasingly defined by tension, with the rapid pace of global economic integration sometimes conflicting with the needs of national democratic systems.

Historically, globalization and democratization were viewed as "two sides of the same coin," with each fueling the expansion of the other. Globalized communication technologies (e.g., the internet, social media) bypass state-controlled media, providing citizens with access to democratic ideas and empowering social movements to organize. Open economies often require transparency and the rule of law to attract foreign investment, which can undermine the opaque structures typically found in autocratic regimes. Membership in global organizations (like the EU or WTO) often demands adherence to certain democratic norms and human rights standards as a condition for trade or aid. Recent reports, including the Global State of Democracy 2026, highlight a "third wave of autocratization" where globalization no longer guarantees democratic growth. Globalization shifts decision-making power from elected national governments to unelected international markets and corporations, creating a "democratic deficit" where citizens feel their votes have less impact on economic policy. While globalization creates overall wealth, it often exacerbates income gaps. This economic frustration frequently leads to populist backlashes, where citizens support leaders who promise to prioritize national interests over global ties, sometimes at the expense of democratic norms. Authoritarian regimes have learned to use the same globalized technologies—once seen as tools for liberation—to conduct mass surveillance and spread misinformation, countering democratization efforts.

A prominent theoretical framework, often discussed in 2026, is the Rodrik Trilemma, which posits that a society cannot simultaneously have economic globalization, the nation-state, and democratic politics. If a country chooses deep globalization and the nation-state, it may have to sacrifice democratic responsiveness to follow global market rules (the "Golden Straitjacket"). If it chooses democracy and globalization, it may need to move toward a form of global governance, weakening the traditional nation-state. If it prioritizes democracy and the nation-state, it must limit its engagement withe global economy to protect domestic interests. For the first time in over 20 years, autocracies outnumber democracies globally. Approximately 72% of the world's population now lives under autocratic rule as Despite declines, some regions like Africa have shown recent advances in credible elections, indicating that the link between global information flow and local democratic demand remains active in some developing contexts.

Democracy, meaning "rule by the people," isn't simple, evolving from ancient Direct Democracy (Athens) to modern Representative/Liberal Democracy (elections, rights, rule of law). C Democracy, meaning "rule by the people," isn't simple, evolving from ancient Direct Democracy (Athens) to modern Representative/Liberal Democracy (elections, rights, rule of law). Contemporary theories like Participatory push deeper involvement, Feminist focus on gender equality, Associationism values group participation, Citizenship theories debate inclusion, and Cosmopolitanism considers global democracy, all challenging purely procedural views for more inclusive, substantive rule by the people. Citizens directly participate in decision-making, like town halls or referendums (Ancient Athens). Citizens elect officials (representatives) to make decisions for them (most modern nations).Combines representative democracy with core liberal values: individual rights (speech, assembly), constitutionalism, rule of law, and minority protections, ensuring power isn't absolute. Stresses deeper citizen involvement beyond voting, emphasizing active engagement in policy-making for better outcomes and empowerment. Critiques traditional democracy for excluding women and seeks to integrate feminist perspectives on equality, care, and power into democratic structures.: Focuses on the importance of voluntary groups and associations (unions, NGOs) in shaping public life and holding power accountable, acting as intermediaries. Explore who belongs (demos), the rights and duties of members, and the responsibilities of the state, moving beyond mere voters to active participants.: Extends democratic principles beyond the nation-state, advocating for global governance and human rights to address issues like climate change and inequality. This debate highlights the tension between mere fair elections (procedural) and ensuring actual participation, inclusion, and empowerment (substantive) for all citizens, which many contemporary theories support.

The tension between state information control and the internet's inherent openness is a defining feature of the digital age, manifesting in continuous conflicts over censorship, misinformation, and the free flow of information. States employ a variety of reactive and proactive strategies to manage online information flows and control the narrative: Internet Shutdowns and Blocking: Governments often use their control over telecommunications infrastructure to intentionally slow down, filter, or completely cut off internet access during times of political turmoil, protests, or elections.

Nations like China use sophisticated tools, including AI-based systems, for real-time content flagging and sentiment analysis to block access to specific websites, social media platforms (e.g., Facebook, Twitter, YouTube), and even search results that are deemed politically sensitive. States implement laws like the EU's Digital Services Act (DSA) or India's IT Rules to mandate content moderation and hold digital platforms accountable for "misinformation," which can also be leveraged for political control. Governments engage in their own online propaganda efforts, sometimes using automated accounts ("bots") to promote state-defined interests, influence public opinion, and drown out opposition voices. Activists, journalists, and everyday citizens face investigation or arrest for their online activities, creating a chilling effect that encourages self-censorship.

he Internet's Force for Openness

The decentralized nature of the internet continuously challenges state control: Users in restricted environments frequently employ censorship circumvention tools like Virtual Private Networks (VPNs) and proxy servers to access blocked content and communicate securely. The speed at which information and events (like protests) can be shared globally makes it difficult for a state to maintain a single, controlled narrative for long. Widespread internet shutdowns and censorship often attract international condemnation from human rights bodies, NGOs, and other nations, leading to potential diplomatic or economic consequences. Promotion of E-Democracy: The internet's open standards and universal access align with principles of transparency and individual liberty, offering platforms for citizen participation and government accountability.

The ongoing conflict manifests in several critical areas:

Sovereignty vs. Global Flow: States assert the right to sovereignty over their digital territories ("digital sovereignty") to enforce national laws and security concerns, which clashes with the transnational and borderless nature of the internet.

Security vs. Liberty: Governments often justify censorship measures under the guise of national security, public order, or fighting terrorism and "fake news," while digital rights advocates argue these reasons are often pretexts for suppressing dissent and basic human rights. As states develop more sophisticated censorship technologies (like deep packet inspection), technology experts and activists create new circumvention tools, in a continuous "cat-and-mouse" game for information control. The balance of power continues to shift as governments adapt their strategies, but the fundamental architecture of the internet as a "network of networks" remains resistant to total centralisation, ensuring the tension between information control and openness persists.

This scenario highlights the significant regulatory challenges posed by the borderless nature of digital phenomena. When digital platforms and cryptocurrencies operate globally, they create conflicts between the territorial basis of national laws and the functional reality of interconnected networks [1]. Jurisdictional Arbitrage: Entities can strategically base their operations in countries with more favorable (or lax) regulations to minimize compliance burdens and avoid stricter oversight in other nations where their users reside [1].A national regulator can issue a ruling, but enforcing that decision against a server or an individual operating in a different country is often difficult, time-consuming, and reliant on complex international treaties and cooperation [1].The result is a fragmented "patchwork" of laws. A single service might be legal in one country but considered illicit in another, creating confusion for both consumers and businesses and hindering seamless global operation [1]. Aggressive national regulations, while intending to protect consumers, can sometimes stifle innovation by forcing companies and talent to move to more permissive jurisdictions, pushing economic activity outside the regulating country's borders [1].

In response, international bodies like the Financial Action Task Force (FATF) work to establish global standards (e.g., anti-money laundering and counter-terrorist financing rules for virtual assets) that national governments are encouraged to implement through their domestic laws [1]. This push toward international consensus is one way to bridge the gap between national jurisdiction and global networks. This ongoing tension between privacy and security is one of the defining challenges of the digital age. It centers on a fundamental conflict between two core societal values: Emphasizes personal autonomy, the right to be free from unwarranted intrusion, and the ability to associate and communicate without constant surveillance [1]. In this view, strong privacy protections are essential for a healthy democracy, free speech, and personal liberty.

Requires governments to protect citizens from threats like terrorism, cyberattacks, and serious crime [1]. In this view, accessing digital communications and data is a necessary, and sometimes the only, way to prevent harm and ensure public safety.

Technologies enable comprehensive monitoring of digital communications (emails, messages, browsing history), creating unprecedented levels of state surveillance capabilities [1].Governments and private entities collect vast amounts of personal data, which can be vulnerable to misuse, breaches, or long-term retention beyond specific investigative needs [1].The widespread use of strong encryption protects individual privacy but also creates "warrant-proof spaces" that challenge law enforcement's ability to access evidence in criminal or terror investigations [1].Democracies continuously grapple with establishing legal frameworks that balance these competing interests, leading to complex debates over oversight, judicial review, and the appropriate limits of state power [1].

The rise of online communities and digital diasporas, facilitated by the internet, creates transnational spaces where people connect globally, potentially weakening singular national identities and traditional civic ties by fostering hybrid, fluid identities tied to homeland, host country, and online groups, challenging the state's monopoly on belonging and potentially diverting engagement from national to transnational/virtual spheres. This phenomenon redefines community beyond physical borders, complicating state cohesion by offering alternative allegiances and platforms for cultural maintenance and political influence, even while creating new forms of digital civic participation.

Key Impacts on State Identity & Cohesion:

Individuals develop "hybrid identities," blending their national origin with host culture and online community affiliations, moving beyond strict national belonging. Digital spaces allow for constant connection to homelands, creating strong transnational ties that compete with national allegiances, potentially reducing focus on local civic duty. Digital diasporas engage in "transnational citizenship," participating politically and culturally across borders, influencing homeland politics and economies online. As communities organize globally online, they can bypass or challenge state narratives, creating alternative sources of identity, support, and political mobilization, thereby complicating the state's role as the primary provider of belonging. Social media becomes new terrain for identity-making and political discourse, allowing for the articulation of plural identities and democratic claims that may not fit traditional state structures. Online transnational communities blur borders, creating a dynamic tension where national identity isn't lost but becomes one layer among many, challenging the traditional, geographically bound nation-state model

Multinational tech giants' vast economic power rivals' small nations, challenging state regulation through market dominance, global reach, and control over digital infrastructure, leading to concerns about antitrust, data privacy, political influence, and effective democratic oversight, with regulators (like the EU with the DMA) trying to curb monopolies and ensure fairness, while tech firms leverage their power to shape policies and bypass national controls.

Some tech firms have revenues or valuations exceeding GDPs of smaller countries, giving them immense financial leverage. Unchecked growth creates near-monopolies (e.g., search, advertising, social media), stifling competition and innovation. They control essential digital spaces (platforms, app stores) that host other businesses, influencing market access. Tech companies actively shape policies, leveraging economic might and data to impact governance and legal frameworks. Their transnational operations and vast data collection allow them to operate across borders, making national oversight difficult. Governments increasingly rely on their technology for public services, creating dependency. Using complex supply chains (e.g., routing through Vietnam) to avoid tariffs and national trade policies.: Influencing public opinion and political outcomes through content control and platform algorithms. Using private data for profit, challenging privacy rights and public values. Investigations into anti-competitive practices (e.g., Google). Laws like the EU's Digital Markets Act (DMA) aim to ensure fairness and contestability. Efforts to implement stronger data privacy and security laws (e.g., GDPR).: Traditional accountability mechanisms struggle with powerful, non-state actors that impact fundamental rights and economic fairness.

In essence, tech giants act as "digital sovereigns," creating new power centers that demand new governance models beyond traditional national regulatory tools to protect public interest and democratic values. The conclusion is that the democratic paradigm is not static; it is undergoing significant stress as it adapts to these new realities. The future of democracy will depend on finding new models that can navigate these complex tensions, likely involving new forms of international cooperation, revised social contracts, and innovative approaches to governance that balance the lessons of history with the imperatives of the digital age. Index funds are investment vehicles (mutual funds or ETFs) that passively track a market index (like the S&P 500) by holding all or a sample of its stocks/bonds, offering instant diversification and low costs due to minimal management, aiming to match market returns rather than beat them. They provide broad market exposure, reduce risk through diversification, and are favored for simplicity and low fees (expense ratios), making them great for long-term, low-maintenance investing.

They hold the same securities as a specific market benchmark (e.g., S&P 500, Sensex, Nifty) in similar proportions.

Passive Management: Fund managers don't pick stocks; they just follow the index's rules, reducing research and trading costs.

Diversification: Owning a piece of many companies (or bonds) within the index, spreading risk. Lower expense ratios (fees) compared to actively managed funds.: Easy to understand and manage, ideal for beginners. Spreads investment across numerous assets at once, reducing risk.

Designed to match Opening a brokerage account lets you invest in stocks, bonds, ETFs, etc., through platforms like online brokers (e.g., Fidelity, Interactive Brokers) or traditional firms, requiring ID (PAN/Aadhaar), bank details, and often linking a Demat account for holding securities, with major types being flexible Taxable Accounts (pay taxes on gains) and Retirement Accounts (tax-advantaged like Roth IRA for tax-free withdrawals in retirement). The process involves choosing a broker, completing an online form with personal info, verification, and funding the account via bank transfer, granting access to markets and tools. Flexible, no limits on deposits/withdrawals, but you pay taxes on profits annually or when selling. Offer significant tax benefits, with Roth IRAs providing tax-free withdrawals in retirement. : Research online brokers (e.g., Fidelity, Interactive Brokers) for fees, tools, and support. Complete an application with your name, address, PAN/Aadhaar, and bank details (for funding/withdrawal). Connect your Demat account (for holding investments electronically) if required by the broker. Transfer money from your bank via ACH or other methods. Once approved and funded, use the broker's platform to buy/sell investments. Access to diverse investments (stocks, bonds, mutual funds, ETFs). Tools for tracking, research, and portfolio management.

Flexibility to add or withdraw funds. Here are some specific, low-cost index fund and ETF tickers from major brokerages, along with key details to help you make a selection.

Total Stock Market (Covers entire U.S. stock market)

Fund Name	Ticker	Fund Type	Expense Ratio	Minimum Investment
Vanguard Total Stock Market ETF	VTI	ETF	0.03%	Price of one share

Vanguard Total Stock Mkt Idx Adm	VTSAX	Mutual Fund	0.04%	$3,000
Fidelity ZERO Total Market Index	FZROX	Mutual Fund	0.00%	None
Schwab Total Stock Market Index	SWTSX	Mutual Fund	0.03%	None

S&P 500 (Tracks 500 largest U.S. companies)

Fund Name	**Ticker**	**Fund Type**	**Expense Ratio**	**Minimum Investment**
Vanguard S&P 500 ETF	VOO	ETF	0.03%	Price of one share
Vanguard 500 Index Fund Admiral	VFIAX	Mutual Fund	0.04%	$3,000
Fidelity 500 Index Fund	FXAIX	Mutual Fund	0.015%	None
Fidelity ZERO Large Cap Index	FNILX	Mutual Fund	0.00%	None
Schwab S&P 500 Index Fund	SWPPX	Mutual Fund	0.02%	None

International Stock Market (Provides exposure to global markets ex-US)

Fund Name	Ticker	Fund Type	Expense Ratio	Minimum Investment
Vanguard Total Intl Stock ETF	VXUS	ETF	0.05%	Price of one share
Vanguard Total Intl Stock Idx Adm	VTIAX	Mutual Fund	0.09%	$2,500
Fidelity Total International Index	FTIHX	Mutual Fund	0.06%	None
Fidelity ZERO International Index	FZILX	Mutual Fund	0.00%	None
Schwab International Index Fund	SWISX	Mutual Fund	0.06%	None
Schwab International Equity ETF	SCHF	ETF	0.06%	Price of one share

Expense Ratio: As noted, aim for funds with very low expense ratios, ideally below 0.10% annually. The funds listed above meet this criteria, with some Fidelity ZERO funds having literally 0.00% fees. Often require an initial minimum investment (e.g., $3,000 for Vanguard Admiral shares) but allow for automatic, fractional-dollar investing, which is great for dollar-cost averaging. You typically buy them directly from the fund provider (Fidelity, Schwab, Vanguard).

Trade on a stock exchange like a stock throughout the day, so you can buy them with no minimum beyond the share price. They are portable across most brokerage platforms. Most brokers now offer fractional shares of ETFs and automatic investing plans for convenience as well.

Both mutual funds and ETFs tracking the same index (e.g., VTSAX and VTI) have nearly identical performance before expenses, so the choice often comes down to account features and personal preference.

o help you in placing a buy order, you can review the recent performance of some of the representative index funds mentioned earlier.

The process for placing a buy order is straightforward, typically involving five key steps within your brokerage platform's "Trade" section. You will need to input the ticker symbol of the fund you selected into the trading interface. For example, you might enter VTI for a total U.S. stock market ETF, VOO for an S&P 500 ETF, or VXUS for an international stock ETF. Choose the action you wish to perform, which in this case would be "Buy". You will select an order type for your trade: A "Market Order" executes the trade immediately at the best available current market price. This is generally sufficient and recommended for beginners purchasing highly liquid, broad-market index funds and ETFs.

A "Limit Order" allows you to set a specific maximum price you are willing to pay per share. Your order will only be filled if the fund's price reaches or falls below your specified limit price. Specify the quantity of your investment:

For ETFs, you typically enter the number of shares you want to buy.

For mutual funds, you often enter the dollar amount you wish to invest. Before the order is processed, a confirmation screen will appear. Double-check all the details, including the ticker symbol, action (buy), order type, and amount, and then confirm the trade to submit your order.

To successfully maintain your index fund investments, adopting a long-term, low-touch strategy is key. The primary approach with index funds is usually "buy and hold", which means resisting the urge to constantly trade based on market fluctuations. The most effective way to maintain discipline is to automate your investment process. Most brokerages allow you to set up recurring, automatic monthly or bi-weekly transfers from your bank account directly into your chosen index fund. By investing a fixed amount of money at regular intervals, you practice dollar-cost averaging. This strategy helps you automatically buy more shares when prices are low and fewer shares when prices are high, which can reduce the average cost per share over time and prevent emotional decision-making. While a "buy and hold" strategy is passive, some periodic maintenance is necessary to ensure your portfolio remains aligned with your long-term financial goals and risk tolerance. Review your portfolio once or twice a year is generally sufficient. There is no need for frequent checking. Over time, market movements can cause your original asset allocation to shift. For example, a strong stock market run might make your stock portion grow from your desired 80% to an unintended 90%, changing your risk profile. Rebalancing involves selling some of the assets that have grown (e.g., stocks) and using the proceeds to buy more of the assets that have shrunk (e.g., bonds) to restore your original, target allocation (e.g., 80% stocks, 20% bonds). This helps you manage risk and maintain a disciplined investment approach.

Social movements in history have played a crucial role in bringing major social, political, and economic changes across societies. These movements emerged when large groups of people collectively opposed injustice, inequality, or exploitation. Historical social movements were often long-term struggles that challenged existing power structures and helped shape modern democratic values.

Social Movement	Time Period	Region	Main Objective	Outcome
Abolitionist Movement	18th–19th Century	Europe & USA	End slavery	Abolition of slave trade and

				slavery
Labour Movement	19th Century	Europe & USA	Workers' rights and fair wages	Trade unions and labour laws
Women's Suffrage Movement	19th–20th Century	UK, USA	Voting rights for women	Women granted voting rights
Civil Rights Movement	1950s–1960s	USA	Racial equality	End of legal racial segregation
Nationalist Movements	19th–20th Century	Asia & Africa	Political independence	End of colonial rule
Peasant Movements	18th–20th Century	Europe & Asia	Land rights and fair taxation	Agrarian reforms

1 Defining Features of Totalitarianism

As suggested by the root of the word, totalitarianism refers to a system in which control of the population is greater—closer to 'total'—than in any other type of system. It is the most extreme version of the subordination of the individual to the state and to a questionable notion of the collective. Totalitarian and authoritarian dictatorships have much in common, including a lack of respect for citizens' rights, for the public accountability of political elites, and for the rule of law. But a totalitarian dictatorship is distinguishable from an authoritarian one in several ways (see Linz 1975).

First, ideology plays a far more significant role in the former than in the latter, even though many observers agree that ideology was less important in Fascist Italy and Nazi Germany than in Stalin's USSR and other communist states. While totalitarian ideology often makes use of the past, particularly national traditions, it is basically radical and future-oriented ('chiliastic' or 'teleological'), whereas authoritarian regimes typically focus more on the past and continuity. It is also often overtly exclusionary, and arbitrarily identifies particular minority groups as 'enemies' of the state and/or the people (e.g., Jews and gays in Nazi Germany, or 'the bourgeoisie' or kulaks [rich peasants] in Stalin's USSR), for whom life could become literally unbearable.

Another difference is that, in theory at least, the single political party plays a more prominent role in a totalitarian regime than in an authoritarian one. Third, authoritarianism relates primarily to a political system, and there is no necessary implication that the state is involved heavily in the economy. In contrast, most theorists of totalitarianism maintain that, while communist states generally controlled the economy much more than did fascist states, the overall level of state interference was much higher in totalitarian states than in authoritarian. Finally but importantly, totalitarianism was seen as a peculiarly twentieth-century phenomenon. This was largely because it was not until then that the technological means for controlling and transporting populations existed. With the rapid development of the means of mass communication, notably the radio and cinema, citizens could be subject to a constant barrage of state propaganda in a manner that was not possible in earlier kinds of dictatorship. This, together with the much greater emphasis placed by totalitarian regimes on state-run education for all, meant that the state's capacity for indoctrination ('thought control') reached qualitatively new levels.

Although there have been several comparative analyses of totalitarianism, the most widely cited are those of Friedrich and Brzezinski (1956, 1965). In the earlier study, these authors identified what they considered to be the six salient features of totalitarian regimes. These were an official, all-embracing, and chiliastic ideology; a single mass party, typically led by one man (the dictator); a system of terroristic police control (high levels of apparently arbitrary coercion); a near-complete monopoly of the means of communication; a near-complete monopoly of the means of armed combat; and central control of the entire economy. In the second edition of their book, this list was supplemented to include a commitment to expansionism and the administrative control of justice. One other distinguishing feature, emphasized particularly by Arendt (1951), is a high level of citizen alienation.

Timeline

This shows milestones of voting laws in U.S. history. This timeline also offers information about the U.S. government denying and granting citizenship to groups of U.S. residents. Citizenship is a requirement of voting in the United States.1789: The U.S. constitution did not establish any specific voting rights, instead states were given the power to regulate voting laws. As a result, most states limited voting to white male landowners.

Representatives were elected by the people, Senators were selected by state legislatures, and the President was elected by state legislature appointed electors.

1790: 1790 Naturalization Law established that only "free white" immigrants can become citizens of the United States.

1848: The Treaty of Guadalupe Hidalgo grants citizenship to Mexicans living in U.S. territories but does not grant voting rights.

1856: All white men can vote—the requirement for property ownership was eliminated. This was a state-by-state change. North Carolina was the last state to remove this requirement in 1856.

1866: Civil Rights Act of 1866 granted citizenship to all persons born in the United States, regardless of color or previous enslavement. This act allowed all citizens of the U.S. equal protection under the law. This act excluded the rights of citizenship to indigenous people who did not pay taxes.

1868: The 14th Amendment extends citizenship to "all persons born or naturalized in the United States." The 14th Amendment enshrined the Civil Rights Act of 1866 as part of the Constitution, protecting it from being overturned by the Supreme Court. The 14th Amendment secured citizenship for freed slaves and black folks but did not include rights of political participation, including voting.

1870: The 15th Amendment granted black men the right to vote -- "The right of citizens of the United States to vote shall not be denied or abridged by the United States of any State on account of race, color, or previous condition of servitude." Some Suffragists opposed the 15th Amendment because it did not extend voting rights to women.

1876: The Supreme Court ruled Native Americans are not citizens as defined by the 14th Amendment, even those that are "tax paying." The decision was offered in Elk v. Wilkins.

1882: Chinese Exclusion Act denies people of Chinese ancestry from naturalizing as American citizens.

1887: The Dawes Act grants citizenship to Native Americans who disassociate from their Nations.

1890: Indian Naturalization Act required some indigenous peoples to apply for U.S. citizenship. In spite of being granted citizenship, indigenous peoples were still denied the right to vote until 1924.

1890: Wyoming becomes a state and the first allowing women the right to vote. Wyoming originally granted women the right to vote in 1873, when it was still a territory. Women's right to vote was not extended to federal elections, only state and local elections. Between 1890 and 1920, several other states extended suffrage to women.

1913: The 17th Amendment gives the power of selecting Senators to the (male) people. Prior to the 17th Amendment Senators were selected by state legislatures.

1920: The 19th Amendment gives women the right to vote.

1922: Supreme Court rules that people of Japanese heritage are ineligible to become naturalized citizens. The same is ruled for Asian Indians in 1923.

1924: The Indian Citizenship Act, also known as the Snyder Act, grants indigenous peoples citizenship regardless of nation affiliation. Previously, indigenous peoples were expect to renounce their tribal affiliations to gain U.S. citizenship.

1943: The Magnuson Act repeals the Chinese Exclusion Act, giving Chinese immigrants citizenship and the right to vote.

1952: The Immigration and Nationality Act of 1952, or the McCarran-Walter Act, granted all Asian-Americans the right to citizenship and to vote. This act also granted citizenship to residents of U.S. territories though not the right to vote in federal elections.

1961: The 23rd Amendment gives residents of the District of Columbia the right to vote for president, but not Congressional representation.

1965: Voting Rights Act is passed.

1971: The 26th Amendment made the minimum voting age 18, previously the minimum voting age was 21.

1986: The Uniformed and Overseas Citizens Absentee Voting Act granted U.S. Military, Uniformed Services, Merchant Marines, and other U.S. citizens living abroad right to vote.

1993: National Voter Registration Act passes, making registering to vote at DMVs and other public assistance centers easier.

2002: The Help America Vote Act requires voter ID for all new voters in federal elections who registered by mail and who did not provide a driver's license number or the last four digits of a Social Security number that was matched against government records. Many states have voter ID requirements. The National Council of State Legislatures (NCSL) provides state by state voter ID laws and requirements.

2013: The Supreme Court overturns Section 4(b) of the Voting Rights Act, no longer requiring states and local governments to notify the Attorney General of changes to local voting laws.

Appendix

Are we facing a paradigm shift?

Democracy research must evolve. Citizens support democracy itself but are growing disillusioned with democratic institutions. Norma Osterberg-Kaufmann and Christoph Mohamad-Klotzbach say we need to rethink our frameworks. Here, they argue for broadening the empirical paradigm – shifting focus from procedural checklists to people's own understandings of democracy – to better grasp today's crisis Contemporary democracy research faces a pressing challenge: how should it respond to the growing gap between citizens' widespread support for the idea of democracy and their deepening dissatisfaction with its practice? Around the world, citizens profess allegiance to democracy, yet trust in democratic institutions is eroding. Elections happen, parties compete, parliaments legislate.

Still, people feel unheard, unseen, unrepresented. This discontent raises a central question: what concept of democracy underlies both our evaluations and measurements of democracy? Is the crisis merely institutional or also mental, cultural, and emotional?

We argue that the crisis of democracy reflects more than failing institutions. It reflects a mismatch between how democracy is currently structured and how people understand and experience it. To confront this, we need to revisit the assumptions driving democracy research itself.

Thomas Kuhn famously defined paradigms as shared frameworks of theories, values, and methods that guide normal science. Paradigm shifts occur when anomalies accumulate – when the dominant framework can no longer explain the world it is meant to describe.

In democracy research, a similar situation is emerging. Much of the field still operates within a narrow liberal-procedural paradigm. Elections, formal institutions, and state structures dominate empirical studies of democracy but they still fail in their task. Why? Elections, formal institutions, and state structures dominate empirical studies of democracy but they still fail in their task. Why?

A narrow empirical lens

Empirical democracy research tends to treat democracy as a fixed institutional structure. Most democracy indices, such as Freedom House, Polity, or V-Dem derive their indicators from liberal Western political theory. They focus heavily on the supply side: elections mainly, additional rule of law, institutional checks and balances. These are seen as universal benchmarks.

Yet this deductive approach often assumes a global consensus around one model of democracy, which Robert Dahl termed 'polyarchy'. Polyarchy sidelines alternative understandings of democracy, and limits engagement with how democracy is perceived and practiced by different populations.

The neglected demand side

While supply-side measures dominate, the demand side – how people understand and evaluate democracy – remains under-researched. Major surveys like the World Values Survey or regional barometers include questions on democratic attitudes, but they often embed polyarchic assumptions. They test support for democracy/polyarchy as defined in the West, rather than exploring how democracy is imagined elsewhere.

To understand the democratic crisis, we must understand how people define democracy. Citizens may reject current democratic institutions not because they oppose democracy, but because these institutions fail to reflect their democratic expectations.

Opening, not overturning, the paradigm

Rather than advocating for a complete paradigm shift, we propose opening the current paradigm to a wider array of perspectives. This means moving beyond a one-size-fits-all model and embracing democracy as a contested concept.

Instead of measuring democracy solely through institutional design, we should examine the principles democracy is meant to serve

Instead of measuring democracy solely through institutional design, we should examine the principles democracy is meant to serve. What is the core purpose of democracy – globally, and across cultures? And how can different institutional forms realise this purpose?

This approach allows us to connect empirical democracy research more directly with comparative democratic theory. It broadens the lens beyond polyarchy to include traditions like republicanism, communitarianism, or indigenous governance models. It also invites us to look beyond the country-state: to local assemblies, citizen juries, expert councils, or other non-state democratic practices.

Rethinking comparative research

Opening the paradigm has major implications for comparative research. It shifts the focus from asking, 'Does this country have free and fair elections?' to asking, 'How do people here understand democracy? What principles matter to them? And do their institutions reflect these principles?'

This dual perspective – bottom-up and top-down – can help generate a more global and pluralistic concept of democracy. We propose a cyclical framework. By starting from individual-level data (citizens' understandings of democracy), we can inductively build a concept of democracy. We can then compare the result with theoretical traditions and re-test it through deductive surveys. The cycle ensures that both normative ideals and empirical realities inform our understanding.

Principles over procedures

Such an approach enables us to assess not only the presence of democratic institutions but their quality and legitimacy on the ground, for the people they concern. Do current institutions fulfil the core democratic principles people care about? If not, reform may be needed – not to abandon democracy, but to bring it closer to what people expect from it.

This shift also affects how we distinguish democracy from autocracy. Rather than ticking off institutional checklists, we can ask whether the core principles of democracy are being fulfilled, however they are institutionalised. This helps us, for example, to better understand why democratic backsliding can occur in democratic regimes and why it is accepted by parts of the electorate who vote for populist-authoritarian leaders or parties.

From Western universalism to global dialogue

Opening the paradigm has broader socio-political implications. If comparative democracy research moves beyond Western-centric models, it can foster an inclusive, global dialogue about democracy's future. Ideas developed in non-Western contexts could revitalise democracy in the West itself.

If comparative democracy research moves beyond Western-centric models, it can foster an inclusive, global dialogue about democracy's future

Of course, this is not without risks. The erosion of polyarchy may raise concerns about democratic backsliding. But ignoring alternative visions only deepens the disconnect between theory and lived experience. What's needed is critical reflection, not defensiveness.

Shift happens

The democratic crisis is not only political, but also conceptual. To understand and address it, democracy research must evolve. We do not call for a revolution in Kuhn's sense, but for a deliberate and thoughtful opening of the empirical paradigm.

By shifting focus from institutional forms to democratic principles, we can reconnect democracy research with the people it ultimately serves. This makes comparative democracy research more relevant, more responsive – and more democratic.

Bibliography

Bermeo, N. (2016).

On Democratic Backsliding

Journal of Democracy. A foundational study on the shift from overt military coups to subtle erosions of democratic norms.

Coppedge, M., et al. (2026).

V-Dem Annual Democracy Report 2026: Democracy Facing New Realities

. V-Dem Institute. This 2026 report tracks the most recent global shifts in democratic vs. autocratic status.

Fukuyama, F. (1989/2026 update).

The End of History?

(Revised Perspectives). Recent scholarship critiques the original "end of history" paradigm in light of rising illiberalism.

Huntington, S. P. (1991).

The Third Wave: Democratization in the Late Twentieth Century

. University of Oklahoma Press. The essential text for understanding the massive global shift toward democracy following the Cold War.

Contemporary & 2026 Research

Fitislis, F. (2023).

Artificial Intelligence (AI) in Parliaments: A Paradigm Shift for Legislatures

. Journal of Legislative Studies. Analyzes how digital technology and AI are fundamentally altering the deliberative process in modern democracies.

Lührmann, A., & Lindberg, S. I. (2026).

Global Challenges to Democracy: Backsliding, Resiliency, and Democratic Theory

. Cambridge University Press. A 2026 publication examining the current defense of democratic regimes against novel authoritarian challenges.

Marchetti, R. (2026).

Postnational Democracy: A Cultural Paradigm Shift in Global Governance

. University of Bologna Research. Explores the shift from state-centric models to "global citizen" models in response to climate change and migration.

ResearchGate (2026).

The Paradigm Shift in the Concept of Good Governance in India

. This recent study details the shift from simple electoral participation to a "welfare state" model focused on service delivery and digital transparency.

Specialized Bibliographies & Databases

Cambridge University Press - Information, Power, and Democracy

: A comprehensive list of references regarding the internet's impact on democratic citizenship.

PhilPapers - Democracy & Government Bibliography

: An extensive, categorized archive of over 7,000 philosophy-focused papers on democratic authority and social choice.

V-Dem (Varieties of Democracy) Dataset: The primary data source used by researchers in 2026 to measure shifts between "electoral democracy" and "liberal democracy".

This bibliography covers the foundational era of democratic thought, tracking the shift from ancient direct participation to the early modern development of the nation-state.

Chapter 1: The Athenian Ideal: Direct Participation and its Limits

Focus: The "Assembly" paradigm and the tensions of an exclusionary demos.

Aristotle. *Politics*. (C. Lord, Trans.). University of Chicago Press. (Essential for understanding the ancient classification of regimes and the definition of a "citizen").

Hansen, M. H. (1991). *The Athenian Democracy in the Age of*

Demosthenes: Structure, Principles, and Ideology. University of Oklahoma Press. (The definitive modern text on the mechanics of the *Ecclesia* and *Boulē*).

Manin, B. (1997). *The Principles of Representative Government*. Cambridge University Press. (Specifically the first chapter, which contrasts the Athenian use of "lot" or "sortition" with the modern paradigm of election).

Ober, J. (2008). *Democracy and Knowledge: Innovation and Learning in Classical Athens*. Princeton University Press. (Explores how the direct participation paradigm utilized collective intelligence).

Pomeroy, S. B. (1995). *Goddesses, Whores, Wives, and Slaves: Women in Classical Antiquity*. Schocken. (Crucial for analyzing the exclusionary limits of the Athenian paradigm regarding gender and labor).

Chapter 2: The Republican Turn: From Polis to Res publica

Focus: The transition to institutional checks, balances, and early representation.

Cicero, M. T. *On the Commonwealth (De Re Publica)*. (J. E. G. Zetzel, Ed.). Cambridge University Press. (The foundational text for the Roman concept of "mixed government").

Black, A. (1992). *Political Thought in Europe, 1250–1450*. Cambridge University Press. (Covers medieval councils and the emergence of "consent" in ecclesiastical and civil governance).

Pocock, J. G. A. (1975). *The Machiavellian Moment: Florentine Political Thought and the Atlantic Republican Tradition*. Princeton University Press. (Traces the shift from Roman civic virtue to early modern republicanism).

Polybius. *The Histories: Book VI*. (Explains the Roman constitution as a paradigm shift from simple democracy to a balance of the "One, the Few, and the Many").

Tierney, B. (1982). *Religion, Law, and the Growth of Constitutional Thought, 1150–1650*. Cambridge University Press. (Links medieval law to the eventual development of constitutionalism).

Chapter 3: The Birth of the Modern Nation-State

Focus: Sovereignty, the Westphalian system, and the centralized power of the state.

Bodin, J. (1576). *On Sovereignty*. (J. H. Franklin, Trans.). Cambridge University Press. (The primary text establishing the modern concept of the absolute, indivisible state power).

Croxton, D. (2013). *Westphalia: The Last Christian Peace*. Palgrave Macmillan. (A detailed analysis of the 1648 treaties that created the paradigm of territorial sovereignty).

Hobbes, T. (1651). *Leviathan*. (R. Tuck, Ed.). Cambridge University Press. (The foundational justification for the state as a necessary "artificial man" to prevent chaos).

Krasner, S. D. (1999). *Sovereignty: Organized Hypocrisy*. Princeton University Press. (Critically examines the paradigm shift of Westphalian sovereignty and its practical limits).

Skinner, Q. (1978). *The Foundations of Modern Political Thought: Volume 2: The Age of Reformation*. Cambridge University Press. (An essential survey of how the concept of "the state" emerged from religious conflict and absolutism).

Online Research Resources

The Avalon Project (Yale Law School): Digital archive of primary documents including the Peace of Westphalia and early English constitutional documents.

Stanford Encyclopedia of Philosophy - Ancient Political Philosophy: Authoritative peer-reviewed summaries of Athenian and Roman political theory.

Online Library of Liberty: A vast collection of downloadable classic texts on republicanism and the birth of the nation-state.

Chapter 4: The Liberal Democratic Paradigm Shift

Focus: The American and French Revolutions as ruptures creating the modern liberal state.

Gottschalk, L. (2026).

Toward the French Revolution: Europe and America in the Eighteenth-Century World

. Irvington Publishers. (Explores the intertwined destinies and global ripples of both revolutions).

Hazen, C. D., & Fiske, J. (2026).

The Age of Revolution: History of the American & French Revolution (Vol. 1&2)

. (A comprehensive anthology analyzing the cultural and ideological ethos that heralded monumental societal changes).

Montesquieu, C. (1748/1785).

The Spirit of Laws (Esprit des Lois)

. (The foundational text for the separation of powers, arguing that liberty requires the distinct distribution of legislative, executive, and judicial authority).

Paine, T. (1791).

Rights of Man

. (A primary text defending the French Revolution and the shift toward individual rights as the basis of government).

The Tobin Project (2024).

When Democracy Breaks

. (A recent scholarly analysis of how liberal institutions are formed and the vulnerabilities inherent in their early design).

Chapter 5: Expanding the Electorate: The Suffrage Revolutions

Focus: The chronological expansion of the "demos" and the removal of property and gender barriers.

Keyssar, A. (2000/2009).

The Right to Vote: The Contested History of Democracy in the United

States

. Basic Books. (A definitive history showing that suffrage was a struggle of marginalized groups and often expanded through the catalyst of war).

Stanton, E. C., Anthony, S. B., et al. (1881–1922).

History of Woman Suffrage (6 Volumes)

. (The primary source for documentation of the women's suffrage movement through the ratification of the 19th Amendment).

Tetrault, L. (2014).

The Myth of Seneca Falls: Memory and the Women's Suffrage Movement, 1848–1898

. University of North Carolina Press. (Critically re-examines the origins of the women's rights movement and how it constructed its own historical narrative).

Weiss, E. (2018).

The Woman's Hour: The Great Fight to Win the Vote

. Viking. (A narrative account of the 1920 ratification and the political maneuvers required to expand the electorate).

White, D. G. (1999).

Too Heavy a Load: Black Women in Defense of Self, 1894–1994

. W.W. Norton. (Essential for understanding the intersectional struggle for suffrage among African American women).

Chapter 6: The Challenge of Totalitarianism and the Cold War Order

Focus: Democracy's survival against fascism/communism and the post-WWII entrenchment of global liberal norms.

Cambridge University Press (2024).

Cold Wars: The United States and the Free World

. (Details how the "Free World" paradigm emerged from the struggle against totalitarian enemies).

Ikenberry, G. J. (2018/2026 update).

The End of Liberal International Order?

(Analyzes how liberal internationalism became the platform for the global order after 1945 and its current erosion).

Joseph, J. (1997/2026 review). *Globalization and the Changing Liberal International Order*. (Reviews the rationalization of liberalism as a dominant global ideology post-1989).

Lührmann, A. (2023/2026).

Democracy and the Liberal World Order Amid the Rise of Authoritarianism

. Belfer Center. (Examines the "new Cold War" between democracy and autocracy in the 21st century).

Mignet, M. (2026 reprint).

History of the French Revolution from 1789 to 1814

. Double9 Books. (A seminal work documenting the collapse of the Ancien Régime and its impact on the broader European stage).

Digital & Archival Resources

U.S. State Department - Cold War Diplomacy: Resource for the use of diplomacy to promote democracy against communist influence.

National Archives - Women's Rights Documents: Primary digital records for the U.S. Suffrage Movement.

Project Gutenberg - History of Woman Suffrage: Full-text digital access to the Stanton/Anthony volumes.

Chapter 7: The Third Wave and Democratic Consolidation

Focus: Post-Cold War democratization and critiques of the "End of History."

Diamond, L. (1997/2026).

Consolidating the Third Wave Democracies

. Journal of Democracy Book. A seminal work on how newly democratic states attempted to stabilize institutions in the late 20th century.

Fukuyama, F. (1992/2026). *The End of History and the Last Man*. Recent 2024–2026 scholarship re-evaluates his thesis, noting that the "end" was a developmental goal rather than an achieved finality.

Mainwaring, S., & Bizzarro, F. (2019/2026). *The Fates of Third-Wave Democracies*. ResearchGate. Analyzes the high collapse rate of regimes that emerged between 1974 and 2012, highlighting the fragility of the electoral model.

Nur, S. (2026). *Third Wave Democratization in Post-Cold War Africa: The Rise of Illiberal Democracy*. ResearchGate. Examines how early 1990s optimism in sub-Saharan Africa shifted toward "liberalized authoritarianism".

Chapter 8: The Digital Rupture: E-Governance and Disinformation

Focus: Technology as both a tool for participation and a threat to the public sphere.

Begoian, H. (2026).

Cyber Citizens: Saving Democracy with Digital Literacy

. Narrates how internet-connectedness and AI-driven misinformation erode human decision-making and civic trust.

Kumar, B. (2026).

Digital Democracy: Navigating India's Future

. National Book Trust. Explores how digital infrastructure like UPI and blockchain can empower citizens while raising privacy and security dilemmas.

Lasquite, J. L., et al. (2026).

Transforming Governance in the Digital Age: A Narrative Review of E-Democracy

. SSRN. Analyzes the vision and challenges of the e-democracy paradigm, using Estonia as a primary model.

Newell, B. C. (2024/2026).

The 2024 Disinformation Election: And What You Can Do to Keep Democracy Intact

. Focuses on how algorithms and deepfakes polarized electorates and how digital literacy acts as a democratic safeguard.

Chapter 9: The Populist Backlash and Democratic Backsliding

Focus: Illiberal democracy and the erosion of institutional compromise.

Erne, R. (2024/2026).

Politicising Commodification

. Cambridge University Press. Examines how vertical EU integration and economic governance have sparked social-movement protests and challenges to democratic direction.

Haidt, J. (2012/2026).

The Righteous Mind: Why Good People Are Divided by Politics and Religion

. A foundational text for understanding the moral psychology behind modern political polarization and the decline of compromise.

Sfetcu, N. (2024/2026). *The Role of Social Media in Democracy, New Public Management and e-Governance*. ResearchGate. Discusses how social media platforms have become "third actors" in the democratic arena, often hollowing out traditional accountability.

Chapter 10: Post-National and Transnational Governance

Focus: Decentralized systems and governance beyond the nation-state.

Alexander, J., & Conrad, A. (2026).

Citizens: Why the Key to Fixing Everything is All of Us

. Argues for a shift from a "Consumer Story" to a "Citizen Story" where institutions empower global residents to solve transnational crises.

Landemore, H. (2026). *Open Democracy*. Reinventing the democratic paradigm by placing ordinary people at the heart of power through randomly selected assemblies, mirroring ancient ideals in a modern, open format.

Weiss, M. (2026).

We the Possibility: Harnessing Public Entrepreneurship

. Focuses on "Possibility Government," where decentralized and imaginative leadership solves urgent global problems that traditional bureaucracy cannot.

Conclusion: The Future of the Democratic Paradigm

V-Dem (Varieties of Democracy) Institute: Use the V-Dem Online Analysis Tools to synthesize historical trends and track the latest 2026 shifts in global democratic resiliency.

Journal of Democracy: Features ongoing 2026 debates on "The End of the End of History" and the future of liberal internationalism.

This index provides a conceptual map of the key terms, figures, and events detailed across the three parts of your study on democratic paradigm shifts, updated with 2026 terminology.

Index

Search Resources for Research:

For primary document verification, visit the Avalon Project at Yale Law School.

To track 2026 backsliding data, access the V-Dem Institute Analysis Tools.

For 2026 updates on digital governance, consult the Journal of Democracy Digital Archive.

Glossary

A glossary of paradigm shifts in democracy highlights the fundamental changes in how political systems, public administration, and societal engagement are conceptualized and practiced. In 2026, these shifts are increasingly defined by a transition away from traditional, state-centric models toward participatory, digital, and network-based systems.

From Government to Governance: A move away from rigid, top-down "command and control" structures toward flexible systems involving non-state actors like civil society and the private sector.

Good Governance: A normative ideal popularized by international institutions (e.g., World Bank) that prioritizes transparency, accountability, and the rule of law over simple administrative effectiveness.

Illiberal Democracy: A shift toward regimes that maintain formal democratic processes (like elections) while actively undermining civil liberties and the independence of democratic institutions like the judiciary.

Deliberative & Participatory Democracy: The transition from purely representative voting systems toward models that emphasize direct public involvement in decision-making and continuous deliberation.

E-Governance & Digital Democracy: The integration of technology to streamline service delivery, increase transparency, and enable new forms of citizen engagement through digital platforms.

Multilateralism to Economic Nationalism: A paradigm shift in global democracy research noting a move from rule-based international cooperation toward protectionist, national-security-centric policies.

Democratic Backsliding: A conceptual shift in political science focusing on the gradual erosion of democratic norms and institutions in established democracies.

Active Citizenship: A redefinition of the role of the individual from a passive voter to an active participant in governance, often facilitated by civic education and local self-governance.

Subsidiarity: The principle that political issues should be handled at the most local or immediate level possible, shifting power from central authorities to local communities.

Varieties of Democracy (V-Dem): A methodological shift in measuring democracy, categorizing regimes into specific types like "electoral autocracy" or "liberal democracy" based on a multidimensional data cube rather than a binary (democracy vs. autocracy).

Part I: Foundations and First Principles (Antiquity to 18th Century)

Chapter 1: The Athenian Ideal

Dēmos: The "common people" as a collective political actor; the root of "rule by the people".

Direct Participation: A model where eligible citizens (adult males) directly debated and voted on laws rather than electing representatives.

Ecclesia (Assembly): The primary governing body open to all citizens, typically requiring a quorum of 6,000 for major decisions.

Sortition: The practice of selecting public officials by lot (randomly) to ensure equality and prevent power concentration.

Exclusionary Citizenship: The "paradigm" limit where political rights were restricted to adult male citizens, excluding women, slaves, and resident foreigners (metics).

Chapter 2: The Republican Turn

Res publica: Literally "the public thing"; the Roman concept of a state belonging to the people, governed by law rather than a monarch.

Representation (Roman): A system where power was shared among elected magistrates, the Senate (aristocracy), and citizen assemblies.

Checks and Balances: The Roman constitutional principle of dividing power among different bodies to prevent any one from becoming tyrannical.

Constitutionalism: The early development of legal frameworks (e.g., the Twelve Tables) that apply equally to different social classes.

Chapter 3: The Modern Nation-State

Westphalian Sovereignty: Established in 1648, the principle that states have exclusive authority over their territory and domestic affairs without external interference.

State Sovereignty: The shift from feudal allegiances to the nation-state as the primary, legally equal actor in global politics.

Absolutism: A system where a monarch holds supreme, centralized authority, often serving as the catalyst for liberal democratic reactions.

Part II: The Great Democratic Waves (18th Century to Mid-20th Century)

Chapter 4: The Liberal Democratic Paradigm Shift

Liberty, Equality, Fraternity: The core trio of democratic values popularized by the French Revolution.

Separation of Powers: A key liberal component ensuring the legislative, executive, and judicial branches remain independent.

Rule of Law: The principle that all individuals and government entities are accountable to laws that are publicly promulgated and independently adjudicated.

Chapter 5: Expanding the Electorate

Suffrage Revolutions: The historical movement to expand the "demos" by abolishing property, racial, and gender qualifications for voting.

Universal Franchise: The right for all adult citizens to vote, a hallmark of 20th-century democratic consolidation.

Chapter 6: Totalitarianism vs. the Cold War Order

Totalitarianism: Regimes (fascist or communist) that seek total control over public and private life, directly opposing liberal democratic pluralism.

Liberal International Order: The post-WWII entrenchment of global rules, institutions (like the United Nations), and norms supporting democracy and human rights.

Part III: The Contemporary Era (Late 20th Century to 2026)

Chapter 7: The Third Wave and Consolidation

Democratic Consolidation: The process by which a new democracy matures, making it unlikely to revert to authoritarianism without an external shock.

Electoral Model: A minimalist view of democracy focusing primarily on the procedural fairness of regular elections.

Chapter 8: The Digital Rupture

E-Governance: The use of digital tools to enhance government transparency, efficiency, and citizen participation.

Disinformation: The strategic use of false information to polarize the public sphere and undermine democratic deliberation.

Chapter 9: Populist Backlash and Backsliding

Illiberal Democracy: A system that maintains elections but restricts civil liberties, media freedom, and judicial independence.

Democratic Backsliding: The gradual erosion of democratic norms and institutions within established democracies.

Chapter 10: Post-National Governance

Multi-Stakeholder Networks: Governance models involving governments, private sectors, and civil society working together on global issues (e.g., climate change).

Transnational Governance: Decision-making processes that occur above the nation-state level, such as in the European Union or International Court of Justice.

www.ingramcontent.com/pod-product-compliance
Lightning Source LLC
Chambersburg PA
CBHW011349230926
51848CB00003B/517